VISION IN CONTEXT

VISION
in
Context

Historical and Contemporary Perspectives on Sight

Edited by Teresa Brennan and Martin Jay

ROUTLEDGE NEW YORK AND LONDON

Published in 1996 by
Routledge
29 West 35th Street
New York, NY 10001

Published in Great Britain by
Routledge
11 New Fetter Lane
London EC4P 4EE

Copyright © 1996 by Routledge

Design: 2^b Group, Inc. NY
Printed in the United States of America on
acid-free paper.

Library of Congress
Cataloging-in-Publication Data

Vision in context: historical and contemporary
perspectives on sight / edited by Teresa
Brennan and Martin Jay.
     p.   cm.
     Includes bibliographical references and index.
     ISBN 0-415-91474-4 (alk. paper),
     ISBN 0-415-91475-2 (pbk. alk. paper)
     1. Image (Philosophy). 2. Vision. 3. Gaze.
     I. Brennan, Teresa, 1952– . II. Jay, Martin, 1944– .

B105.I47v57 1995   95-42441
128.3—dc20   CIP

ACKNOWLEDGMENTS

The editors would like to thank the Belle van Zuylen Institute of the University of Amsterdam, which organized the conference and lectures on which this book is based. We also thank the *rector magnificus* of the University of Amsterdam, Professor Peter de Meijer, for his personal vision in this and other projects and Elisabeth Lissenberg for many kinds of support. Special thanks to Kate Brennan and Kwok Wei Leng, for their intelligent and tireless assistance in preparing the manuscript, and to Kevin Bruyneel. We would like to thank Cathy Gallagher, who has contributed to this book in many intangible ways and Tom Conley who, apart from being an exemplary contributor, selected and took most of the photographs in this volume. Teresa Brennan would also like to thank the Institute of Commonwealth Studies of the University of London for a Robert Gordon Menzies Fellowship and the Philosophy Department of Melbourne University for its collegiate hospitality.

All photos for chapters 4, 6, 14, and 15 were taken by Tom Conley.

Vision in Context: Reflections and Refractions

Martin Jay

The new fascination with modes of seeing and the enigmas of visual experience evident in a wide variety of fields may well betoken a paradigm shift in the cultural imaginary of our age. What has been called "the pictorial turn" bids fair to succeed the earlier "linguistic turn" so loudly trumpeted by twentieth-century philosophers.[1] The model of "reading texts," which served productively as the master metaphor for postobjectivist interpretations of many different phenomena, is now giving way to models of spectatorship and visuality, which refuse to be redescribed in entirely linguistic terms. The figural is resisting subsumption under the rubric of discursivity; the image is demanding its own unique mode of analysis.

The linguistic and the discursive have not, to be sure, been simply replaced by the pictorial and the figural but rather in complicated ways infiltrated by them. As the title of a recent book suggests, "viewing texts" and "reading pictures" are now chiasmically intertwined.[2] No longer is it possible for psychoanalysts and those influenced by them to say, as Lacan famously once did, that "the unconscious is structured like a language," for Lacan's own later ruminations on vision can be mobilized to undermine or at least radically add nuance to this claim. What has been called "the optical unconscious" now appears as a new dark continent ripe for exploration.[3] The "other" of textuality, the referential object supposedly banished by self-sufficient diacritical systems, has returned to haunt many texts. Perception, in short, has come back in postobjectivist, postpositivist, even postphenomenological forms.

These forms reflect, however, the lessons of the linguistic turn, which taught us to attend to the constituted rather than the found quality of seemingly "natural" phenomena. Naive mimesis has been displaced by a far more sophisticated version, which goes beyond the simple notion of imitative mirroring or specular duplication.[4] At a time when the constructed nature of the body in general has become a commonplace of contemporary scholarship, "the eye" and "the gaze" (or "the look") have been opened to historical and cultural interpretations, which undermine their allegedly universal character. Whole theories have been built on distinctions between "the gaze" and other types of seeing, such as "the glance," or on distinctions between "panoptic," "virtual," and "mobilized" gazes.[5] Culturally specific "visuality"—or what the French film critic Christian Metz called different "scopic regimes"—has displaced "vision" per se as the central concern of scholars in many different disciplines.[6] New attention has been paid to scientifically and technologically generated "techniques of observation," which are shown to be dependent on culturally inflected visual practices and able in turn to influence later ones.[7] Scholars in fields as disparate as philosophy and anthropology now probe their disciplines' past and interrogate their present to unveil the hidden effects of visual metaphors and visual practices on their most fundamental assumptions.[8] More obviously visually oriented disciplines such as art history, film studies, and the history of photography have suddenly gained a central place in the humanities as a whole as their lessons seem applicable to issues far from their original field of inquiry.[9] The work of leading critics in these fields, such as Rosalind Krauss, Michael Fried, Victor Burgin, Stephen Heath, Benjamin Buchloh, Kaja Silverman, Craig Owens, Hal Foster, Miriam Hansen, and Joel Snyder, now rapidly produces a ripple effect through neighboring disciplines.

The pictorial turn has taken place, observers have been quick to note, against the backdrop of the seemingly exponential increase of images in Western culture, an increase that has unleashed panegyrics of postmodernist praise and jeremiads of antimodernist anxiety.[10] The rehearsing of ancient iconoclastic polemics over the seductive power of images has been widely remarked.[11] The political implications of this hypertrophy of visual stimulation have engendered vigorous debate, which has led to historical investigations of the entanglement of the political and the visual in many previous eras and cultural contexts. One need only mention Michel Foucault's work on surveillance and the panopticon, Guy Debord's critique of the "society of the spectacle," and John Berger's exploration of the "ways of seeing" to signal the widespread fascination with this theme, which has informed disciplines from political theory to postcolonial studies.[12]

Perhaps nowhere have the problematic implications of certain scopic regimes been as rigorously probed as in the area of gender, where the notion of the objectifying "male gaze" emerged only a few years ago in the work of critics like Laura Mulvey, Griselda Pollock, and Mary Ann Doane as one of the primary mechanisms by which oppressive patriarchal relations seemed to be maintained. It is a mark of the rapid and proliferating discussion of visuality that these relatively recent efforts now seem somewhat dated as more complicated and nuanced notions of gendered spectatorship have been advanced. If anything is clear about the vigorous and ongoing discussion of how to situate "sexuality in the field of vision," to borrow the title of Jacqueline Rose's influential book,[13] it is that we are still very much at the dawn of a collective exploration that shows no signs of reaching an easy consensus.

Indeed, as the chapters in this collection powerfully demonstrate, the pictorial turn is only now beginning to produce work that complicates and adds nuance to the conclusions reached by pioneering efforts in this area. First, we must remark the attention to historical specificity that informs several—if not all—of the contributions. Rather than offering sweeping generalizations about the ocularcentric character of all of "Western culture" or the "Cartesian perspectivalism" that dominates the modern era, they carefully discriminate among discrete and often contradictory moments in that heterogeneous history. Thus, Simon Goldhill successfully challenges the conventional assumption that the privileging of *ekphrasis*, the picturing of set pieces from another medium such as poetry, defined virtually all of classical visual practice. He shows instead that at least three distinct moments can be discerned in which alternative scopic regimes—or at least discourses of viewing—prevailed: the democratic city-state of fifth and fourth century b.c.e., in which the viewer was identified with the collective gaze of citizens participating in the polis; the Hellenistic Alexandria of the ca. third to first centuries b.c.e., in which the individual expert (*sophos*) analytically viewed art from the past based on the exercise of a capacity for knowledge-producing *phantasia*; and the Second Sophistic Era of the Roman Empire (ca. the second to fourth centuries c.e.), in which the desiring eye came to be the source of serious concern, a concern that later had its impact on the Christian suspicion of the eye. In all of these cases, Goldhill demonstrates the complex imbrication not only of the visual and the rhetorical but also of the visual and larger institutional structures of the ancient world.

Similarly, Janet Martin Soskice shows that the medieval church's ambivalent reservations toward the physiological vision of the actual eyes in comparison to the "intellectual visions" of the soul drew on an implicit hostility to the body, which had roots in gnostic thought and carried explicit gender implications. Insofar as women were generally associated with "lower" corporeal functions than men, the distrust of visual experience was a sign of patriarchal bias. Interestingly, it also betokened a diminution of the importance of the Incarnation, in which God had taken on the fleshly identity associated primarily with women. Although Soskice acknowledges the continuing importance of visual stimulation in Christian worship during the Middle Ages,[14] her analysis of devotional writings demonstrates the abiding power of the iconoclastic impulse inherited from certain gnostic sources. Soskice concludes that modern feminists might need to rethink their general suspicion of vision in light of its tainted pedigree.

Tom Conley's examination of Holbein's celebrated painting *The Ambassadors* (1533) situates it in the transitional era that Teresa Brennan has called the onset of the "age of paranoia," when the aggressive and dominating ego emerged to control a world it perceived as hostile and threatening. Conley does not read the painting as a depiction of a conflictual optical field—the conventional perspectival image of the figures crossed by the anamorphic distortion of the skull at their feet, which unsettles the putative unity of visual experience. He argues instead that the viewer is rigidly fixed at the intersection of the two planes, giving his ego what Lacan would have called a "puncti-form" character. The effect of fixation, Conley contends, is reinforced by Holbein's introduction of written material—emblems, alphabets, and marginalia in maps—which can be compared with the appearance of the letter in the unconscious, an appearance that Lacan argued freezes the endless circulation of indeterminant meanings in previsible language. But in a final rumination on anoth-er reading of Holbein's work, that of the French novelist George Sand in the 1840s, Conley finds some resistance to this fixating process that calls into question the success of the punctiform cre-ation of the paranoid ego.

Close attention to the ambiguities of visual experience is also evident in Peter de Bolla's account of eighteenth-century British theories of spectatorial subjectivity, which challenges con-ventional wisdom about the Enlightenment's dominant scopic regime. He shows how certain Lacanian insights into the complicated cross-fire of visual experiences were anticipated by the metaphorics of vision in the works of such writers as Adam Smith and were acted out—or subtly contested—in the visually charged space of Vauxhall Gardens. De Bolla contends that Smith's *Theory of Moral Sentiments* was based on a notion of visual sympathy in which ethical behavior was derived from the ability to see oneself through the eyes of others or, even more radically, the eyes of an idealized "impartial spectator." From one perspective, the triangulated logic of this self-dis-placement recalls the participatory spectatorship Simon Goldhill located in the democratic Athenian polis. From another, less positive vantage point it evokes the mimetic triangulation of desire whose more sinister implications were famously limned by René Girard.[15] In fact, de Bolla's account of the struggle for mastery over the site of spectatorial authority in Vauxhall Gardens, a homosocial struggle between men over the right to gaze at a woman and the right to turn oneself into an object of desire, shows how complicated and indeed contradictory visually charged inter-actions could be during this period. What de Bolla dubs the "heterotopics of the visual field" thus contains the potential for both consensual and conflictual outcomes.

Gillian Beer's discussion of the late-nineteenth-century discourse on visuality shifts attention away from viewing subjects, visual fields, and the objects on view to the more general dialectic of visibility and invisibility. She argues that invisibility in particular became a contested territory for scientists and spiritualists, who were troubled by its implications for knowledge and belief. Whereas Christians such as John Henry Newman could celebrate an invisible world of eternal truths, later scientists, following the pioneering work of Hermann von Helmholtz, became anxious about their inability to make visible what lay beneath the threshold of normal human sight. Beer shows that this anxiety was shared by many outside the narrowly defined scientific community. Indeed, the time-honored scientific project of enlightenment, the uncovering of hidden truths, was called into question by the new realization that waves of energy could never be seen by even the most powerful optical tools. Beer concludes that the metaphoric implications of this realization were significant for gender relations, as women writers—and certain gay men—could identify with the invisible, oceanic flows that male-dominated, visually determined science could not see. Luce Irigaray's well-known opposition between female sexuality based on touch and smell and male sex-uality based on sight, as well as her identification of women with fluids and men with solids, was thus both anticipated and subtly challenged by the nineteenth-century appropriation of the lessons of recent scientific discoveries.

Whereas these historical accounts of the complex and often conflicting dynamics of visuality provide a cautionary check on prematurely ambitious generalizations about the implications of vision per se, or even the homogeneity of specific scopic regimes, the remaining chapters in this collection, which deal with contemporary themes, have no less unsettling implications. Stephen Melville's consideration of the current theoretical debate about vision notes an often occluded tension between essentially Sartrean and Lacanian positions. Sartre's dark analysis of the reifying power of the gaze is grounded in a pessimistic appraisal of the impossibility of reciprocal recognition that stresses the asymmetry in any dyadic interaction. Lacan, Melville argues, opens up a more triangulated relationship in which viewer and viewed themselves are always in a more impersonal visual field. In Lacanian terms, the Symbolic is not radically apart from the Imaginary but in fact actually subtends or is at least equiprimordial with it, a point missed by those who overemphasize Lacan's early writings on the mirror stage. Again there is no symmetrical reciprocity, but a less sinister outcome follows from the intervention of the inhuman field in the broken dialectic of gazes than Sartre would have assumed. For the grounds of human sociability are established precisely by this third term, which is not available for recognition in the Hegelian sense of mutual regard but rather for "acknowledgment," by which Melville means an act that takes time and is based on belated understanding. Melville further points out that whereas Sartre's visual ruminations were not dependent on a consideration of painting, Lacan's, like Maurice Merleau-Ponty's before him, were deeply indebted to precisely such a consideration. For the latter two, human seeing is thus always situated in a world of objects that present light in all its materiality, as Goethe suggested in his critique of Newtonian optics, not a world in which objects merely exist in the visual field created by a monocular gaze. Melville concludes by arguing that a Sartrean dialectic of uncompleted recognition is itself dependent on a reductively spectatorial notion of theory, which ignores the imbrication of the visual and the linguistic, whereas the Lacanian alternative, dependent as it is on the nontheoretical experience of painting, paradoxically provides a more complex appreciation of the intertwining of saying and seeing. Unlike Conley, who emphasizes the congruence of the seen and the spoken in fixing the punctiform subject, Melville stresses the tension between them.

Melville's attempt to mobilize Lacanian arguments for a more benign appreciation of visuality—"giving oneself over to visibility and its coding," he claims at one point, "is the hesitant means to freedom"—brackets the question of gender, which exercises most of the other contributors to the collection. For example, in his discussion of Ian McEwan's novel *The Comfort of Strangers*, Ernst van Alphen discerns a homosocial interaction between male characters in which their women counterparts implicitly play the role of the inhuman third suggested by Melville's reading of Lacan. But here the triangulation involved is that of Girard's mimetic desire, where competitive rivalry through the struggle for the right to gaze supplants the more benign reciprocity of Lévi-Strauss's exchange of women (benign, that is, from the point of view of the men). Unlike Melville, who rejects a notion of vision based on Lacan's early work on the mirror stage, van Alphen appeals precisely to the mirror as a way beyond the hostile homosocial exchange of women. In his view, the mingling of images of male and female characters in a mirror somehow undercuts the dominating logic of the gaze and produces the healthier visual experience of the glance, which undoes the rigid separation of sexual difference. Without that undoing, van Alphen suggests, all that is possible is homosocial rivalry based on the objectification of women and the abjection of homosexual desire. What Peter de Bolla detected in the Vauxhall Gardens in the eighteenth century is thus repeated in the visual interaction described in a twentieth-century novel.

The male gaze, the mirror, and the process of abjection also appear in Helga Geyer-Ryan's exploration of nationalist hostility based on the permeation of rigid borderlines, but these ideas form a very different constellation. In her account, xenophobia is based on a perceived assault by foreigners against the fragile national identity that is a displaced and enlarged version of the unified body-self Lacan claims is grounded in the mirror stage. The penetration of that identity, Geyer-Ryan argues, with a nod to Kristeva, leads to the threat of a regression to an even earlier, more archaic stage, that of the abjection of the mother's body. Men, she claims, are more prone to the aggressive rejection of abjected others than women because of their experience of oedipal rivalry, the more powerful repression of their incestuous desire, and their more radical decorporealization in the Symbolic realm.

Against the reifying power of the male gaze, which subtends xenophobia as well as other aggressive and paranoid behavior, Geyer-Ryan calls for a polyscopic proliferation of visual practices that correspond to a deterritorialized, nomadic sense of space. She concludes, however, by acknowledging that some sense of ego integrity and bodily unity, as well as some identification with a larger *Heimat*, is necessary. Indeed, women may be threatened by too weak an ego and too diffuse a body image even if men suffer from the opposite problem. Some presumably visually reinforced boundary-setting is thus necessary even in the most nomadic of spatial orders, a conclusion that implicitly jibes with the recent argument of Jean-Luc Nancy that the temporal process of founding a political space is a prerequisite to freedom.[16]

The male gaze remains the target of several contributors, but others speculate on the implications of women's vision or possible participation in alternative scopic regimes. Cathryn Vasseleu provides a strikingly original reading of the French feminist Luce Irigaray's meditations on sight. Rejecting the conventional assumption, operative for example in my *Downcast Eyes*, that Irigaray considers the privileging of sight to be inherently hostile to women, Vasseleu shows that in her more recent writings Irigaray has explored a positive role for a nonheliocentric, non-Platonic version of illumination. By focusing on Irigaray's complicated and ambivalent appropriation of certain ideas from Emmanuel Lévinas, Vasseleu is able to find in her work a "genealogy of photosensitivity," which uncovers an erotic dimension of illumination that includes women's experience.

Arguing against the connoisseurship tradition of purely aesthetic taste in art history, Irit Rogoff likewise urges awareness of the multiple contexts of spectatorship, the gendered (as well as ethnic and class) status of who is looking and the nature of the desire involved in even the most seemingly disinterested act of spectatorship. Every gaze is sited, she insists; every viewer occupies a position in a cultural field. Rogoff provides a number of telling examples to show that the "objects" of art history must themselves be understood as inevitably constructed, at least in part, by their particular beholders.

A similar emphasis on the concrete specificity of the spectator is evident in Renée Hoogland's examination of the film *Basic Instinct*. Hoogland claims that the apparent right to look given to lesbians in recent popular culture is often tacitly undermined by the medium's underlying visual dynamics, which allow lesbians to function only as the abject other in the construction of heterosexual male identity. Implicitly distancing herself from Gillian Beer's conclusion that women can and have made a virtue out of their invisibility, she claims that the invisibility—or exclusively degraded visibility—of lesbians in particular simply reinforces the dominant heterosexism of Western culture. Invoking queer theorist Judith Butler's deconstruction of fixed sexual identities, Hoogland argues not only that lesbians should become more visible in positive ways but also that their own "visionary" capacities can provide a valuable model for a new viewing subject.

An even more complex economy of looking and perversion is suggested by Parveen Adam's detailed analysis of Michael Powell's film *Peeping Tom*, an analysis less of its characters than of the ways the film works to produce meaning. Here the issue is not so much the gender of the film's spectator as the complicity of *all* viewers in the structure of fascination produced by the film's rendition of a murderous voyeur's attempts to film his victims as he kills them. Adams distinguishes between the normal pleasure of looking, based in the Imaginary, and the perverse *jouissance* solicited by the murderer's horrible deeds. Following Lacan, she claims that the search for such *jouissance* is a response to the appearance of the Real in the Symbolic, or, more precisely, the indirect manifestation of the Real as an impossible-to-attain *objet petit a*. That object is sought as an antidote to the castration anxiety felt by the voyeur, who both disavows his lack and desperately tries to make it up.

In a series of steps too complicated to rehearse now, Adams argues that the spectator is caught up in, but ultimately separated from, the murderous voyeur's failed attempt to achieve the fulfilment he seeks. That attempt is carried out through a process in which the voyeur also becomes an object on view, an exhibitionist open to the gaze of two women in the film. He seeks, in other words, to capture on film the terrified look of the women at the moment he kills them, the look being in fact the version of the *objet petit a* that he hopes will provide what he lacks. The impossible aim of the pervert, Adams argues, is to make his own vision and the look of the other coincide. But one of the women is blind—and therefore has no look of her own to be captured—and for this reason, among others Adams details, the project fails. In complicated and indirect ways, this failure calls into question the spectator's complicity in the voyeur's project, thwarting his or her own parallel search for an impossible jouissance.

The moral of the story is that we too are unable to elude castration; we too cannot provide what we lack by merging our subjective vision with our place as objects in the visual field of the other. The voyeur ultimately commits suicide in the film; the spectator is saved a similar fate not only by the blind woman's resistance to the role he has assigned her but also by the other woman's refusal to accept her own image in a mirror as a petrified thing. Both women defeat the project of turning them into positive realizations of the *objet petit a*, which might then function to realize the voyeur's perverse *jouissance*. If gender enters Adams's argument, it is not at the level of the film's spectator, whom she describes in neutral terms, but rather at that of the interplay of the characters and their gazes. Here, paradoxically, it seems that women defeat male power—or at least the search for *jouissance* produced by disavowed castration anxiety—not by becoming spectators but rather by resisting the male desire for their becoming precisely that!

Still more complexity is added to our understanding of the relations between vision and sexuality by Mieke Bal's semiotic consideration of Proust's *Remembrance of Things Past*, in which vision is understood as a mode of narration rather than an actual medium of perception.[17] Instead of asking for the frank acknowledgment of homosexuality—exemplified by Hoogland's call for lesbians to be both visible and the inspiration for visionary spectatorship—or seeing it as an abjection in the service of male homosocial exchange—as do Peter de Bolla and Ernst van Alphen—Bal explores the ambiguous implications of remaining "in the closet," at least on the level of narrative epistemology. She identifies one visual practice in the novel with the taking of snapshots (either metaphorically by the focalizing narrator or literally by a character in the novel), which involves not merely a vulgar recording of the events of everyday life but also an implied ontology. The snapshot, she tells us, signifies a belief in superficiality and presence; Marcel's photos of Albertine thus imprison her in an ontology of atemporality and depthlessness. Or rather, they create a tension between her visual representation and her inaccessible self.

As a woman, a lesbian, and someone who literally flees her lover, Albertine perfectly embodies all the fugitive qualities—the qualities of the "closeted gaze"—that suggest an irreparable gap between knowledge and being, epistemology and ontology. A modified version of the same dynamic is at work in the depiction of another closeted homosexual, Robert de Saint-Loup, whose surface rather than depth is also on display. Unlike the snapshots that try to fix Albertine, those that describe him are arranged in a series, like the chronophotography of Eadweard Muybridge or Étienne-Jules Marey. Whereas the woman is shown as a passive, if ultimately elusive, victim of Marcel's snapshooting gaze, the man is allowed a more mobile identity, albeit not one that mimics the apparently lifelike movement of the cinema. Instead, Bal compares it to a contact sheet, which eschews the illusory effects of mainstream movies. The movement it does produce, she concludes, is like the *écriture* that Derrida defines as a process of interminable spacing. That is, the narrative depiction of visual experience produces a clearer understanding of writing, the spatialized temporality that is also a figuration of desire.

Insofar as desire is unfulfillable and writing always inadequate to the perfect expression of meaning, the gap between the gaze and its object—a permanently "closeted gaze"—is thus a figure of a larger pattern. Or rather, to adopt Bal's terminology, it is a "disfigure," a rhetorical device invested with multiple meanings. These meanings never cohere into one pattern, a refusal that parallels the self-division of visuality and desire described by Lacan. Like the famous unshown photograph of his mother in Roland Barthes's *Camera Lucida*, something is both concealed and revealed, seemingly "out," yet still with one foot in the closet. For the temporal deferral that is the motor of narrative to work, the gaze in the text, like desire in general, must remain permanently unable to achieve its sought-after object.

Is it possible, let me ask in conclusion, to soar above these essays and provide a sovereign overview of the argumentative pattern they reveal? Can we find a figure in this bewildering carpet of attempts to explore the multiple contexts of visuality? Is there a common denominator running through such seemingly disparate investigations of theories about vision, general visual cultures, specific visual artifacts like movies, and the role of visual metaphors in written texts? Although there are certain recurring themes and a frequent overlapping of arguments, the answer, it seems fair to conclude, is that no single gestalt presents itself, no matter how high the altitude of our bird's-eye view. Instead , we find ourselves in a heterotopic space without a single totalizing vantage point. The "pictorial turn," like the "linguistic turn" before it, shows itself to be richly varied and irreducible to one dominant model.

The essays dealing with discrete historical periods clearly support this conclusion, as they almost all give us a sense of the inadequacy of any sweeping generalization about hegemonic scopic regimes. But the answer is no less compelling in the more theoretically and present-minded essays, even if we note the extraordinary consensus on the part of virtually all of the contributors concerning the most productive theoretical approach to vision. In the wake of Teresa Brennan's effort to think about "history after Lacan," most of these essays are, we might say, trying to understand "visuality after Lacan."

But as anyone who has tried to summarize the Lacanian legacy in this area can well attest,[18] there is no straightforward and integrated account to be derived from Lacan's transcribed seminars and written texts. Although one might argue that the later ruminations in *The Four Fundamental Concepts of Psychoanalysis* somehow supersede the earlier ones on the "mirror stage," Lacan himself never explicitly rejected his first attempts to understand ego formation and aggression in largely visual terms. Understandably, the contributors are thus able to find inspiration in different Lacanian arguments about vision. Yet even when certain Lacanian texts are privileged over others, the results are by no means always uniform. Thus, for example, in considering the mirror-stage argument, Helga Geyer-Ryan employs it as a way to explain the creation of fragile national identities, which can be threatened by external penetration that produces regression to an even more archaic stage of abjection. Ernst van Alphen, on the other hand, implies that the mirror can serve in the present as a site of transgendered identity fusion in which one boundaried self is assimilated to another with an essentially benign effect.

For those who turn instead to Lacan's later thoughts on the chiasmic intertwining of the eye and the gaze in a heterogeneous visual field, the implications are no less contradictory. Thus, Tom Conley sees the punctiform subject produced at the onset of the "age of paranoia" as fixed at the point of chiasmic crossing, a fixation reinforced by the written material introduced into paintings such as *The Ambassadors*. In contrast, Stephen Melville presents a triangulated account of the centrifugal forces that dissolve any subjective unity. From his perspective, the nonreciprocity and lack of mutual recognition produced by the introduction of an "inhuman" third element in visual experience is welcome evidence of the social and the cultural that needs to be acknowledged in order to get beyond the interpersonal duel of raw gazes demonized by Sartre. Here he approaches Peter de Bolla's reading of Adam Smith's claim that an imagined impartial spectator is the ground of social solidarity, with the important difference that Smith's concept was based on a universalizing gesture of identification that the Lacanian triangulation denies.

Melville's stress on the role of language in the composition of the social and cultural—the Symbolic and the Imaginary are not for him radically different stages—also invites comparison with Mieke Bal's semiotic reading of Proust on vision. Her presentation of the "closeted gaze" as a mode of imperfect sight crossed by the temporality of language accords as well with Melville's notion of "acknowledgment," which is based on the passage of time. Perhaps the one difference is that Bal emphasizes the forward-looking force of desire, whereas Melville stresses the way in which understanding happens only *après-coup*, after the fact.

Although Bal is more attuned to the gender workings of visual interaction than Melville, she also avoids simply equating male power with the right to see. Bal's implicit critique of voyeur theory as essentializing and her praise for the ambiguities of the closet suggests a certain distance from Renée Hoogland's defense of the lesbian's visionary gaze and goes beyond Irit Rogoff's call for responsible gazing as an awareness of gendered subject positions in art history. Bal is perhaps more in tune with de Bolla's account of the mobile gaze in Vauxhall Gardens, in which power can come from exhibitionist as well as spectatorial roles. Her ideas also seem compatible with Parveen Adams's indifference to the gender of the film spectator and her analysis of the ways in which the woman who refuses to look thwarts the perverted yearning for a *jouissance* based on the capturing of the other's look. Bal also appears less inclined than de Bolla or van Alphen to focus on homosocial gazing, in which women are merely mediated objects in a male competition for power; instead she foregrounds the more direct workings of homosexual desire of both genders.

There is no obvious agreement among the contributors over the social implications of visibility and invisibility. Hoogland, for example, bridles at the absent or demonized images of lesbians in the dominant cinema of our day, and Janet Soskice worries about the gnostic, antimaterialist baggage carried by the denigration of vision that sees women's bodies in particular as corrupt and unworthy of visual affirmation. For these two contributors, to be on view, at least in certain ways, can be a check against being ignored or forgotten. As in Simon Goldhill's depiction of the participatory spectatorship of the ancient polis, seeing and being seen are not understood as absolute alternatives. Vasseleu's presentation of Irigaray's recent ruminations on illumination support a similar conclusion.

In contrast, Gillian Beer finds that invisibility—and a concomitant privileging of other senses—has been, at least at one point in recent history, a means for women to bypass the dominant scopic regime of the West. Like both Plato and the sophists, who distrusted the realm of appearances, late-nineteenth-century scientists and those who pondered the implications of their wave theories of light, heat, and sound abandoned belief in a world that could reveal its secrets to the inquiring eye.

In short, we have a welter of competing interpretations of the meaning and implications of vision and visuality. Choosing among them, moreover, is no easy task, as it is not clear what would count as evidence for or against one or the other. Evidence, after all, is a word derived from the Latin *videre*, which suggests it may be based on a visual metaphor whose innocence can no longer be assumed. As is the case with Lacan's suggestive, if not always fully coherent, theories, on which

so many of these essays depend, a certain leap of faith is required before one account can be accepted as superior to another. Indeed, the assumption that Lacanian theory, however it is understood,
can be applied with equal assurance to a sixteenth-century painting and a twentieth-century film
rests on an undefended belief in the persistence and universality of visual experience that is tacitly
questioned by the historical transformations of visuality demonstrated by many of the contributions to this collection. The familiar nature/culture conundrum remains unresolved in the contexts
of vision, as it does in so many others.

If a metaphor borrowed from another sense is permitted, what we hear in reading these
diverse and stimulating pieces is the sound of ground being cleared for a possible new paradigm,
but it is still too early to tell what that paradigm's shape will be and whether or not it will be coherent and unified. The linguistic turn, after all, produced many different, even conflicting, variations;
the pictorial turn, if these essays are any indication, promises to be no less productive and probably even more unpredictable.

1   W. J. T. Mitchell, "The Pictorial Turn, *"Picture Theory: Essays in Verbal and Visual Representation* (Chicago, University of Chicago Press, 1995). Mitchell's work has contributed powerfully to this trend. See, for example, his *Iconology: Image, Text, Ideology* (Chicago: University of Chicago Press, 1987).

2   Claude Gandelman, *Reading Pictures, Viewing Texts* (Bloomington, Ind.: Indiana University Press, 1991).

3   The term was coined by Walter Benjamin in his "A Short History of Photography," *Screen*, no. 7. (Spring 1972). It serves as the title for Rosalind E. Krauss's latest book (Cambridge, Mass.: M.I.T. Press, 1993).

4   More sophisticated versions of mimesis are advanced by theorists such as Theodor W. Adorno, *Aesthetic Theory*, ed. Gretel Adorno and Rolf Tiedemann, trans. Christian Leenhardt (London: Routledge & Kegan Paul, 1984); and Philippe Lacoue-Labarthe, *Typography: Mimesis, Philosophy, Politics*, ed. Christopher Fynsk, intro. Jacques Derrida (Cambridge, Mass.: Harvard University Press, 1989).

5   Norman Bryson, *Vision and Painting: The Logic of the Gaze* (London, Macmillan 1983); Anne Friedberg, *Window Shopping: Cinema and the Postmodern* (Berkeley: University of California Press, 1993).

6   See the essays in Hal Foster, ed., *Vision and Visuality* (Seattle: Bay Press, 1988), and Chris Jenks, ed., *Visual Culture* (London: Routledge, 1995).

7   Jonathan Crary, *Techniques of the Observer: On Vision and Modernity in the Nineteenth Century* (Cambridge, Mass.: M.I.T. Press, 1990).

8   For philosophy, see David Michael Levin, ed., *Modernity and the Hegemony of Vision* (Berkeley: University of California Press, 1993); for anthropology, see Lucien Taylor, ed., *Visualizing Theory: Selected Essays from V.A.R., 1990–1994* (New York: Routledge, 1994).

9   See, for example, the two collections edited by Norman Bryson, Michael Ann Holly, and Keith Moxey, *Visual Theory: Painting and Interpretation* (Middletown, Conn., Wesleyan University Press 1990) and *Visual Culture: Images and Interpretations* (Middletown, Conn., Wesleyan University Press 1994).

10 For an example of the former, see Jean Baudrillard, *Simulacres et simulation* (Paris: Galilée, 1981); for the latter, see Jacques Ellul, *The Humiliation of the Word*, trans. Joyce Main Hanks (Grand Rapids, Mich.: William B. Eerdmans, 1985).

11 See, for example, Mosche Barasch, *Icon: Studies in the History of an Idea* (New York: New York University Press, 1992).

12 For an example of the former, see Yaron Ezrahi, *The Descent of Icarus: Science and the Transformation of Contemporary Democracy* (Cambridge, Mass.: Harvard University Press, 1990); for the latter, see Robert Young, *White Mythologies: Writing History and the West* (London: Routledge, 1990).

13 Jacqueline Rose, *Sexuality in the Field of Vision* (London: Verso, 1986).

14 For more evidence of the importance of visual stimulation, see Margaret Miles, *Image as Insight: Visual Understanding in Western Christianity and Secular Culture* (Boston: Beacon Press, 1985).

15 René Girard, *Deceit, Desire and the Novel: Self and Other in Literary Structure*, trans. Yvonne Freccero (Baltimore: Johns Hopkins University Press, 1965).

16 Jean-Luc Nancy, *The Experience of Freedom*, trans. Bridget McDonald (Palo Alto: Stanford University Press, 1993). Nancy claims that "the foundation of foundation that is freedom is the very experience of founding, and the experience of founding is nothing other than the essence of experience in general.… Is not the model of all foundation the founding of the ancient city—the marking of the outline of the city limits?" (p. 84). But he then adds, in order to distinguish his position from that of Hannah Arendt, that "this spatiality is not so much a given free space…as it is the gift of a spatio-temporality… [whose] description could be borrowed from the description of nomadic space in another thinking, distanced from the thinking of being and whose distance itself here signifies the free space of thinking" (p. 145).

17 For another semiotic interpretation of vision, based on a reading of Lacan, see Joan Copjec, "The Orthopsychic Subject: Film Theory and the Reception of Lacan," *October* no. 49 (Summer 1989), pp. 53–71.

18 For my own efforts, see *Downcast Eyes: The Denigration of Vision in Twentieth-Century French Thought* (Berkeley: University of California Press, 1993), Chapter 6.

PART ONE

Historical Perspectives

It all—always—begins with Homer. In the *Iliad,* Helen, that warred-over object of desire, comes to the walls of besieged Troy and is observed and wondered at by the assembled Trojan elders. King Priam asks her to name particular Greeks whom she sees ranged against the city, and the face that launched a thousand ships identifies the warriors she has deserted. Priam's gaze distinguishes the leading princes of the Greek host: the bodily form of excellence and the social status of prince—mutually implicated categories[1]—are visible signs, visible attributes, paraded for recognition. This privileged scene of viewing (the *teichoscopia*) establishes an economics of display that is rehearsed throughout the epic: physical and social worth is constructed in and by the gaze of others. So Achilles at the height of his destructive rampage cries out to his victims, "Look at me! Do you not see how beautiful, noble and great I am?" (*Il.,* 21.108). Even the *Odyssey's* games of disguising its hero lead to his splendid, epiphanic appearance, flanked by his father and son, at the epic's close. The hero is ineluctably linked to the modality of the visual.

The Homeric poems and their public presentation of the body of the hero retained a unique position throughout Greek culture for more than a thousand years: education, cultural capital, and literary and artistic worth find their source and resources there. What is more, not only does Greek artistic representation return repeatedly to the display of the heroic body for the establishment of its visual regimes, but also the celebrated description of the Shield of Achilles in *Iliad* 18 heads a tradition of writing about visual art that leads toward the classical turn of Vasari, Lessing, and beyond. It has thus been easy to construct a (white, unbroken) image of the Classical Tradition of writing about viewing and vision. So Stephen Bann, who may stand, together with Norman Bryson and John Hollander[2] (whom he quotes), as an icon for the most interesting contemporary exploration and appropriation of ancient writing about viewing (art), states: "Writing about the visual arts in the classical period took place within the terms of the convention usually known as *ekphrasis*, and though the rules applying to this convention were not absolutely rigid, it is possible to state its main presuppositions with some confidence."[3] It is the aim of this chapter to question each of the central claims of this starting position and to challenge its confidence. First, I will attempt to show that to treat "the classical period" as an unbroken tradition (from Platonic mimesis to Philostratus's *Imagines*) ignores fundamental paradigm shifts in the culture and philosophy of viewing over what is a more than seven-hundred-year span. In the space available here, I will visit three paradigmatic moments—the classical city of the fifth-fourth century b.c.e.; Hellenistic Alexandria (ca. C3-1 b.c.e.); and the Second Sophistic (ca. C2-4 c.e.).

These three moments are chosen not because of any commitment to Foucauldian "rupture" but in order to maximize difference for the sake of rhetorical clarity. Second, the idea that writing about the visual arts can safely be limited to the trope of *ekphrasis* significantly distorts what might be called "the discourse of viewing." Not only is there an extensive tradition of writing on optics,[4] but also ancient writing on tourism, theater, desire, epistemology, etc., repeatedly invokes and analyzes accounts of viewing and observation. To extract the description of a painting from its social and intellectual context necessarily misrecognizes it as a historical or cultural artifact. In the first section of this chapter I will focus on the cultural and political context of viewing; in the second, on an intellectual and specifically philosophical frame; in the third, on the novel's narrative engagement with viewing. In the best of all possible worlds these elements would not be so separated (refracted). Since part of my claim, however, is that the range of writing that should be brought to bear on the topic of viewing has been extensively undervalued, each of my limited snapshots will have to be taken as exemplary fragments of a wider possible history. Third, the continuing belief that *ekphrasis* is most profitably to be analyzed under the rubric of rhetoric, and specifically the rhetorical tradition that opposes *narratio* and *descriptio*, seems to have contributed to this restriction of scope in the discussion of viewing.[5] I shall argue that writing about viewing is (also) a major contributing factor in the *construction of the viewing subject*, and it is within such terms that the discourse of viewing (art) should be approached.

These are somewhat grandiose claims, especially when stated so baldly. What is more, this chapter will be able only to sketch in outline what should be a much longer study. I offer these refracted views of ancient viewing, however, as markers of and stimulus to further discussion.

IN THE GAZE OF THE CITIZENS

The view from the walls of Troy and the display of the heroic body as a sign of worth remain an integral and privileged element in the cultural imagination of the classical city. Yet the fifth-century polis fundamentally restructured the space for display and the technologies of representation—as it did the signs and signals of worth. It is the classical city, and Athens in particular, that provided the frame for Plato's theories of mimesis and his analysis of epistemology and vision.

The establishment of democracy depended on a physical and conceptual reorganization of sociopolitical space. Cleisthenes' reforms (which began the development of democracy)[6] divided the territory of Attica and the citizen body into a series of demes (a localized social and political unit), and each deme was further assigned to one of ten tribes, which functioned as essential divisions of the citizen body in ceremonial, political, and religious events. Each tribe was made up of demes from the coast, the inland region, and the town itself. Since most political appointments were made by lot from a list drawn up to ensure equal representation from each tribe, there was a compulsory geographical spread that diffused power throughout the territory of the state and spread the opportunities of office to the largest possible range of candidates. Although this sense of a possible tension between coast, country, and town is enacted, on the one hand, in a series of writings that both praise the simple delights of country life and disparage the boorishness of rustics and, on the other, in the rituals and ceremonials that articulate the boundaries between town and country,[7] it is in the city itself on which I wish to focus attention. The *agora* (marketplace) formed the central locus for most cities in Greece (along with the military and religious complex of the acropolis), and I shall be returning to this site shortly. First, however, I want to concentrate on the three major public institutions by which Athenian culture was recognized as supremely Greek, supremely democratic, and supremely Athenian, namely, the assembly, the law-court, and the theater.

Now, classical Greek society was a performance culture that valorized competitive public display. The gymnasium, with its display of bodies in the contests of manhood, and the symposium, with its performance of songs and speeches, became the key signs of Greek culture itself as Hellenism spread through the Mediterranean in the wake of Alexander's conquests. The assembly and the law-court, however, the unique institutions of democracy, constituted a special type of performance culture. For the law-court and assembly were the major political institutions of the state, the city's major sites of conflict and debate, and its citizens' major route to positions of power. Both law-court and Assembly involved large citizen audiences, public performance by speakers, and voting to achieve a decision. Democracy made public debate, collective decision-making, and the shared duties of participatory citizenship central elements in its political practice. To be in an audience was not just a thread in the city's social fabric, it was a fundamental *political act*. So Athenian political ideology proudly highlighted democracy's commitment to putting things *es meson* "into the public domain to be contested," and the historian Thucydides had Cleon, a leading politician, call the Athenians in a telling phrase *theatai tôn logôn,* "spectators of speeches" (3.38). The pervasive values of performance in Greek culture together with the special context of democracy and its institutions meant that to be in an audience was above all to play the role of democratic citizen. The political space of democracy was established by the participatory, collective audience of citizen spectators. *Theoria*, the word from which "theory" comes, implies, as has often been noted in contemporary criticism, a form of visual regard; what is less often noted is that *theoria* is the normal Greek for official participatory attendance as spectator in the political and religious rites of the state.

This sense of participatory collective spectatorship is nowhere more evident than in the *theatron*, the theater, or "place for viewing." The dramatic festival of the Great Dionysia, the major theatrical occasion of the year, brought together the largest single collection of citizens in the political calendar. The audience was a visual map of the city. Citizens sat in the wedges of seats according to their tribal divisions, with special seats reserved for the executive council of the city, for priests and for other dignitaries of the state, and for foreigners. So, too, other social groups were specifically distinguished. The audience represented—in all senses—the formal sociopolitical divisions of the state. On stage, before the plays started, extensive rituals were performed that projected and promoted both an ideal of citizen participation in the state and an image of the power of the polis of Athens.[8] The civic occasion was used to glorify the polis of Athens—and to construct a highly charged moment for the display of individual status before the citizens' gaze. Plays were funded by individuals (*chorêgoi*) who gained great political capital by their conspicuous beneficence before such a large audience. The performance of these *chorêgoi* became a standard subject in the contests of the law-court, where citizens further competed for honor and position. In short, the theater was a space in which all the citizens were actors as the city itself and its leading citizens were put on display. Spectacular viewing.

The institutional spaces of the democratic city thus established the citizens' gaze as the field in which position was contested and made the collective, participatory spectator the role of the citizen. The celebrated imperial decoration of Athens—led by Pericles and his Parthenon—was corollary to this process. On the one hand, the Parthenon itself, as figurehead of the program, funded by and thus sign of Athens' imperial expansion, is decorated over the barbarian wildness of the Centaurs and Amazons but also with an extended, idealized representation of the civic body of Athens performing the ritual processions of the Panathenaia (a festival of the city as a totality [*pan*-]). As the citizen spectator processed 'round the Parthenon to its entrance, the engagement as spectator in the frieze's procession is an encouragement to associate with this idealized mimesis of democracy.[9] Significantly, this was the first time in Greek temple sculpture that the citizen body was so imaged.

The Stoa Poikile, or Painted Stoa, shows a similar exemplary construction of a political space for viewing as a citizen. This colonnade along the agora was elaborately decorated, first with major paintings showing Athenian military triumphs over the Spartans juxtaposed with scenes from the capture of Troy: the affiliation of glorious present to glorious past. Second, there was inscribed a famous epigram on the victory of the Greeks—led by Athenians—over the Persians at Marathon, a victory that was central to Athenian self-projections. These military images were buttressed with captured military equipment dedicated in the Stoa. Third, there was (at least) a statue of Solon, a founding figure of democratic ideology. Again, a novel architectural and artistic experiment was designed to construct a political and military surround for the work of the agora, to turn the citizen's gaze toward his military and political obligations (and history).[10]

At this same time, the new intellectuals (usually known by the misleadingly disparaging term "sophists") began an inquiry into vision itself. Democritus's materialist optics, for example, based on the reception in the eye of *eidola*, "little images" emanating from an object, established the notion of a physical ray connecting viewer and viewed, a notion that founded an extensive intellectual tradition of optics as *"une analytique du regard"* (to use Simon's phrase).[11] Similarly, the sophists' attack on the primacy of perception permanently linked the clarity of sight to the falseness of appearance. Since in Greek the word "to know" (*eidenai*) is semantically and morphologically cognate with the word "to see" (*idein*), the *"analytique du regard"* is always already an anatomy of the subject's claim to know. The paradoxes of such connections are explored most famously in Sophocles' *Oedipus Tyrannus*,[12] but the concern with vision, knowledge, and the boundaries of the subject are a repeated, self-reflexive concern of fifth-century theater.

Indeed, what makes the classical city's culture of collective citizen viewing so productive and interesting is precisely the extensive overlap between the different spaces for viewing and discussing viewing that I have been outlining. Theoretical analyses of scene-painting in the theater precede Plato's interest in art and mimesis; the performance of citizens in the theater is discussed on the stage of the law-court; the victory of Marathon is a staple of political ceremony as it adorns the *agora*; the imaging of pot-painters and the theater interpenetrate[13]—and examples of this complex interplay of visual fields can be multiplied. The fifth-century enlightenment is, in short, a reformulation and rearticulation of the viewing subject within the frames of the political collective.

This sketch—and here it can be no more than such impressionism—provides a necessary frame for a remarkable but little-known text. The figure whose physical ugliness (but spiritual grandeur) paradigmatically redefines (philosophical) worth (and erotic engagement) is Socrates. In Xenophon's *Memorabilia*—far less studied than Plato's accounts—two juxtaposed discussions (3.10, 3.11) give a less Platonic but perhaps more instructive insight into Socrates' engagement with viewing in the city. In the first passage (3.10), Socrates visits a series of craftsmen—a painter (Parrhasius), a sculptor, and an armorer—and convinces each in turn that what makes their products significant is the way in which each modifies the mimesis of what is seen, in the case of the painter and the sculptor by idealism and a desire to represent a noble character or soul and in the case of the armorer by proportion and comfort. Agnes Rouveret discusses this challenge to art as (mere or even Platonic) mimesis of the visible and wonders whether this "dialogue...is not a precious testimony of the moment when painting conceived as an image resembling the visible world, imposes new figurative problems on aesthetic reflection and new criteria of appreciation that lead it to play a pioneering role in the exploration of sensible appearance."[14] The move away from understanding representation simply as the reproduction of bodily image opens the range of questions invoked by "inner vision."

This view of art as striving beyond the visible toward the ethical, however, is immediately followed in the *Memorabilia* by a remarkable sequence that surprisingly has not entered contemporary art-historical writing.[15] Socrates goes with some friends to visit a beautiful woman, Theodote, who is being painted by an artist. Socrates is prompted to ask an extraordinary question that goes to the heart of the public, visible construction of status: "Ought we be more grateful to Theodote for letting us see her beauty, or she to us for looking at her?" It will depend, he adds, on whom the act of looking has benefited more. The logic of the formulation of status within the gaze of the citizens underlies this question (even as the woman as object of the gaze introduces a new level of complication. What is it *proper* to see of a woman?). Socrates goes on to argue that since she wins admiration now and praise in the future while the viewers are just titillated, desiring but unsatisfied, Theodote should be more grateful to be observed than the men should be for their view of beauty. (This is agreed by all: as Foucault has argued, not being the master of one's desire is always a threat to the Greek, male subject). Socrates, however, continues to explore Theodote's position in the economics of exchange. He discovers that she relies on admirers for her livelihood, and he compares her body at length to a hunting net that lures the gaze of men—whom, he adds, she will be able to gratify in return. (There is an elaborate wordplay informing this passage: *charis* means "thanks," "grace," "beauty." "Where is the *charis* in looking at a beautiful woman?" is the opening question; now it is the beautiful woman's ability to gratify (*charizesthai*) a man that guarantees her role in the exchange).

Theodote is impressed and asks Socrates to stay and help her hone her skills of entrapment, but he, "poking fun at his own avoidance of public life, replied, 'It's not very easy for me to find the time for it. I have a great deal of public and private business that keeps me occupied. I have girlfriends too, who will never let me leave them…'" The girlfriends turn out to be his philosophical companions (all male). Socrates' ironic account of his position in civic life is complex: highly visible but not directly engaged in formal public life—a position he himself mocks; an older man pursued by his pupils, whom he calls his "girlfriends"—what exchange is taking place in this educational encounter? What is he doing to his pupils that makes them into "girlfriends" who will not let him out? Indeed, when Theodote asks to borrow his love charms, Socrates replies significantly, "Certainly not! I don't want to be drawn to you; I want you to come to me." His flirtatious liaison with beauty seduces, performs a power game, requires its—*her*—submission to him (as *she* will not be titillated but unsatisfied). It makes him master of the situation, the scene of viewing. The observed woman feels not merely gratitude but attraction as Socrates finally emerges as the object of desire in the dialogue—the dialectics of *charis* inverted. The ironic exchange uncovers a shifting and unstable (self-)positioning within the frame of the public regard as Socrates, the male and master, attempts to control the scene of viewing and desire—at the cost of representing himself as the object of desire, surrounded by his "girlfriends." The dialogue *represents* the *process of negotiation* within the realm of public regard. Much as Plato repeatedly explores the uneasy relation between sight and knowledge at an epistemological level, so in its very different way this Xenophonic dialogue mobilizes the different modes of exchange—words, teaching, gratitude, desire, vision—to explore the construction of the subject in the gaze of the citizens. This highly self-reflexive and self-aware discussion of Socrates as subject and object of the public view allows us to see something of the complexity of this process within the visual regime of the democratic city.

DISPLAYING AN ANALYTIC OBSERVATION

The second moment on which I wish to focus is Hellenistic Alexandria.[16] In this vast polyglot metropolis, a new city, the culture of viewing underwent a radical shift. The great public institutions of the fifth-century polis did not exist, nor did the founding category of citizenship in any comparable sense. Though public ceremonials may have been grand, they occurred firmly within the hierarchical political system of the royal palace and the celebration of its own controlling power. (For this and other reasons Hellenistic culture has all too often been treated as a handmaiden to classical Athens or as a precursor to Rome.) However, not only was there a profusion of writing about art, particularly in epigrams and other literary forms, but also the relation between art and the viewer changed in a fundamental manner. For it was in Hellenistic Alexandria that the museum, the practice of collecting art (both privately and under royal patronage), and the practice of commenting on art as the works of a (classical) past were set in place as the new privileged experience of viewing. If in the fifth-century democratic polis the viewer was to be found in the collective gaze of the participating citizens, the archetypal Hellenistic viewer was the philosophically and rhetorically trained expert (*sophos*) expressing his individual analytic pose before the great art of the past.

This new idea of viewing can be seen in, say, the much-reviled series of twenty-nine extant epigrams, each of which dramatizes a response to a famous classical work of "realist" sculpture, *Myron's Cow*.[17] None of these epigrams, it must be stressed, *describes* the *physical* work of art. Each poem focuses on the fictionalized onlooker and plays an increasingly baroque game with the *topos* of the work's impression of life-likeness, or rather, with the possibilities of imaging that impression. Each poem dramatizes the moment of looking as a moment of interpreting, reading—seeing meaning. The archaeological uncovering of a sedimented world of significance, the pointed articulation of the striking new sense, structures the viewing of the *sophos*. So, typically, for Plato the younger seeing an amethyst ring carved with a figure of Dionysus is to see a paradox, since "amethyst" etymologically means "against drunkenness," whereas Asclepiades, seeing a similar amethyst carved with an image of "drunkenness," claims it is a proper link of form and image because it is a ring designed for the queen's hand, where "even drunkenness is sober."[18]

This ekphrastic gesture of the *sophos*, however, with customary Hellenistic literary self-awareness, also repeatedly discusses the process of interpretation as it is performed. This process is seen first in the explicit markers of the *sophos* reading: there are numerous riddles, numerous riddling images where false steps and clever guesses are expressly articulated. ("Let's see... Is this the message?...Or is it not so? Now I'll think I'll get it... That was a superb voiceless image..."—a running commentary on reading extracted from one brief poem by Antipater.)[19] Second, this self-reflexivity is seen in the increasing use of a technical vocabulary from art criticism in poetic responses to art. These gestures of self-aware interpretation emphasize that such ekphrastic poems represent not merely a work of art but *the poet as seeing subject*. The self-conscious and self-reflexive dramatization of viewing—seeing oneself seeing—is a fundamental element of Hellenistic *ekphrasis*. As the professional exegete in the museum becomes the model reader, so Hellenistic poetry signals a consciously changing interaction between the seeing subject and the object of his critical gaze.

This dramatization of response is implicitly and explicitly value laden. So, for a most explicit example, Dioscurides dramatizes a passerby's encounter with the tomb of Sophocles so that the grave's guardian statue can assert that the two best plays of Sophocles are the *Electra* and the *Antigone*.[20] At a more general and implicit level, the mass of epigrams—a major though scarcely discussed part of Hellenistic cultural activity; enough survive to fill six volumes of Loeb—create and police the position of the Hellenistic viewer by promoting and projecting a way of viewing the monuments, literature, and art of the past—a view for which the very form of the epigram with its evident commitment to the discrete, pointed, and surprising image is fundamental.

What I wish to emphasize in this section, however, is a more specific intellectual background that has largely been overshadowed by the pull of Plato and his analysis of mimesis. For the way that Hellenistic epigrams seek by force of poetic *sophia* to reveal and articulate the concealed significance of the objects of their gaze is also linked to a changing philosophy and physiology of vision. This chapter is not the place for an exposition of the place of philosophical and rhetorical training in Hellenistic society (made familiar to many by Foucault's history of sexuality) or for a general account of the different Hellenistic philosophy schools. But I do want to draw attention to one broad area of thought that provides a fundamental frame for what I have been calling the "viewing of the *sophos*," and that is the set of ideas invoked by the word *phantasia*. In later Greek writing it means "imagination" and is so used in art history. But in Stoic and Epicurean writing of this period, it means "impression" or "presentation." It is a key term in articulating the relations between sense perception, cognition, and understanding and the possible criteria for judging the accuracy and authority of perceptions and knowledge.[21] In Stoic epistemology, "to see something …is to have a certain kind of thought generated in a certain way";[22] to think or speak presupposes *phantasia*, that is, a person's "mind must be affected by something, have something presented to it. *Phantasia* is this affection, 'something which reveals itself and its cause.'"[23] Thus, much later, Longinus writes (15.1) that the term "*phantasia* is used generally for anything which in any way suggests a thought productive of speech." Longinus goes on to point out that in rhetorical and aesthetic theory the term further specifies that state of emotion or enthusiasm by virtue of which a speaker can *see* and make his audience *see* what he is talking about—thus assimilating *phantasia* closely to what is called *energeia* in rhetorical theory since Aristotle. The Stoic and Academic positions contest the degree to which "clear impressions represent all the relevant features of an object,"[24] the degree to which "certain cognition of things" is possible for the *sophos*, and the conditions of possibility of "true impressions." The debates in this area are notoriously complicated—Sextus Empiricus (7.241) was the first of many scholars to declare that "*phantasia* in Stoic theory is hard to expound." There are two brief observations I want to make here, however, that are relevant to my main argument.

The first is that both the Stoic evaluation of the viewer's intellectual comprehension of the objects of vision and the Stoic association of truth and *phantasia* marked a significant distance from Aristotelian and Platonic theories of mimesis (a move that must be seen as fundamental to the Western ideas of representation[25]). The developing culture of Hellenistic viewing was contemporaneous with a major shift in the discussion of the epistemological status of viewing. It was a discussion that had extensive reverberations. For example, although Epicurean ideas of *phantasia* were perhaps less richly developed (and indeed the Stoic concept became dominant), Philodemus, a major figure of Epicurean aesthetics, reported a fascinating debate focused on the perception of music that went back to Speusippus and even earlier,[26] on the differences between what he calls *aisthêsis epistêmonikê*, and *aisthêsis autophnês*, which can be glossed "sense perception endowed with cognitive capacity," and "natural, simple perception". *Aisthêsis autophnês*, "natural perception," is in humans inasmuch as they are alive and are in contact with a physical external world; *aisthêsis epistêmonikê*, "sense perception endowed with cognitive capacity," implies, however, a perception already endowed with *logos*, reason, a "scientific" or "interpretive" perception. This debate has broad implications for understanding the whole range of sense impressions and aesthetic experience,[27] including sight. If Plato constantly worked to separate the faculty of vision from true knowledge, Hellenistic philosophy reestablished a necessary link between sight and true knowledge.

Secondly, the deployment of *phantasia* in these debates was used to theorize the comprehension of the physical and the ethical world (as the gap between perception and understanding is differently constructed and contested). At stake in these contestations of the viewing of the world were secure knowledge, secure ethics, and the role and authority of the *sophos*—his viewing—in the interpretation of the world. In other words, the integral part *phantasia* played in Hellenistic philosophy betokened a debate that worked to create, explore, and legislate the viewing subject—as, in its different way, did ekphrastic poetry.

Phantasiai, "presentations," then, "are wholly involved in the soul's desire to see, to believe, to interpret";[28] nowhere more clearly than in the impressions of *eros*, the desiring soul. So the language of viewing and desiring is redefined within this new sense of vision. Here is Meleager:

> One single, total object of beauty I know; only one thing my greedy

> Eye knows, to see Musikos: I am blind to the rest.
> Everything makes a presentation of him in me. Do my eyes see
>   To gratify my soul, the flatterers?

The blindness of the lover to all but his loved one—a well-known idea, of course—is imaged as a constant and exclusive *impression* or *presentation* (*phantasia*). As *phantasia* is used in philosophical discussion to connect the physics of vision and the process of conceptualization, so here the poet via the language of *phantasia* questions whether his eyes merely see or are already part of an erotic economy of persuasion, pleasure, and doubt. Do they flatter to gratify (*charis*) his soul? Do his eyes seduce his mind, like a lover? The question the poem poses is the relation between desire and the viewing subject—a question of the lover's control over vision. This question may occupy a similar locus to the dialogue of Xenophon I discussed earlier, but its formulation redefines the lover's gaze within the terms of the Hellenistic *sophos* and his philosophically trained understanding of perception.

Such an argument is not at all designed to suggest that the epigrams I have mentioned are the product of a close engagement specifically or solely with Stoic—or Epicurean—philosophy, nor, of course, that severally or collectively they are to be seen as making an incisive, committed, or systematic contribution to a philosophical debate. Rather, there is a weaker—but crucial—connection, that of a shared educational and intellectual background between different writers: I am suggesting that these epigrams are to be appreciated as the products of *sophoi* in the context of contemporary *sophia*. Consequently, to discuss *ekphrasis* without a recognition of the importance of *phantasia* to contemporary thought, without, that is, a recognition of the implicit siting of such ekphrases within theories of language and representation, will necessarily impoverish our understanding of the cultural context of their production. These epigrams are, in short, a constitutive factor in the production of a Hellenistic *discourse of viewing*. As Baxandall writes, seeing is a theory-laden activity.[29] The philosophy of vision, the poetry responding to art, and the cultural frame in which art and poetry are perceived together mark a changing *discourse of viewing* in the Hellenistic period.

THE DESIRING EYE

My third, and most briefly treated, moment is the so-called Second Sophistic, a highly influential renaissance of Greek intellectual life, particularly in the East, as Christianity was beginning to dominate the Roman empire. It was the period in which Philostratus, Callistratus, and Lucian each wrote works called *Imagines*; Pausanias composed his *Travels Around Greece*; Longus's *Daphnis and Chloe* and Achilles Tatius's *Leukippe and Cleitophon*, two of the greatest of ancient novels, each began with extensive descriptions of works of art (and, in the case of Achilles Tatius, went on to include other set-piece descriptions, including the first Western analysis of a diptych of paintings as a significant pairing); Heliodorus's great novel, the *Aethiopika*, was similarly replete with the practice of viewing, represented through the lens of technical art history and the traditions of writing about art. It is not by chance that this period has provided the material for much of contemporary writing about art in the ancient world.[30] Equally, it was not by chance that there is in contemporary analysis little sense of this period's ekphrastic writing as being in dialogue not merely with the past of the philosophical tradition and Hellenistic culture but also with other genres of composition.[31]

Rather than turn once more to the viewing of the *sophos*—Lucian or Philostratus—I will merely introduce here two passages from the novels that have scarcely entered the art-historical canon. Both are about the physiology of the eye, and both demonstrate the spread and manipulation of ideas about vision beyond the strictly "art-historical" writings of Philostratus or, say, the optics of Ptolemy. Once again, my aim is to underline the range of questions that bear on the issue of a discourse of viewing.

In Heliodorus's *Aethiopika*, the heroine, Charicleia, has seen the hero and has fallen in love, which, as is only proper for a proper young woman, takes the form of an undiagnosed physical sickness. Calasiris, the prime mover of the plot,[32] suggests to her father that she may be the victim of the "evil eye." For, he explains, we are surrounded by air, and when a man looks on beauty maliciously, the foulness he exudes into the air with his breath can infect his neighbor. "Conclusive proof of my point," he continues, "is furnished by the genesis of love, which originates from visually perceived objects, which, if you will excuse the metaphor, shoot arrows of passion, swifter than the wind, into the soul by way of the eyes. This is perfectly logical, because of all our channels of perception, sight is the least static and contains the most heat, and so is the most receptive of such emanations; for the spirit which animates it is akin to fire, and so it is well suited to absorb the transient and unstable impressions of love" (3.7). Now, Plutarch in his *Tabletalk* (680cff) has a remarkably similar explanation of the evil eye, which may imply that the two writers have a common source or that Heliodorus is citing Plutarch, or both. But most importantly the layers of quotation, together with the technical vocabulary of materialist optics as well as the standard metaphorical language of desire (explicitly—and with disingenuous coyness—marked as metaphorical by the speaker), signal this passage as a rhetorical tour de force—and one whose design is evident. For Calasiris is here misleading the girl's father prior to aiding her elopement. The quotation—blinding the father with science—plays with the ideas of clear sight and malice as it is uttered to be misinterpreted. As the girl falls in love at first sight, the desiring eye is given a physiological account that on the one hand grounds the language of viewing, art history, and tourism through which the hero's and heroine's trip 'round the Mediterranean is expressed and on the other plays a role in the narrative of the novel as a lure, a distraction of the father's attention in order to aid the plot of the lovers' elopement. So, when the narrator turns to describe a jewel carved with the figure of a shepherd and his sheep on a rock and writes, "The rock was a real rock, no illusion (*mimêma*), for the artist had left one corner of the stone unworked to produce the effect he wanted: he could see no point in wasting the subtlety of his art to represent a stone on a stone" (5.13), this playing with the categories of mimesis and verisimilitude, culture and nature, has been prepared for by the development of the technical language of perception theory that preceded it. In Heliodorus, seeing is not merely theory-laden but laden with the history of theory, as the narrative's scenes of viewing, and commentary on viewing, and manipulation of the language of viewing interrelate.

A similar but more lascivious strategy is evident in the work of Achilles Tatius, an author whose text is a most wonderful bricolage of strange sights, high theory, and lovers' melting glances. Cleinias, cousin and confidante of the hero who has fallen in love, counsels the hero that the opportunity to look upon his love is greatly to be prized: "This pleasure is greater than consummation. For the eyes receive each other's reflections and they form therefrom small images (*eidola*) as in mirrors. Such outpourings of beauty flowing down through them into the soul is a kind of copulation at a distance. This is not far removed from the intercourse of bodies—it is in fact a novel form of intimate embrace...." (2.9). If theory proposes a materialist model of vision, Achilles Tatius, with typically sly wit and brilliant manipulation of the possiblities of the technical language of vision and desire, rewrites the penetrating and longing gaze as a form of copulation—if not quite intercourse, at the very least an intimate embrace. (For Achilles Tatius, narrative is a space for playing with the gaps between theorizing and experience.) As Theodote in Xenophon's *Memorabilia* is led to feel gratitude for being looked at (and eventually to desire her observer), so Achilles Tatius's Cleinias reverses the logic of the gaze and eroticizes it in a quite different (though not unrelated) way. The theorized story of the eye is here part of erotic discourse. In Achilles Tatius's novel, which juxtaposes theatrical spectacles of false executions, art-historical expositions of how to read pictures, tourist accounts of the city of Alexandria, and paradoxographical accounts of the wildlife of Egypt, this anatomy of the desiring eye is one threat in a wildly kaleidoscopic and baroque narrative of the range of interactions between the knowing eye and the variety of the world. As much as Philostratus's professional account of a trip 'round the art gallery, the narrative of Achilles Tatius, which traces the sights of the Mediterranean, produces a very particular image of the viewing subject.

Differentiating within the "Classical Tradition," then, extending the range of writing on viewing (art) beyond a few well-known texts on painting, and widening the scope of inquiry beyond the "rules" of a rhetorical tradition are all necessary strategies if the history of writing about viewing (art) is to develop in a properly nuanced way and if the discourse of viewing is to find its place within a history of the construction of a viewing subject.

Heliodorus and Achilles Tatius were—somewhat bizarrely from this distance—both claimed as bishops by the successful Christian church, and their works continued to be read.[33] The culture of viewing continues to develop and change, however, and I shall end merely by quoting the Christian homiletic writer who enjoins a virgin even when washing "never to observe her own body." From Achilles exhorting the world to "Look at me!" via the different articulations of the viewing subject and the object of the gaze, finally we can close with the patriarch exhorting the female not to look even at herself—and the beginnings of Christianity's long involvement with the normative relations between vision and the subject.

1 On the conceptualization of Homeric bodies, see, e.g., J.-P. Vernant, "Mortals and Immortals: The Body of the Divine"; "A 'Beautiful Death' and the Disfigured Corpse in Homeric Epic," both conveniently translated in Froma Zeitlin, ed., *Mortals and Immortals* (Princeton, 1991).

2 Norman Bryson, *Vision and Painting—The Logic of the Gaze* (New Haven and London, 1983); *Looking at the Overlooked* (London, 1990); John Hollander, "The Poetics of Ekphrasis," *World and Image* 4; 1 (1988). See also J. Hillis Miller, *Illustration* (London, 1992); W. J. T. Mitchell, *Iconology: Image, Text, Ideology* (Chicago, 1986).

3 Stephen Bann, *The True Vine: On Visual Representation and the Western Tradition* (Cambridge, 1989), p. 32.

4 Interestingly discussed by Gérard Simon, *Le regard, l'être et l'apparence dans l'optique de l'antiquité* (Paris, 1988).

5 The standard modern account remains Jean Hagstrum, *The Sister Arts: The Tradition of Literary Pictorialism and English Poetry from Dryden to Gray* (Chicago, 1958); but see also R. Lee, *Ut Pictura Poiesis: The Humanistic Theory of Painting* (New York, 1967); Mario Praz, *Mnemosyne: The Parallel Between Literature and the Visual Arts* (Washington, 1970); H. Buch, *Ut Pictura Poiesis: Die Beschreibungsliteratur und ihre Kritiker von Lessing bis Lukács* (Munich, 1972); the articles of Hamon and Beaujour in *Yale French Studies* 61 (1981), dedicated to the topic of description; and *Word and Image* 2, 1 (1986) and 4, 1 (1988), both on *ekphrasis*.

6 For Cleisthenes' reforms, see W. G. Forrest, *The Emergence of Greek Democracy* (London, 1978); and P. Vidal-Naquet and P. Lévêque, *Clisthène, l' Athénien* (Paris, 1964).

7 See Robin Osborne, *Figures in a Classical Landscape* (London, 1987); François de Polignac, *La Naissance de la cité grecque* (Paris, 1984).

8 For a description and analysis of these rituals, see Simon Goldhill, "The Great Dionysia and Civic Ideology," in J. Winkler and F. Zeitlin, eds., *Nothing to Do with Dionysus?* (Princeton, 1990).

9 See Robin Osborne, "The Viewing and Obscuring of the Parthenon Frieze," *Journal of Hellenic Studies* 107 (1986): 98-105.

10 For a recent attempt to read the Stoa Poikile, see David Castriota, *Myth, Ethos and Actuality: Official Art in Fifth-Century Athens* (Madison, Wis., 1992).

11 Simon, *Le regard*, p. 187.

12 See, for convenient discussion and bibliography, Simon Goldhill, *Rading Greek Tragedy* (Cambridge, 1986), pp. 199–221.

13 For a fine recent analysis of this process, see Froma Zeitlin, "The Artful Eye: Vision, Ecphrasis and Spectacle in Euripidean Theater," in Simon Goldhill and Robin Osborne, eds., *Art and Text in Ancient Greek Culture* (Cambridge, 1993).

14 Agnes Rouveret, *Histoire et imaginaire de la peinture ancienne* (Paris, 1989), p. 18.

15 For a full account of this passage, see my article, "The Reciprocity of the Gaze: Seducing Socrates' Girlfriends," in Paul Cartledge, Paul Millett, and Sita von Reden, eds., *Kosmos: Order, Individual and Community in Classical Athens* (Cambridge, forthcoming).

16 The following section is based on my article, "The Naive and Knowing Eye: Ecphrasis and the Culture of Viewing in Hellenistic Alexandria," in Goldhill and Osborne, eds., *Art and Text in Ancient Greek Culture*.

17 The poems are to be found in the *Anthologia Palatina* 9.713–744; 793–798. Grow and Page, the standard editors of the poems, typically call it a long and tedious series" and along with art historians do not ask the basic question of *why* there are so many poems on this subject in this form.

18 *Anthologia Palatina* 9.748; 9.752.

19 *Anthologia Palatina* 7.427, discussed fully in Goldhill, "The Naive and Knowing Eye."

20 *Anthologia Palatina* 7.37.

21 The relevant texts can be found in A. Long and D. Sedley, *The Hellenistic Philosophers*, 2 vols. (Cambridge, 1987), index *sub phantasia*. I have particularly learned from A. Long, "Language and Thought in Stoicism," in A. Long, ed., *Problems in Stoicism* (London, 1971); H. Sandbach, "*Phantasia Kataleptike*," in *Problems in Stoicism* (London, 1971); M. Burnyeat, "Can the Sceptic Live His Scepticism," in M. Burnyeat, ed., *The Skeptical Tradition* (Berkeley, 1983); G. Watson, *Phantasia in Classical Thought* (Galway, 1988); and in particular M. Frede, "Stoics and Skeptics on Clear and Distinct Impressions," in *The Skeptical Tradition*. G. M. Rispoli, *L'artiste sapiente: Per una storia della fantasia* (Naples, 1985) has the most useful historical overview of *phantasia* with regard to artistic concerns. Claude Imbert, "Stoic

Logic and Alexandrian Poetics," in M. Schofield, M. Burnyeat, and J. Barnes, eds., *Doubt and Dogmatism: Studies in Hellenistic Epistemology* (Oxford, 1980) is important as the first full-length article that attempts to bring together philosophy and literature for this period; it is unfortunately quite unreliable in detail and unconvincing in conclusion.

22 Frede, ibid., p. 67.

23 Long, "Language and Thought in Stoicism," p. 82. The quotation within the quotation is Aetivus iv 12.1, also discussed by Sandbach, *"Phantasia Kataleptike,"* pp. 10–11.

24 Frede, "Stoics and Skeptics," p. 72.

25 Imbert, "Stoic Logic," p. 183, notes "how un-Platonic [Stoic] aesthetic theory is"; see also J.-P. Vernant, "The Birth of Images," in Zeitlin, ed., *Mortals and Immortals*; Rouveret, *Histoire et imaginaire*; *phantasia* in Plato and Aristotle is discussed well by Watson, *Phantasia in Classical Thought*; M. Schofield, "Aristotle on the Imagination," in G. E. R. Lloyd and G. Owen, eds., *Aristotle on Mind and the Senses* (Cambridge, 1978); M. Nussbaum, *Aristotle's* De Motu Animalium (Princeton, 1978), pp. 221–269; and most recently A. Silverman, "Plato on Phantasia," *Classical Antiquity* 10 (1991): 123–147.

26 The most important source is Sextus Empiricus, *Adv. Math.* VII, 145–146, on which see M. Parente, "Speusippo in Sesto Empirico, *Adv. Math.* VII, 145–146," *Parola del Passato* 24 (1969): 203–214. See G. M. Rispoli, "La 'sensazione scientifica,'" *Cronache Ercolanesi* 13 (1983): 91–101 for a good discussion of the relevant fragments of Philodemus's *On Music* and their relation to philosophical traditions.

27 Well brought out by Rispoli, ibid., and Parente, ibid.

28 Imbert, "Stoic Logic," p. 215.

29 Baxandall (1985) 107 on the culture of Piero della Francesca: "Seeing was 'theory-laden.'"

30 On Philostratus, see Norman Bryson, "Philostratus and the Imaginary Museum," in Goldhill and Osborne, eds., *Art and Text in Ancient Greek Culture*; Bryson, *Looking at the Overlooked*, pp. 17-59; Bann, *The True Vine*, pp. 27-40; on Pausanias, see J. A. S. Elsner "From the Pyramids to Pausanias and Piglet: Monuments, Travel and Writing," in *Art and Text in Ancient Greek Culture*; on Achilles Tatius and Heliodorus, see Shadi Bartsch, *Decoding the Ancient Novel: The Reader and the Role of Description in Heliodorus and Achilles Tatius* (Princeton, 1989); and

Simon Goldhill, *Foucault's Virginity: The History of Sexuality and Ancient Erotic Fiction* (Cambridge, 1994); on Longus, see Froma Zeitlin, "The Poetics of *Eros*: Nature, Art and Imitation in Longus' *Daphnis and Chloe*," in David Halperin, John Winkler and Froma Zeitlin eds., *Before Sexuality* (Princeton, 1989).

31 A notable exception to this is Zeitlin, ibid.

32 See John Winkler, "The Mendacity of Calasiris and the Narrative Strategy of Heliodorus' *Aithiopika*," *Yale Classical Studies* 27 (1982): 93-158.

33 The evidence for this is usefully collected by Ebbe Vilborg, *Achilles Tatius: Leucippe and Cleitophon* (Stockholm, 1955), pp. 163-169.

3 **Sight and Vision in Medieval Christian Thought**

Janet Soskice

In the Tertia Pars of the *Summa Theologiae*, Thomas Aquinas addresses the question, "Should the angel of the announcement have appeared bodily to the Virgin?" Aquinas takes it *as read* that Mary, as reported in the account of the Annunciation in Luke's gospel, actually and physically saw the angel. Indeed, this seeing is what creates the theological problem. "It would seem not," he continues, for "Augustine notes that *intellectual vision is better than physical vision* and this is especially true in the case of the apparition of the angel.... Thus if it was right to have the divine conception announced by the best kind of messenger, it should follow that he present himself in the best kind of vision. So then the angel of the Annunciation should have appeared to the Virgin in an intellectual vision."

Aquinas knows and accepts, as a commonplace for medieval theology, the Augustinian teaching that physical (or corporeal) visions come a poor third after spiritual and intellectual visions. Aquinas knows the best class of vision should not be corporeal and confronts what he takes to be Luke's clear testimony that, in what is one of the most important of Christian miracles, Mary actually saw the angel of the Annunciation. His resolution is that "the angel appeared bodily to the blessed Virgin. This fitted in first with the message itself, since he came to tell of the incarnation of the invisible God. It was appropriate then that an invisible being assume a visible form."[1]

This excerpt displays a central ambivalence in Christian attitudes toward vision from the patristic through the medieval periods and beyond. The medievals received from Platonism, and later Aristotelianism, philosophical systems that privileged vision above the other senses. But this primacy of vision was qualified, particularly in matters epistemological, by at least two important reservations. The first was the accepted inadequacy of all the senses, including vision, to obtain the most important kind of knowledge, viz, knowledge of God; and the second is the importance accorded to "the Word." These reservations were shared by Judaism and Islam. A twist peculiar to Christianity, but important for aesthetic theology and philosophy during this period, was the centrality of the doctrine of the Incarnation. This doctrine asserts that God became incarnate as a man—not as the mere appearance of a man, as some gnostics held, but as a real man born of a woman, dying on a cross, touchable, audible, and, notably for our purposes, visible. The belief that God had assumed a human nature meant that the physicality of the body, including the senses, could not be despised.[2] The Incarnation was seen by Christian theologians as further affirmation of the created order described in the first books of Genesis as "good." God Incarnate in Christ, they believed, could really be seen with the eye while nonetheless remaining a mystery. This set of theological convictions lies behind early apologia for the icons, the intellectual and visual ancestors of Western representational painting, which had the temerity to present an image of the invisible God.

The doctrine of the Incarnation also informs the remarks of Aquinas with which I began. Despite Augustine's cautions about the deceptiveness of sight, Aquinas argues that especially in the case of the Annunciation, it was appropriate that Mary actually corporeally *saw* the angelic messenger because the angel brought the message that God was to become flesh and as flesh visible. (The Dominican translator adds a personal comment: "A rather striking example of Mr. Marshall McLuhan's favorite thesis on communication, the medium is the message."[3]) With his usual concision Aquinas tosses a stick of dynamite beneath both an extreme apophantism that would deny we can say anything positive of God and gnosticisms ancient and modern that would deny the importance of the physical body. But his remarks are at the same time totally consonant with the theological and mystical tradition that he inherited: the belief that God became flesh means that the physical senses no less than the physical world may not be despised.

The New Testament texts themselves (and indeed those of the intertestamental writings) were significantly influenced by Platonism. This influence is most apparent in the Johannine writings, which make boldest use of the synaesthetic image "visible Word": The Word became flesh and dwelt among us, full of grace and truth; and we beheld his glory, glory as of the only Son from the Father" (John 1.14). And: "That which was from the beginning, which we have heard, which we have seen with our eyes, which we have looked upon and touched with our hands, concerning the word of life—the life was made manifest and we saw it" (John 1.1-2).

A certain privileging of vision clearly suited Christianity's gospel of incarnation, but the tendency was not exclusive to Christian writings of this time. Philo of Alexandria, a Hellenized Jew writing in the first century c.e., accords what seems in Jewish terms a bizarre priority to sight and vision in matters to do with the knowledge of God. As David Chidester has pointed out, Philo's commitment to the superiority of sight was reflected throughout his work. Particularly in his extended analysis of creation, the *De opificio mundi*, he was preoccupied with the visual mode, explaining the entire process of creation in terms of visual correspondence: God fashioned the visible world in direct correspondence to an intelligible pattern. Philo compared the creator to an architect, "keeping his eye upon his pattern and making the visible or tangible objects correspond in each case to the incorporeal ideas."[4] In order to put vision foremost, in his *De decalogo* Philo insists that the law of God was given to Moses in a theophany whereby those present "seemed to see rather than to hear them."[5] This preference for vision fits oddly, of course, with the Jewish texts Philo expounded, with their privileging of the Word and horror of idolatry. One of Philo's more curious exegetical strategies was to suggest that the idolatry of the golden calf had to do not with a visual idol but with hearing, since the calf supposedly was made of earrings. Philo's purpose was to show how the religion of the Jews was fully consonant with, and even anticipated, the wisdom of Plato and the Greek philosophers. He was a somewhat idiosyncratic figure whose work was to have more influence on Christianity than on Judaism.

Within Christianity the importance accorded to sight among the senses during this period, such as it was, cannot be attributed to the influence of Platonism alone. As has already been suggested, beliefs intrinsic to the new religion had a bearing. For instance, despite a constant predilection, Christianity in this period was not in its orthodox variants "dualistic," nor was the human body despised. Indeed, Trinitarian orthodoxy was hammered out in the early centuries in the face of gnostic preferences for a fully "spiritual" religion that did despise the concept of embodiment. The gnostics known to Plotinus did "hate the nature of the body" and "censure the soul for its association with the body."[6] This position, though tempting during the early days of monastic asceticism, was untenable within Christian orthodoxy precisely because of the doctrine of the Incarnation (if God took a human body, the body cannot be all bad) and Christian belief in the resurrection of the body (*not* the immortality of the soul, with which such resurrection is frequently confused).[7] Augustine argued that far from being a trap for the spirit as the Manichees with whom he once kept company believed, the body is God's good creation and the means by which we come to know God. Following the lead provided in Genesis, the theologians argued that the creation was divinely ordered and totally good. Sin and evil were deprivations and not positive forces in themselves.

The fine line patristic theologians had to follow is demonstrated by Athanasius's fourth-century text, the *Contra Gentes*, a polemical work attacking idolatry that indirectly tells us a good deal about early attitudes toward vision and visibility. Idol worshipers are deluded, Athanasius argues, and not just those crude idol worshipers who honor bits of rock and animals and things made by human hands but also the most sophisticated "idolaters" who worship the cosmos. Their mistake is to give the honor due to the creator to the creatures. One can see how easy it would be for Athanasius at any stage in his argument to fall into disparagement of the creation. He avoids this by insisting that the whole of creation was created by and through the Word of God, who is one with the Father. This statement serves at the same time as an apologia to the Jews, who might well say that Christians themselves are the greatest idolaters since they worship a man. Athanasius's reply, which makes him a key figure in the development of Trinitarian orthodoxy, is that the Word through which all things were made is no creature but one with the Father. The human race was made in God's own image, through his Word, and thus human beings were their vision not clouded by sin, should see the glory of the creator in the creation. Instead, "misusing the individual faculties of the body, delighting in the contemplation of the body and regarding pleasure as a thing good in itself," they become blind to their true being in God, and their pleasures and senses are distorted. At some point, human beings began to do everything in reverse: "So they put their hands to the opposite use and worked murder, they turned their ears to disobedience and their other members to adultery instead of legitimate procreation..." Tongues, hands, sense of smell, and stomachs, he adds, also err in similar ways. It is "as if a charioteer, mounting in the stadium, were to disregard the goal to which he was supposed to drive and, turning away from it, were simply to drive his horses as hard as he could."[8]

In so doing, people cease to be rational and to differ from the irrational animals who see but without understanding. Human beings, however, judge with their reason what they see with their eyes: "The eye can only see, the ears hear, the mouth taste, the nose smell, and the hands feel; but what is to be seen or heard, and what one must touch or taste or smell, is no longer for the senses but for the soul and its intellect to determine.... Certainly the hand can grasp a sword and the mouth taste poison, but it does not know that they are harmful unless the mind determines so."[9] In short, the senses are the means by which we know the world, but they can be disordered. In Athanasius's favorite and notably auditory image, the senses are like the strings of a well-tuned lyre, and the musician (an understanding mind) plays upon them.

It is within such a context that Augustine's influential demotion of corporeal vision, as invoked in my opening quotation from Aquinas, can be understood. In the *De Genesi ad Litteram* Augustine explains his low regard for corporeal visions by a mixture of common sense, philosophy of perception, and biblical citation. Corporeal vision is worth little without some understanding of what is seen: "And so Joseph, who understood the meaning of the seven ears of corn and the seven kine, was more a prophet than Pharaoh, who saw them in a dream; for Pharaoh saw only a form impressed upon his spirit, whereas Joseph understood through a light given to his mind."[10]

Intellectual vision trumps dreams and corporeal ones. Balthasar, the king, saw the figures of the handwriting on the wall and retained an image of it after its disappearance (this is to behold "spiritually" in Augustine's sense). But it was left to the prophet Daniel to discern the *meaning* of this vision by means of intellect. "These and other similar facts make it abundantly clear," says Augustine, "that corporeal vision is ordered to the spiritual, and the spiritual to the intellectual."[11] Corporeal visions are less reliable not least because they may be deceptive—the result of illness, or tricks of the Devil, or the result of pain, or simple illusion as "when an oar in the water appears to be broken." Before we accuse Augustine of antiocularism we must note that he continues, "The same may be said when the soul takes one object for another that has a similar colour, sound, odour, taste, or touch.[12] All the senses can be deceived, and yet they all may guide us truly and must be trusted, "for the mind employs the senses through the agency of the body, and anyone who supposes that they can never be trusted is woefully mistaken."[13] For Augustine as for Athanasius, vision, like all the senses, must be ordered and well used if it is to disclose the beauty of creation and its truth.

It is now known that Judaism in the first centuries c.e. was not as aniconic as is frequently supposed. Excavations at Dura-Europas discovered synagogue murals from about 230 c.e. that mark the Jewish liturgy in a narrative sequence: Moses and the burning bush, Moses on Mount Sinai, Joshua and Jericho, the visions of Ezekiel. The Jewish rejection of images was rejection *not* of any representation at all but specifically of any representation of God. A Christian house church of the same period and at the same site shows the Good Shepherd and sheep, Adam and Eve, the healing of the paralytic, the woman at the well—images we suppose significant in liturgical practice.[14] These *historiae* were not simply illustrations of biblical stories but unified visual accounts of the Christian reading of Old Testament "signs." Like most early Christian art, they had to be read with an understanding mindful of received biblical typologies.

Aidan Nichols contrasts this early Christian "theology in images," which may have some continuity with Jewish practice, to the full-scale "theology of images" that arises later and is more a more distinctly Christian phenomenon. This latter has its foundation in the high patristic writings on Christ, the image of the invisible God. In the face of gnostic deprecations of the material world, theologians like Irenaeus stressed the Visible Word. The Word is not a divine instrument nor a celestial messenger but truly God and, as Word incarnate, God who is seen.[15] The invisible God could not be pictured, but the "invisible God made visible in Christ must be imaged, for God in the Incarnation had taken human form, had come to humanity through human agency."[16] The iconoclast controversy circled around such arguments.

In 725 c.e. the iconophile bishop of Byzantium, St. Germanus, could write, "We feel ourselves urged on to represent what our faith really is, to show that he (the only Son) is not united to our nature in appearance only, in some shadowy way…but has become man in reality and in truth…. For this reason…we represent the character of his holy flesh in the icons, and we venerate and revere them with due honour since they lead us to remember that lifegiving incarnation of his, before which all language must fall." Also in the eighth century, St. John of Damascus wrote, "I boldly draw an image of the invisible God, not as invisible, but as having become visible for our sakes by partaking of flesh and blood."[17]

At least in his defense of icons, St. John of Damascus is an unrepentant (and triumphalist) privileger of vision: "The ancient Israel did not see God, but we (the Christian Church as the new Israel) behold the glory of the Lord by means of the face that has been revealed to us. And through the use of our bodily senses…we perceive his express image…everywhere. Through it we sanctify the primary (sense)—for the primary one among the senses is the sense of sight—just as by means of the words (of God) we sanctify hearing."

It can readily be seen that for the iconophile theologians and for the tradition of veneration of icons that followed them, the icons are not illustrations of the Bible but themselves holy objects. They are emblems of the Incarnation insofar as they re-present the mystery of the invisible God made visible for the sake of humankind, partaking of flesh and blood. The icon is in its own way a transformation, remaining wood and paint yet being image and saint at the same time. The physicality of the surface—the wood, the pigments—is an emblem of the physicality of the God whose veneration the icons serve. Aesthetics are informed by theological conviction. The icon is furthermore not passive to the gaze. If anything, and explicitly with the icons of the Virgin and Child, it is the worshiper who is looked upon. In the early icons no attempt is made at naturalism—frequently the Virgin stands in a field of gold, the supernatural color, and faces us in a posture of prayer. Far from being subject to our gaze, the female figure of Mary commands regard from the worshiper for the Christ Child who appears on her lap or in a circle on her chest.

It is not surprising that the Annunciation should have become such a favorite with early Western painters (and before them the painters of icons). Nor did this trend occur because everyone likes a mother with a baby. The story of the Annunciation in Luke's gospel is the manifesto for religious art—a visible God in a certain sense demands to be represented visually. Eastern icons spreading along trade routes in the centuries after the iconoclast controversy made an early impact on Western art, with the Virgin and Child as a favored subject. These paintings show their theological character clearly. In Simone Martini's *Annunciation* (circa 1333), now in the Uffizi, the words themselves flow in golden letters from the angel's mouth to Mary's ear. This representation is not be taken simply as a visual aid for the uneducated (who would not in any case benefit unless they could read and indeed read Latin since this is the language the angel speaks). Rather, it is a deliberate and painterly representation of a religious belief—the Word becomes flesh. Here we can truly see the fleshed-out words as they proceed across a shining golden space.[18]

But it is the Madonnas and Childs of the Quattrocento that remain exemplary of their theme—the Bellinis, Fra Angelicos, and Botticellis. In the dignity and humanity of these very real mothers and children we breathe the air of the Renaissance. Despite the elaborate surrounds, we think, these are real mothers dandling real babies. It is of painterly theological importance that we see them so, yet we misunderstand them if we do not also read them as standing in a tradition of theological representation that goes back to the icons. Bellini's Madonnas, despite the more naturalistic approach, gaze from the paintings in the same contemplative manner as many before.[19] As with the icons, the Renaissance Madonnas stand in idealized surroundings, now not so much otherwordly as "this world perfected," the ideal calm of the new creation. We can still feel the universal theophanic harmony of medieval aesthetic theory, beauty as "a pure intelligible reality, as moral harmony and metaphysical splendor,"[20] but perhaps only with difficulty, for we have (mostly) lost the religious and metaphysical convictions that those who first saw these paintings had. Indeed, our experience of the paintings comes not from dimly lit churches and their place in liturgy but from books of reproductions and art galleries where we may see whole rooms full of Madonnas and Childs—more like refugee camps for women and babies than the original context of veneration in which they were painted. To us and our "idolatrous" gaze these are more like figures on a screen than personages who command our attention.

It is not possible with a topic of such importance to human life as vision to do give a "boo-and-hurrah" account of the period and sources upon which this chapter touches. As Martin Jay shows in the early chapters of *Downcast Eyes*, we can find almost every attitude toward sight and vision at almost any time. Selective and partial citation can support almost any possible attitude.

Although we read that the Christian tradition is "antiocularist" or more generally antisensual, the position is hard to defend against the splendors of medieval cathedrals, polyphonic music, or early Renaissance painting. European theologians of this time for the most part followed a patristic lead in believing that just as all the senses may be deceived, so may they all bring us into the presence of God if rightly ordered. Vision, even if privileged, must admit its inability to comprehend that which is most worth knowing and "seeing": the glory of God. The body and the senses are not to be despised: yet they must be well ordered and even so can give only a fragmentary and pale guide to the glories that are to be known in the resurrected body. Much of the apparent denigration of the senses, including vision, in devotional writings of this period are rhetorical invocations of the "greater" sensual powers that were held to be in store for the resurrected body. Hence the predilection in so much devotional writing for synaesthetic images that both invoked the power of the senses and described their limitations, at least for the purposes of knowing God. Augustine, though cautious in his approval of physical sensuality, is a well-rounded sensualist in his spiritual imagery:

> But when I love you, what do I love? It is not physical beauty nor temporal glory nor the brightness of light dear to earthly eyes, nor the sweet ointments and perfumes, nor manna or honey, nor limbs welcoming the embrace of the flesh; it is not these I love when I love my God. Yet there is a light I love, and a food, and a kind of embrace when I love my God—a light, voice, odour, food, embrace of my inner man, where my soul is floodlit by light which space cannot contain, where there is sound that time cannot seize, where there is a perfume no breeze disperses, where there is a taste for food no amount of eating can lessen, and where there is a bond of union no satiety can part. That is what I love when I love my God.[21]

Is this passage a disparagement of the senses or not? Its rhetorical power rests on the evocation of the senses, and any reader of Augustine's *Confessions* will be well aware of how much Augustine has known the sway of beautiful words and sounds and the love of women. It is by knowing the power of these things that we can sense what Augustine wants to say about the love of God. In a passage that is very nearly a summary of the *Confessions* Augustine says,

> Late have I loved you, beauty so old and so new. And see, you were within and I was in the external world and sought you there, and in my unlovely state I plunged into those lovely created things which you made. You were with me, and I was not with you. The lovely things kept me far from you, though if they did not have their existence in you, they had no existence at all. You called and cried out loud and shattered my deafness. You were radiant and resplendent, you put to flight my blindness. You were fragrant, and I drew in my breath and now pant after you. I tasted you, and I feel but hunger and thirst for you. You touched me, and I am set on fire to attain the peace which is yours.[22]

This synaesthetic imagery might be read as a denigration of the senses, but it might also be read as one of the most powerful prose invocations of the powers of the senses in Christian Latin literature. This sensual style is very apparent in medieval devotional texts and notably in those, when we begin to get them, written by women.

Although it is impossible and indeed undesirable to search for a monolithic attitude to sight or vision, what one can say of patristic and medieval aesthetics is that they were, to a very great extent, theologically motivated and informed and that this if anything differentiates them in crucial ways from the aesthetics of modernity. We might also say that something seems to happen between the high Middle Ages and early modernity that affects not only the rise of modern science but the shape of theology, and I can only just begin to shape suggestions as to what this event might be.

Umberto Eco charts a move in the late medieval period away from a metaphysics of divine participation toward more humanist conceptions that emphasize relations between the knower and the known. Thus, "for Albertus (Magnus), beauty is objectively present in things without the help or hindrance of men. The other kind of objectivism considers beauty to be a transcendental property also, but a property which is disclosed in relation to a knowing subject. This is St. Thomas Aquinas's kind of objectivism. It represents a substantial move in the direction of humanism."[23] According to Eco it was Duns Scotus who developed the idea that beauty involves an act of judgment in a decisive way, especially with his stress on the absolute particularity of an individual (*haecceitas*). The individual is seen as having beauty as an aggregate of its many properties. The move is away from the organic and participational model toward a nominalist emphasis on particulars. Metaphysical beauty becomes impossible: in "a universe of particulars, beauty had to be sought in that uniqueness of the image which is generated by facility or genius."[24]

In *Sources of the Self* Charles Taylor charts a parallel epistemological shift in early modernity from participational theories of knowledge (in which, in knowing, the mind becomes one with the object of thought) to procedural strategies. Descartes, says Taylor, is interested in certainty and especially the certainty of science. For Descartes, and not only for him, rationality becomes a property of private thought rather than a vision of reality.[25] It is achieved by method, albeit one guaranteed in Descartes's system by a trustworthy God.

I am straying into territory covered by other chapters in this collection, but a few theological comments may not be out of place. In the Renaissance, and somewhat paradoxically, vision achieved a fillip within religion because of the importance of the printed word and a new iconoclasm that took place. In Calvin's texts we find the phrase "the Word," which in patristic writings refers to Christ, moving ambiguously between reference to the second person of the Trinity and to the Bible. The humanist revolution of which Protestantism was part was convinced of both the desirability and the feasibility of returning to sources undefiled by the later (corrupt) readings of the Papal church. This quest for a purified reading of the Word informed early science in its analogous aspiration to "read" the Book of Nature. Just as Holy Scripture might be thought to have one meaning that scholarship can discern, so might the natural order. Francis Bacon's science is known to be informed by his puritanism, both appealing to living experience over and against received tradition.

It is also worth remarking that the period that saw the rise of the modern sciences was also, and perhaps especially in Britain, the period that saw the doctrine of the Trinity under attack and deism in the ascendent. In deism God is no longer the one whom the believer can caress, taste, or smell but instead Newton's "intelligent Agent."[26] This distant and diffident God who, having created the world, watches it from afar is the ideal template for his regent, modern man. Not surprisingly, man was soon to discover that he could dispense with the divine hypothesis and do his "God's-eye viewing" for himself.[27] This doctrine is perhaps the early modern theological background of the gaze.

In feminist critical theory "God" gets short shrift as a bit player who is little more than a pretext for the authority of man and men, the divine guarantor of the veracity of the insights of the Cartesian subject. The "cogito," self-engendered through the denial of the other, the external world, and even in the last instance his own deceiving senses, speaks in the place of and with the authority of God, dividing fact from value, male from female, civilized from primitive, self from other. However, there is never a genuine other, always just the "economy of the Same." But a theologian might object, and indeed should object, that this version of "God" is not the only one to be found in the Western Christian tradition and indeed looks remarkably like a well-known philosophical fiction, the *causa sui*. At most this "God" is a binity where the second partner is man himself. Indeed, man is the senior partner, establishing God as another self and guarantor of his projects. This is indeed a culture of narcissism where the one (man) gazes on the other he has made

(God made in man's image).[28] This concept of deist idolatry is damaging not least for what it does to "man" fashioned in the image of the divine viewer.[29]

A deist drift in Christian thought in the early modern period no doubt informed the development of modern science for better and for worse. Ilya Prigogine and Isabelle Stengers point out with some fairness that it was theologians as much as scientists who favored the mechanical model of the universe in the seventeenth century. Man was, for many of them, "emphatically not part of the nature he objectively described" but rather dominated from the outside.[30] With God as guarantor of his interrogations of a mute and passive Nature (notoriously rendered in Baconian science in female imagery) man could, as it were, see things from a "God's-eye view." But this is a disembodied vision forgetful of the materiality of the eye and aligned to a disparagement of actual seeing as primitive and even misleading. In occupying the gaze of a deist God, man ceases to be any *body* at all, and so indeed do women occupying this Enlightenment space.[31]

> The question whether, in his [Lacan's] logic, they [women] can articulate anything at all, whether they can be heard, is not even raised.... And to make sure this does not come up, the right to experience pleasure is awarded to a statue. 'Just go look at Bernini's statue in Rome, you'll see right away that St. Theresa is coming, there's no doubt about it."
>
> In Rome? So far away? To Look? At a statue? Of a saint? Sculpted by a man? What pleasure are we talking about? Whose pleasure? For where the pleasure of the Theresa in question is concerned, her own writings are perhaps more telling.[32]

Irigaray is piquing Lacan, who after all has not escaped the ocularcentrist (phallogocularcentrist?) tendencies of Western philosophical thought. So what happens if we let Teresa speak for herself? In her *Vita* she tells us that her Jesuit confessor tried to wean her from her corporeal visions. She clearly knows the Augustinian teaching and knows that corporeal visions are less noble than other sorts, but she hangs on to them. It is tempting to see Teresa as a late scion in the tradition of the medieval women mystics about whom Caroline Walker Bynum has written with such interest—women who claimed not only to see visions but in them to drink milk from Christ's breast, or blood from his wounded side, or to taste the circumcised foreskin of the infant Christ, sweet as honey, in their mouths. Bynum argues that medieval piety, and especially female piety between 1200 and 1500, was especially somatic: "This was so not only because medieval assumptions associate female with flesh, but also because theology and natural philosophy saw persons as in some real sense body as well as soul."[33] Although the alignment of the female with the physical could be used to the detriment of women, it was also the basis by which women were regarded, by both men and women, as being closer to Christ, the *embodied* God. Women disproportionately spoke of sensory and indeed sensual religious unions whose erotic overtones were clear to their contemporaries and to the women themselves. Part of this somatizing tendency was no doubt due to the fact that women, deprived for the most part of formal Latin education and thus the educated "grammar" of theology, invoked powerful experiences that validated their testimony. Nonetheless the "tendency of women to somatize religious experience and to give *positive* [my emphasis] significance to bodily occurrences is related to what is generally recognized...to be a more experiential quality in their mystical writing."[34]

Bynum continues, "Women regularly speak of tasting God, of kissing Him deeply, of going into His heart or entrails, of being covered with His blood." The thirteenth-century lowlands mystic Hadewijch can write of a union with Christ,

> After that he came himself to me, took me entirely in his arms and pressed me to him; and all my members felt his in full felicity, in accordance with the desire of my heart and my

humanity. So I was outwardly satisfied and fully transported. Also then, for a short while, I had the strength to bear this; but soon, after a short time, I lost that manly beauty outwardly in the sight of his form. I saw him completely come to naught and so fade and all at once dissolve that I could not longer distinguish him within me. Then it was to me as if we were one without difference.[35]

For those interested in gender reversals, Hadewijch also uses this sensual language while, following the tradition of courtly love poetry, styling herself as the (male) suitor of God as female, Lady Love.

So I remain on Love's side
Whatever may happen to me after that:
The pain of hunger for her, the joy of satisfaction in her,
   No to desires, or yes to delight.
The valiant lover himself strikes before Love strikes:
   Thus he comes bravely to combat.
He who dares to fight Love with longing,
Whatever cruelty he meets with,
Shall possess her immensity.[36]

Lacan's remarks about Saint Teresa are after all, not very original. A cardinal contemporary with Bernini made the same salacious comment. But why should Bernini's statue misrepresent Teresa? Why should she *not* know her God in her body, with eyes, ears—with all her senses? Why should not the Virgin Mary have seen the angel of the Annunciation with her eyes and not only as an intellectual vision? The cardinal's comments already indicate a kind of squeamishness that, while putatively worldly, actually disdains the body. Yet we must ask, what have women to gain from despising the body or any of the senses, even that of sight? In the periods that this chapter discusses, true denigration of vision is usually attendant on denigration of all the senses. Commonly it appears as some form of gnosticism that denies the importance of the body as a means of knowing God, or anything at all. And almost always, gnosticisms that denigrate the body bode ill for women, who historically are associated with bodiliness. Feminists do well to criticize the gaze but should hesitate over the historical record before vilifying sight.

Modern philosophical debates echo older theological ones.[37] Nietzsche is one of the best modern critics of the West's residual gnostic tendency to despise the body, a tendency which has not disappeared with the eclipse of religion but just become harder to spot. Of the philosophers Nietzsche says,

All that philosophers have handled for millennia has been conceptual mummies, nothing actual has escaped from their hands alive. They kill, they stuff, when they worship, these conceptual idolaters... Now they all believe, even to the point of despair, in that which is. But since they cannot get hold of it, they look for reasons why it is being withheld from them... 'We've got it,' they cry in delight, 'it is the senses! These senses, *which are so immoral as well*, it is they which deceive us about the *real* world. Be a philosopher, be a mummy, represent monotono-theism by a gravedigger-mimicry!—And away, above all, with the *body*, that pitiable *idée fixe* of the senses! infected with every error of logic there is, refuted, impossible even, notwithstanding it is impudent enough to behave as if it actually existed!'[38]

"Truth," says Irigaray, "is necessary for those who are so distanced from their body that they have forgotten it."[39] There is more than one way to forget that we are bodies.

Thomas Aquinas, in the quote with which I began, is mindful that demoting physical vision will frustrate a central tenet of his religion—belief in an incarnate and visible God. Nietzsche, who one would think had little in common with Aquinas (and who indeed might himself be surprised to find they shared any convictions), nonetheless makes a consonant point in the passage I've just cited—the senses are 'immoral' where the body is an object of contempt.

3.1 Hugo Van der Goes, Madonna and Child, ca
1468, detail (Frankfurt, Städel-Institut)

3.2 Bernini, Saint Teresa, on cover of Jacques
Lacan, Encore (Paris, 1972).

1   Thomas Aquinas, *Summa Theologiae*, Blackfriars trans. (London: Eyre and Spottiswoode, 1969), pp. 3a, 30, 3.

2   This statement should not be taken as implying that Judaism in any way held the body in contempt. Some of the sects early Christianity encountered certainly did, however.

3   Aquinas, *Summa Theologiae*, p. 77.

4   David Chidester, *Word and Light: Seeing, Hearing, and Religious Discourse* (Urbana: University of Illinois Press, 1992), p. 35.

5   Ibid., p. 30.

6   Michael A. Williams, "Divine Image—Prison of Flesh: Perceptions of the Body in Ancient Gnosticism" in Michel Feher, ed., *Fragments for a History of the Human Body*, Part One (New York: Zone, 1989), p. 129.

7   "Orthodox" and "orthodoxy" here name those who, so to speak, won. It was not clear at this stage which set of beliefs might eventually triumph.

8   Athanasius, *Contra Gentes* (Oxford: Clarendon, 1971). p. 13–14.

9   Ibid., p. 85.

10 Augustine, *The Literal Meaning of Genesis (De Genesi ad Litteram)*, trans. J. H. Taylor (New York, 1982), book 12, ch. 8.20.

11 Ibid., p. 193.

12 Ibid., p. 215.

13 Augustine, *City of God*, book 19, ch. 19.

14 See Aidan Nichols, O.P., *The Art of God Incarnate* (London: DLT, 1980); John Dillenberger, *A Theology of Artistic Sensibilities* (London: SCM, 1986), p. 16. Both authors draw on the important work of Sister Charles Murray, *Rebirth and Afterbirth: A Study of the Transmutation of Some Pagan Imagery in Early Christian Funerary Art* (Oxford: BAR, 1981).

15 Op. cit., chapters 2–5.

16 Dillenberger, *A Theology of Artistic Sensibilities*, p. 57.

17 Jaroslav Pelikan, *Imago Dei: The Byzantine Apologia for Icons* (New Haven: Yale University Press, 1990), p. 113.

18 See Peter Levi and Christopher Lloyd in Bruce Bernard, ed., *The Queen of Heaven* (London: Macdonald and Orbis, 1987).

19 Julia Kristeva's article on these Madonnas, interesting though it is, almost entirely overlooks their theology. See "Motherhood According to Giovanni Bellini," in *Desire in Language* (New York: Columbia University Press, 1980). For a feminist and theological account of fourteenth-century Tuscan painting, see Margaret R. Miles, *Image as Insight: Visual Understanding in Western Christianity and Secular Culture* (Boston: Beacon Press, 1985), esp. chapter 4.

20 Umberto Eco, *The Aesthetics of Thomas Aquinas* (London: Radius, 1988), p. 6.

21 Augustine, *Confessions*, trans. Henry Chadwick (Oxford: Oxford University Press, 1991), p. 183.

22 Ibid., p. 201.

23 Eco, *The Aesthetics of Thomas Aquinas*, p. 26.

24 Ibid., p. 89.

25 Charles Taylor, "Inwardness and the Culture of Modernity," in Axel Honneth et al., eds., *Philosophical Interventions in the Unfinished Project of Enlightenment* (Boston: MIT, 1993), pp. 97–98.

26 In a letter to Bentley in 1692 Newton wrote, "I am compelled to ascribe the frame of this System to an intelligent Agent." Cit. Michael Buckley, *At the Origins of Modern Atheism* (New Haven: Yale University Press, 1987) p. 130. Buckley's book is an excellent account of the theologians' contribution to their own downfall during this period.

27 I use noninclusive language deliberately here since the scientific agent of the period was almost inevitably styled as "male."

28 See Teresa Brennan, *History After Lacan* (London: Routledge, 1993).

29 Criticism of this idolatrous God is at the heart of Jean-Luc Marion's *God Without Being*, where Marion follows Heidegger's critique of the "onto-theological constitution of metaphysics." As causa sui, the God of modern philosophy is, as Heidegger says, an idol before which we can neither pray nor dance. Heidegger, cit. Marion, *God Without Being* (Chicago: The University of Chicago Press, 1991) p. 35.

30 Ilya Prigogine and Isabelle Stengers, *Order out of Chaos* (New York: Bantam Books, 1984), p. 50.

31 Martin Jay notes that Mary Wollstonecraft claimed for herself a God's-eye view in order to "survey the world stripped of all its false delusive charms." Cit. Jay, *Downcast Eyes: The Denigration of Vision in Twentieth-Century French Thought* (Berkeley: University of California Press, 1993). p. 524.

     Roughly the same point that humanism put "man" in the place of "God" is made by Alice Jardine in *Gynesis* (Ithaca: Cornell University Press, 1985), p. 82. And notably, it is also made with regard to painting by Roland Barthes in describing the gaze of the guild masters in seventeenth-century Dutch guild portraits: "In this perfectly content patrician world, absolute master of matter and evidently rid of God, the gaze produces a strictly human interrogation and proposes an infinite postponement of history." Barthes, "The World as Object," in Norman Bryson, ed. *Calligram: Essays in New Art History from France* (Cambridge: Cambridge University Press, 1988), p. 114.

32 Luce Irigaray, *This Sex Which Is Not One* (Ithaca: Cornell University Press, 1985), pp. 90–91.

33 Caroline Walker Bynum, "The Female Body and Religious Practice," in Michel Feher, ed., *Fragments for a History of the Human Body*, Part One (New York: Zone, 1989), p. 162.

34 Ibid., pp. 167–168.

35 Ibid., p. 168.

36 From "Love's Blows," stanza 10 in *The Complete Works of Hadewijch,* trans. Mother Columba Hart, O.S.B. (London: S.P.C.K., 1980), pp. 242–243.

37 For a valuable critique of the notion of the "naked" self from the gnostics through Lacan, see Rowan Williams, "'Know Thyself': What Kind of an Injunction?" in Michael McGhee, ed., *Philosophy, Religion and the Spiritual Life* (Cambridge: Cambridge University Press, 1992).

38 Friedrich Nietzsche, *Twilight of the Idols*, trans. R. J. Hollingdale (London: Penguin, 1968), p. 35.

39 Irigaray, *This Sex Which Is Not One*, p. 214.

One of the wagers that Teresa Brennan places before the readers of *History After Lacan* (1993a) involves specifying the moment when the Western ego becomes a fixed and inviolable form. When it does, she argues, the modern age—what she elsewhere calls the age of paranoia—begins. It is our age, marked by the singularly aggressive and expansive character of the ego, and it owes many of its woes to the historical moment of its formation. Extensive analysis can show that masculine dominance, characterized by fear of the other as a threatening force, a drive to colonize, and a need to establish economies of expansion and exploitation, came with the era of the ego. We could say that the same parabola of development can explain the condition of rampant global degradation.

Elsewhere Brennan argues that the unprecedented violence that we witness being enacted against the planet, *geocide*, in fact has its foundation in the fantasy of egocentered control. Massive ecological destruction does not, like a low dose of sulfuric acid, merely "come with the rain."[1] The foundational fantasy of mastery over the world "increases as the material means to control the environment increase. In other words, in that active agency is the ability to do things according to one's own direction, to impose direction" its psychical omnipotence increases in proportion to its actual social, technological control. (Brennan 1993b: 109–110).

Brennan adds that the agency of the visible has the paradoxical effect of abetting the ego in its drive to establish itself in the world but that it gets detached from the environment in which it originates. The ego "imposes direction" on the environment, but it does not heed "natural rhythms and their own logic" (1993b:110). As the ego gains ascendancy, the resistance offered by the world decreases at those points where the ego uses its fantasies to serve as a guarantee for its attachment to reality. Commodities, simulacra, manmade objects, and visual debris become the stuff of founding fantasies in the continuous labor of psychogenesis and subjectivity. These commodities close the "subject off to the movement of life, [and] they are also visual tangible evidence of a different physical world that, however fantasmatic its origin, makes the subject more likely to see what it has made, rather than to feel itself to be connected with, or part of what has made it" (1993b:110). Parts of Brennan's argument hinge on the sense of closure and isolation that come with a subject's increased investment in visual forms that serve as substitutes for the messier, more vital condition of the environment that gave rise to the ego. It is as if what the visible had promised to the ego in its earlier phase of development is eagerly mistaken for exactly that which it is not. "The visual hallucination that denied feelings of unpleasure is not a concrete thing, and the various senses that otherwise connect the subject with the world stand back in favor of the visual sense" (1993b:111) or, in other words, *on prend des vessies pour des lanternes*: we are duped, we pull the wool over our eyes, or, literally, we mistake bloated bladders for illuminated lanterns.

Both here and in *History After Lacan* Brennan marks the visible with a double valence. On the one hand, it is absolutely crucial to the constitution of a healthy consciousness from the very beginnings of its development. In a certain way she reminds us that sight, as Guy Rosolato has eloquently argued (1993), offers the subject's initial movement into and retreat from the physical world: the infant looks into and about things in its earliest moments of life after birth, and it closes its eyelids to discover the first protective barrier given to the baby body. Unlike voice, sight does not come from without, beyond any control, but from within; it allows the world to be felt, but it gives us the initial means of feeling somatic motion, of tasting, testing, and coping with the world. But on the other hand, visual process has been associated with forces of containment, indivisibility, and fantasy of self-control. The visual is considered in line with the feeling of paranoia that Lacan has often associated with vision and that is seen in the formation of sexual difference.

The assignment or "fixing" of social and sexual roles, which entails the creation of subjectivity, is clearly related to the impact of artificial perspective that allows what is seen to be aligned with the "subjective standpoint of a beholder" (Panofsky 1991:69); in the perspectival plan, point of view becomes autonomous but also a function of a central vanishing point marked in the image to which the viewer's gaze is attached. The effect of the visual mechanism extends itself so decisively in the early modern world that when a subject obtains his or her "point of view" from alignment with a vanishing point, "all objects in the representational space depend on the point of view, or rather, they seem exact only if one occupies the point of view" (Langer 1990:193).[2] In a nutshell, visibility becomes a controlling agency by virtue of a systematic means that manuals of vision in the wake of Filippo Brunelleschi and Leon Battista Alberti (e.g., Jean Cousin, Sebastien Serlio) took care to codify. Through perspective subjectivity can claim itself to be entirely objective all the while it works in concert with the conquest of space. It is not by chance that Samuel Edgerton (1975), in reproducing the terms of these manuals for lay readers, was impelled to note that the invention of moveable type, artificial perspective, *and* the conquest of the New World were together the most decisive events of the early modern period.

Here we should note that Jacques Lacan's ambivalence toward optical mechanisms of the early modern age may in fact—like Brennan's (1993a:61–62)—be symptomatic of the fear of what happens when the era of the ego begins. The establishment of the self in space brings forth what Lacan calls "passification," an intolerably ironic condition in which individuals feel that they have been told that what is best for them will be found right where they are. Aggression is fostered as a consequence of imposed passivity. The reaction serves as a destructive response to—but not a solution for—the decisions that lead subjects to get settled in the areas they occupy.

The guarantee of truth in visible things—things that are not also invested with language— plays a major role in passification. In a short and telling analysis of closed and extended fields of visibility, Norman Bryson (1988:86–113) notes how Lacan conceives of visibility "within a conceptual closure" (87). In his notorious reading of Hans Holbein, Lacan uses the double point of view that we discern in *The Ambassadors* to emblematize the dynamics of the psychoanalytical process. The individual who lives under the illusion of self-sovereignty in the system of Brunelleschian perspective remains free to "choose" a point of view that, once taken, will tell exactly how and where he or she can move in and about space. In Lacan's example the opposite holds sway. Before a multiplicity of objects depicting the five senses, figures of science, discovery, and refinement are arranged in a careful scatter on a table and a buffet supporting the thrust of two ambassadors' arms placed on a heavy wooden support. The viewer cannot fix an ideal position. He or she gathers multiple entries into the space of the painting—the curve and lines of the mosaic floor, the handle of the lute that leads the eye to behold what almost seems to be a great matrix, the melonlike bottom of a lute, or the globe to the right that begs the eye to grasp its handle—but realizes that the statesmen, Jean de Dinteville (to the left) and Lazare de Selve (to the right), cast a penetrating stare that defends the painting from anyone risking a symbolic venture into its confines.

At the intersection of the sightlines of their gaze the viewer is—as the passive voice of this sentence might confirm—set in place. But the celebrated anamorphic death's-head in the lower center, with its vector of mobile force moving from the lower right to the upper left of the painting, parallels the vectors of the handle of the lute and Jean de Dinteville's cap. It indicates to the viewer that he or she is also being displaced by transverse lines. Not only is a single point of view predetermined; another simultaneously throws the viewer into an impossible condition of being beside oneself, as a subject both of the gaze of others and as a function of death that drives its memory-image squarely into our faces. For Lacan the painting reenacts the blinding pain of our birth into a pregiven symbolic condition. In Bryson's gloss the psychoanalyst tends "to privilege the genetic and formative moment" of subjectivity and not "the long and diverse elaborations of adult life" (1988:105) that are better likened to what he calls an expanded field of vision. In comparison, the ink flung in Ch'an painting revives our pleasurable awakening onto a decentered, almost "all-over" perspective that scatters to the wind all vanishing points and other illusions of subjectivity.[3] Lacan is instructive, Bryson concludes, in showing us how power makes use of the social construct of vision and visuality and how it "disguises and conceals its operations in visuality, in myths of pure form, pure perception, and culturally universal vision" (1988:108).[4]

Bryson and Brennan meet where they find in Lacan a tantalizingly instructive model that compares perspectival centering to the formation of the ego. In what follows I would like to show that the commanding example of Holbein's painting does not fall into Lacan's study of psychogenesis in any stray manner. Holbein in fact underpins the relation between the mapping of the ego and its formation and control in a specifically *lettered* condition that can exploit visibility in two ways: either as conquest or, in a spendthrift and self-consuming fashion, in wit. If the history of the visible is related to ego formation as Lacan explains it through the example of *The Ambassadors,* it must also pervade other areas of subject-formation. In recalling Edgerton's remarks about the modern era beginning when the moveable type, artificial perspective, and oceanic travel to the West were meshed, we can surmise that Holbein internalized all of those elements and that in their conflation in the painting Lacan calls constitutive of ego-formation we witness the consciousness of subjectivity being mobilized. Holbein's painting would seem to be an accretion of these three innovations, for, apart from the perspectival trick of the *memento mori* that flashes through the picture, we witness a record of instruments of mapping used to navigate travel beyond the sight of coastlines (globes with gores that followed Martin Behaim's invention of 1491); evidence of printed books, and, possibly, scrolled maps or portolan charts. Not least, the carpet that drapes over the table that exhibits the upper tier of objects displays a diapered design of squares enclosing what appear as cruciform or x-like letters. We behold crisscrossings that betray a configuration assigning equal value to all points upon its surface, an "equipollent" design that is used for centuriation, or a mode of expansion that deploys geometry to conquer space.[5] The juxtaposition of new inventions within the frame of the standardized allegory of the five senses or the *memento mori* invests a conquering drive to live in the midst of the attributes of transience and death. But these are only preliminary impressions gained from the pleasure of scanning a painting whose profusion of detail invites various haptic readings. Before seeing how the internalization seems to work, we can first return to Lacan.

In the discussion of the gaze and anamorphosis Lacan hints that the "*objet a*" has a punctiform character. The gaze penetrates; it is what has since been called the "punctum" in discussions of those areas in photography where something inassimilable, something that resists meaning, that is maddenly enigmatic, keeps returning to nag us (Barthes 1980). It is as if the subject is created when he or she is "subjected" to the imprint of a graphic puncheon.

Schématisons tout de suite ce que nous voulons dire. Dès que ce regard, le sujet essaie de s'y accommoder, il devient cet objet *punctiforme*, ce point d'être évanouissant, avec lequel le sujet confond sa propre défaillance. Aussi, de tous les objets dans lesquels le sujet peut reconnaître la dépendance où il est dans le registre du désir, le regard se spécifie comme insaisissable. C'est pour cela qu'il est, plus que tout autre objet, méconnu, et c'est peut-être pour cettre raison aussi que le sujet trouve si heureusement à symboliser son propre trait êvanouissant et *punctiforme* dans l'illusion de la conscience de *se voir se voir*, où s'élide le regard (Lacan 1973:79; emphasis placed on *punctiforme*). (Let's immediately schematize what we mean. At the moment of this gaze the subject attempted to get adapted to it; he becomes this punctiform object, this vanishing point of being, with which the subject confuses its own deficiency. Thus, of all the objects in which the subject can recognize the dependency where he [or she] is found in the register of desire, the gaze is specified as what eludes all grasp. That is why it is, more than any other object, mistaken, and that is perhaps also why the subject takes such blithe pleasure in symbolizing his own vanishing and punctiform line traced in the illusion of the consciousness of *seeing himself be seen*, in which the gaze is elided.)

The subject is objectified through the transmission of visual energies that confuse the play of the gaze with an effect of printed impressions. The Freudian vocabulary of the "Mystic Writing Pad" seems to be transposed into a scopic register that moves both horizontally and vertically but now with more unpredictable mobility than what is implied by the incision of "tracks" on a wax ground in Freud's famous figure of the mind in his essay of 1925. But if the multiple effects of projecting, of casting, and of receiving impressions through the play of the gaze are conveyed by the emblem of *The Ambassadors*, it may be that the text is working through the creation of the ego on the basis of a play of coextensive discursive and visual registers.

In other words, in the allusion to Holbein, "punctiform" objectification is not limited to anamorphic painting. Also evoked are the same artist's emblems, historiated alphabets and marginalia in cartographical images. The multiple binds imposed upon the subject in the visual effects of anamorphosis bear strong analogy to what seems to be ubiquitous in Lacan's sense of the history of ego-formation extending into other of the painter's works of the early 1500s. Now we can get back to Holbein: the large death's-head in the *The Ambassadors* cuts into a matrix of printed signs of mortality that take the form of tripartite emblems, *Simulachres & historiées faces de la mort*, published in French in 1538, and an alphabet of historiated initials from the 1520s that circulated in bookshops throughout much of the sixteenth century.[6] Both works are incisively "punctiform" insofar as they divide the gaze of the beholder. The letters and woodcuts are "read" in a lexical fashion, as concretions of discourse about prehensions of death, at the same time that they are seen as framed compositions that use figural and spatial means to produce "caricatures" (literally, bodies incarcerated in visual or textual surrounds) of death. In both works Holbein seems to be claiming that the combination of sight and reading in the mixed medium of the historiated initial and emblem constitutes a division basic to the formation of the ego. Beholders are drawn to these works because their decipherment enacts the very division tied to what determines the subject, or, in Lacan's words, "*l'intérêt que le sujet prend à sa propre schize est lié à ce qui la détermine—à savoir, un objet privilégié, surgi de quelque séparation primitive*" (Lacan 1973:78) ("The interest that the subject takes in his own splitting is linked to what determines the latter, that is, a privileged object that surges forth from some primitive separation"). In the case of the historiated alphabet, the subject is the visualized letter floating in the frame of a death personified in a perspectival field. The letter occludes the depth of the image but also, because it masks the landscape beneath, *hastens our desire to penetrate it*. Inversely, the woodcuts that serve as inscriptions for the biblical devices seem to accrete into visual form the Latin mottoes that are suspended above.[7]

In both the initials and the woodcut images we stand at the threshold to the fixing effect of visuality in the field of writing. The one confirms but also attenuates the other. Both works are narrative in that they begin with creation and end with the last judgment. In the alphabet the initial letter A (figure 4.1) is indirectly taken to be the character that typically serves as the "compass" or geometer's instrument that maps out the world (Tory 1529; Desmoulins 1509 in Lecoq 1987:96). It also comprises the "angle," originary corner, or *anguish*, that opens visibility itself.[8] Yet in the overall allegory the A also underscores the mortal silence of writing that does *not* translate into music the notes of a clarion played by a skeleton to the percussive accompaniment of a drum that its companion hits with his baton of bone. There follows, from B to Y, a portrayal of death that inhabits all walks of life before Z foregrounds the zigzag path that good subjects must follow on their ascent to salvation (figure 4.2). The Z sums up the paradigm by entirely anamorphic means. It is "read" in a direction contrary to the alphabet since the humans who wish to gain access to the light of heaven over the globe begin at the lower right-hand bar; move to the opposite end (man "naked" before judgment); ascend the transverse line upward toward the archangels; and then continue, as if following the path marked in the children's game of Parchesi, to the sacred world. The letter sums up the narrative path of the alphabet by reversing the direction that prevailed. It invests images of death into a child's world of transitional, dialogical "objects" that move between abstraction and visibility. It causes fear and it inspires; it promotes a double bind both in its thematic or narrative order and in its pictural and lexical register. The project of the dance-of-death alphabet amounts to the story of the coming of judgment and apocalypse. The child who gets "lettered" begins from accession to vision, A, before encountering all of the standard areas of symbolic life as denoted in the castes and commerce depicted in the margins, seeming "spandrels" of each image-form, between the letters and their surrounds. At the end, Z, all is done, and there remains only the lightning flash of an image of the path that was followed until then and that now ends in a blitz. The letter of death, as it were, is undone by the wit that is supplied through the narrative or discursive elements that occupy each letter and that are inferred from the parataxis of their sequential but unlinked arrangement.

The emergence of visibility in Holbein's alphabet is not far from what Lacan notes about the "instance of the letter in the unconscious." In his essay (1966), the letter inspires a subject to fix his or her relation to visibility through the coagulation of interdeterminate impressions into a "punctiform" object, "*par quoi l'on voit qu'un élément essentiel dans la parole elle-même était prédestiné à se couler dans les caractères mobiles qui, Didots ou Garamonds se pressant dans les bas-de-casse, présentifient valablement ce que nous appelons la lettre, à savoir la structure essentiellement localisée du signifiant*" (501) ("by which we see that an essential element in speech itself was predestined to flow into moveable type, Didots or Garamonds, being pressed into lowercase, justly presentify what we call the letter, that is, the essentially localized structure of the signifier").[9] In that same context, as most readers remember about this canonical piece of writing, the analyst invokes the *points de capiton* to figure the sites where the letter dominates "*dans la transformation dramatique que le dialogue peut opérer dans le sujet*" (503) ("in the dramatic transformation that dialogue can operate within the subject"). Lacan hints that the dialogic condition in which an endless flow of shards or rings of perceptions and discourse circulates in the subject will get *fixed* when the letter makes visible its own form and meaning. At that point a firm symbolic meaning—invested in the iconography of the letter as well as in its place in an ordered concatenation of speech or writing—finds a site that determines the subject.

Lacan's instance of the letter seems to be the very drama that is being played out in Holbein's historiated letters and the dance-of-death alphabet. This drama has more decisive spatial effects in the work that appends cartographical representations. Holbein also completed an impressive surround to the world-map of Simon Grynaeus's *Novus Orbis* (Basil 1532, ill. in Nordenskiöld 1973 rprt, plate XLII, fig. 3 detail).[10] In the spandrels of the world map Holbein depicts daily activities that characterize (or render quasi-timeless) the inhabitants of the four continents. On the upper left Africa is typified by plate-tongued Ubangis below a pachyderm, the quarry of a hunter who arches his bow at the beast from behind a tree. Asia, to the right, is personified by Persians hunting adjacent to a grove of exotic shrubs and vines *en espalier*. Europe below is seen as a seaside port next to finely wrought columns, and the New World is shown inhabited by nude cannibals butchering flesh on a table, roasting arms and legs over a fire, and hanging disparate bodily parts from branches woven into a primitive wigwam. In each instance, except perhaps for the vast and mobile seaside of the European port (in front of which, however, a ram is about to be slaughtered), murder and ritual sacrifice are celebrated. The expansive view of the world is accompanied by images that are "destined" to evoke fear of death and dismemberment. Violence, celebrated as the basis of both religion and the identification (and hence the conquest) of space, is given marked emphasis. Holbein points to something invisible that confuses the project of self-vanishment into *another* space with fantasies of anthropophagia, mutilation, and ritual sadism that are said to bind the four compass points of the world. An invitation to rove in and about the names and places of a physical mass of new and infinite variety is countered by an allegory that associates deadliness with the quadrature of a spatial frame. The Copernican theory of the earth rotating on its own axis is antedated through the image of angels at the upper and lower meridian who turn the globe around by a crank and windlass held in their hands.[11] The doubly bound inflection marks the experience of seeing the map as a fearful but precarious and delicious optical venture into new spaces. What was ambivalent in the letters and the emblems seems to converge upon the world within in scenes of absolute, invisible abjection coming from without.

It would be wrong, however, to reduce Holbein's four drawings to morbid themes of conquest and dismemberment. The allegorical scenes constructed to typify the four continents are comparable to the wit of table-talk—what Bakhtin (1968) called *propos de table licentieux*—that antedates ethnic jokes. They are smutty, tendentious, and loathesome, to be sure, but they also obtain pleasure. The fact remains that their structure as a "simple form," no matter whom they satirize, is in itself wittier than its content, its destination, or its ideology. Here Holbein is at once Erasmian and Freudian to the extent that the wit of his invention rivals the violence of its signification.[12] Implied in Holbein's work is that any nation or continent can be distorted for any allegorical end, but that *his* distortions are livelier than any veracious rendering of the geographical world seen on the map. The pleasure we derive from the spandrels and the proto-Copernican design of the windlass exceeds the truth of the cartographical commodity of expansion of ego control.

With Holbein's experience of the printed letter and cartographical caricatures in mind, we can now return to *The Ambassadors* and the movement, noted above, that vectors from the lower right-hand side to the area about Jean de Dinteville's head on the upper left. It would appear that writing *inheres* in the visual field by virtue of a certain "worldliness," or sense of expanding geographical borders, that is condensed in the emblematic design of the *Simulachres*, the dance-of-death alphabet, and the cartographical materials executed in collaboration with Sebastien Münster. The death's-head skull in the anamorphic perspective is paralleledl by the barlike shape of the cap that Dinteville wears. It bears the likeness of a "personal badge or device" of the sitter (or stander), who may have gone by the nickname "Morette" (Chamberlin 1913, vol. 2: 38 and 49). The punctiform "little death" would be the skull on the cap that gazes at us as does the ambassador. But in the articulation of the general form of the cap in respect to the nonrepresentational bar below, what we discern as the transverse bar of a perspectival Z becomes a new piece of wit, namely, a far-and-near and large-and-small articulation of *two* death's-heads, or a shifting perspective of minuscule and majuscule renderings of a sign spatializing the picture through linguistic means. The Z, the letter of death, is calligraphically a figure that at once traces and sums up the itinerary between the point of Dinteville's skull and the foregrounded image in anamorphosis. Where a drama of death is enacted or narrated along visual lines it is also summed up or mapped out in the redundancy of the skulls as initial and end points of an extended rebus.[13]

The two death's-heads and their oblique frames serve as cardinal, controlling points but also as units of wit that both patronize and totemize the ambassador. Dinteville is likened to one of the skeletons of the alphabet and is thus underwritten, as it were, by a linear design that the viewer supplies as the invisible integument, the *skeletos*, holding erect the robust body that the future archbishop displays. Far from being merely a sign of shock value or the sign of the limits of visibility, the death's-heads are tantamount to verbal icons of worldly mockery.[14] The placement of the two figures in miniature and oblique form, in addition to heralding the artist's talent for heeding detail, also refers to the geographical dimension of the letter, the objects in the picture, and the subjacent theme of overseas travel. Close analysis and historical research have shown that the glove adjacent to Dinteville inscribes, next to the major cities and nations in Europe, the toponym "Polisy," "an obscure village in Burgundy," next to which the other French centers noted are Paris, Lyon, and Bayonne (Chamberlin 1913, vol. 2: 38). Holbein executes with the toponym what he does with the skulls. The near and small is *in* and *of* of the far and large. The irony of a miniature inscription confirms and preempts that of the whole. The artist, furthermore, rivals the cartographer insofar as he sets a personal, motivated place name on a map that would otherwise be an arbitrary register of points and places garnered from the gazetteer accompanying Ptolemy's *Geographia*.[15]

In Lacan's reading of Holbein's painting it may be that the "other" death's-heads—the one figuring on Dinteville's cap, the toponym of Polisy on the globe, and the correlative of the anamorphic bar to the shaft of a spatialized letter—confirm how the subject is created and how the primary skull "with its invocation of the nothingness of death expresses this subject trapped in a visual field it cannot master" (Jay 1993: 364). But they may also determine where Lacan's own language, his wit, interrupts the power of the gaze and thus, as an *unspoken complicity with the speech* of Holbein's verbal and pictorial wit, counters the truth of the gaze and the punctiform drive that he is simultaneously establishing.

What Lacan derives from Holbein about the constitution of the ego has strong and varied resonance in the later fortunes of the artist's work. We would not do justice to the modern character of Holbein's reception in our age if his work were taken to be emblematic only of subject-formation. The Erasmian wit that characterizes the paintings, the alphabet, and the cartographical marginalia becomes, I should like to argue, a site of rivalry. Lacan's wit battles with that of the humanistic *renovatio* that discovers an unconscious reservoir of illumination in the careful scatter of words, letters, and carved impressions of contemporary life. For Holbein they are not quite fixed in an expansive ideology and remain, like Rabelais's writing of the 1530s, of utopian dimension. They attest to an infinite animation and expansion of things under the force of wit. Lacan, it appears, pushes the threshold of *The Ambassadors* far enough forward to imply that its fixating qualities, however latent, signal the coming of the "world-picture" or the establishment of the subject in an assigned and confined space.[16] Lacan virtually steals the wit of the work by translating it into the volatile and sublime areas of his own style with its mix of literature, enigma, and conceptual forms.

Holbein inspires a dialogue of rivalry. For this reason a test case of the fortunes of Holbein in the frame of a mobile reading of pictures and images can be found in what the feminist George Sand made of them in her literary campaigns of the early 1840s. In the preface-manifesto to *La Mare au diable* (1844), an engrossing tale of lovers of different age and origin who venture through the enchanted forests of the Berry, later to live happily ever after, the novelist invoked Holbein's *Simulachres & historiées faces de la mort* to show adepts of literary "realism," of whom

Honoré de Balzac was a leader, that fiction did *not* have to subscribe to the pain and travail of lives destroyed by social contradiction. She argued that the stuff of fables and fairy-tales can better inspire readers to live well and to espouse the joys of life than to fall victim to the crushingly depressive effects of realism.[17]

It is Holbein who conveys the latter in his unremitting picture of the laborer, dressed in tatters, who holds the handles of a plow being drawn by what Sand figures as four emaciated nags whose ribs and pelvic bones almost pierce through their gaunt hides. The plowman tends to his fields, like Sisyphus, in the unending toil of turning the soil moistened only by the sweat of his brow. The picture elicits expressions of outrage, of disgust, even of loathing implicitly aimed, on the one hand, against specifically *male* proponents of realism and, on the other, against three hundred years of history that have left agrarian France with a legacy of poverty and toil.[18] Something or someone has to be blamed. In the vituperation aimed at Holbein Sand's rage also seems to be directed against an unnamed coalition of "realism," the masculine ethos, capitalism, and agencies that use visibility to fix the ego in place.

A close examination of Sand's *reading* of Holbein's picture shows that Lacan's institutions might have strong grounding in both the science of perception and early modern history. The apparent genius of the artist (and of his masterful engraver, Hans Lützelburger) is translated into the undulations of the furrows that lead deep and far into a landscape that seems without end. The four horses that pull the plow seem to follow the row of lines, nineteen traces or tracings of figural writing, that converge toward a shade below a northern French and Bernese-style barn (a broad and flatly sloped roof over a wide foundation) in the distance. They turn slightly to the right, as if either to heed the whip that the sprinting skeleton brandishes with its right arm or, on another visual register, to aim themselves toward the great steeple set over the crossing in the distance of the transept and nave of a stout country church. There we behold a site radiant with the light of day or of God; an aura is produced from diverging lines, marking dawn or dusk, that cut into the sky above. The horses seem to labor irrespective of all these signs in their midst, proving that "life goes on" despite the imprecations of both the church and the allegory of death. The scene is understated enough to allow the reader to invest into the picture both the superscriptive motto from Genesis 1, *In sudore vultus tui vesceris pane tuo*, and the quatrain below: "By the sweat of your brow/You'll live your measly life./After long labor and toil now/Comes death with its knife."

The writing seems to enhance the reader's perception of the space of the woodcut. The furrows indicate a scene laced with writing-memories that confuse, as does a good deal of medieval iconography, the analogy of drawing, tilling, incising, scripting, inseminating (Kuhn 1967: 109 and passim), and producing things that will multiply and grow in both printshops and countrysides. The writing above and below the emblem forces the eyes to move, like the horses themselves, toward points of vanishment that are apparently coordinated with the figure of death. Surely enough, the death's-head figures at the center like a white blob, a circle of *nothing* at the center of the image. It resembles a stone, perhaps, or a rock that might be what the plowman avoids as he turns the soil under the blade of the plow. The skull appears not merely as a skull but also as a commanding sign of what *cannot be represented* in the picture. Below the skull, hanging from the skeleton's neck, is an hourglass set at a coordinate position just below the crossing of the diagonals that stretch from the four corners of the frame. It is set immediately below the skull and suspended above the haunches of the horse set between the skeleton and the laborer that thrusts its hindquarters and raises its cropped tail. It pushes ahead and defecates as it pulls the plow. A vertical sightline is established between the white, stony back of the death's-head; the hourglass; and the stool that falls earthward. The apparent "gravity" of the image is demonstrated by the vertical descent connoted by the sand in the hourglass and the stony scat about to plop into the soil. A visual allegory and a lusty, earthy joke about the cycles of life seems to be written into the woodcut: the stone of the skull is pulverized into the sand of time that passes through the sphincter of the glass that is transformed into the organic waste that fertilizes the soil, assuring the coming of new life thanks to human labor.... It moves contrary to the flow of the image that goes up and away onto the horizon, all taking place in the blitz of our view of the picture.

Why, then, would George Sand be repulsed by the abject realism of the miniature? Is it because she fixes on the peasant's tattered trousers or the bare feet that touch a cold and unremitting earth? Because the horses seem as gaunt as the skeleton who eggs them on? Is Holbein's wit too much for serious ideology? As we saw with Lacan standing before *The Ambassadors*, Sand may also be seen, betrayed, or even *translated* by the picture.[19] Its own bind of writing and of illusionistic perspective might inspire a reaction by which the implied *sand* at the vanishing point of the image convokes her own name and aligns it with the manure of realism just below. The dialogue of the *Berrichonne* writer and the early modern landscape is therefore one that tends to "fix" the name of the feminist into a relation of productive negation. The name that she sees written into the landscape at a *point de fuite*, a point of escape from which there is no escape, elicits a denial of the discovery of itself in the field of the image. In the rebus we behold a negative device of the kind that Holbein fashioned for his clients and for Jean de Dinteville. Sand inverts the wit of the artist's process into a social program because the name is fixed and fixated, like an emblem, into an image to which the author is attracted but which she must vigorously reject. The name in the image inspires a contrary effect in the tale that is a negative subscription to the pictorial component of the emblem. If the relation of Holbein's picture to the name fixes Sand with the sand of the hourglass of death, it nonetheless promotes a woman's liberation through a praxis that rewrites fairy-tales.

In the remobilization inspired by the presence of Sand's name in the picture of the plowman we reach a point where, in the words of Teresa Brennan, history begins to be rewritten "after" Lacan, both according to his intuitions of the early modern age and in the wake of ego-formations that it is our responsibility to call into question. Summing up, we can say that Holbein's relation to visibility in Lacan is as decisive to the *Ecrits* and the *Seminars* as are their hypotheses to the era of the ego or the age of paranoia. There are at least three levels of interaction between the painter and craftsman's work and what the analyst calls the emergence of the modern period. The most common, which Malcolm Bowie and Norman Bryson have studied in terms of the splitting and self-distancing in the closed relation of the gaze between the viewer and the environing world, concerns the genesis of a subject that is mapped into a network of visual relations. These are apparent in what Lacan observes about the acute angularities of vision and signs of transience and death. They are drawn into the play of sight and sightlines in *The Ambassadors*, in the obliquely drawn figure of a *memento mori* that slashes through a world celebrating space and time that are respectively shrinking and accelerating. A second and broadly intertextual relation exists between Holbein's historiated alphabets and the analyst's pronouncements on the instance of the letter in the unconscious. In the *Ecrits* (1966:523ff) Lacan alludes to the divided character of the letter as a concrete instance of a double bind that inheres in perception. The nascent subject is impelled to invest abstraction into a lexical dimension of writing, but the figural ground of the historiated initials juxtaposes topical images of everyday life—what expressly seems to be a timeless theater or meticulous chronicle of activities in bourgeois and nobiliary worlds—with those of death and destiny. A "punctiform" quality results: whereas a perspective on daily labors of the peasants, gentry, and upper social orders is given within the surrounding frame, the alphabetical shapes at once occlude the images and invite the spectator to construct abstract analogies that the surrounding context or the letter reroute through the logic of conundrums or rebuses. The latter area of play, which comprises a model for a Freudian *Bilderschrift*, indicates how Holbein and his contemporaries seem to be producing a medium that uses wit, based on conflations of visual and lexical orders, to create an unconscious (a prescience of death in all human activity, especially in the "fixing" of visibility in writing). That same unconscious is a subject of play, variation, and creative reconstruction rather than a strict mode of control. The third relation emerges from Holbein's cartographical marginalia and in the woodcuts in the *Simulachres & historiées faces de la mort*. The *danse macabre* sets a stage for allegories that fail to master the paradox of the visible evidence of invisibility that would be the "sight" of death in scenes, again, of all ways and walks of life. The efficacy of the paradox is such that its visual approximation both celebrates the labors of early modern life and imparts a sense of destiny that plays, on one register, on Erasmian satire and comedy to promote an ideology of religious reform. On another register, it moves toward but also—because of its strongly marked linguistic context—retracts from its consequence, which would produce subjectivity, by locating the viewer in a closed spatial perspective. Holbein's perspective, because it is infused with language, is not entirely closed. Its wit establishes a field of play and dialogue within itself and with its later viewers and readers.

1 A reader is tempted to explore the amphibole of "ego" and "geo" (and the near-homonym "eco") through "ecology," the science of the self taken up in Brennan's work. Goux (1985) speaks of the *égo-centrique* domain in the Cartesian ethos, in which an inaugural sense of the self becomes the basis of a discipline of conquest and control. Brennan's arguments are aimed at having the *ego* recover a *geo*morphic condition of expanded consciousness of complexity and diversity.

2 Langer's remarks sum up an alert reading of deistic relations that define the social condition of the poet in the European Renaissance. He shows that the writer is obliged to map out, through the performance of poetry, the very conditions of social difference that determine class differences and subjectivity. Langer shows that discourse and visual forms are of similar nature. Deixis, the configuration of speech that establishes both points of speech (the positions of interlocutors) and content (what can be stated in respect to these points or subject positions), is already imbued with the fixing quality of visual perspective. At the conclusion of his study Langer is almost destined, despite the pleas made for subjective freedom for the poet throughout the study, to compare deixis and perspective. The development of the analytical trajectory is thus as symptomatic as the analyses themselves.

3 In a comparison of a fly from Robert Hooke's *Micrographia* (London, 1667) and Ch'ien Hsüan's *Early Autumn*, Samuel Y. Edgerton, Jr. (1991:2–3) rearticulates Bryson's comparison by showing how the anatomical drawing of the drosophila portrays a dead fly, whereas the Japanese artist depicts the "gossamer lightness" (4) of insects that fly. Edgerton sets out to correct radical relativists (he cites Bryson), who see linear perspective as a means to affirm political power (e.g., the male gaze, denigration of women, police-state surveillance, and "imperialist 'marginalizing' of the other"), by showing that "pictures in perspective permitted human beings to see the world just as God conceived of it at Creation" (5). Edgerton indeed universalizes his comparison at the point that he plays God with his reader. The Lacanian dimension that betrays the passage—its ego-flytrap, as it were—may be located in what it does not develop (the expanded field of the gaze in Ch'ien Hsüan's drawing); in its point of departure equating science with death; in the marvelous confusion of the signifier *fly* in the text, with its analog of the two insects' wings in the two pictures that are seen as "dead" in Hooke and "living" in Hsüan (the "gossamer lightness of *flying* insects …").

4 Malcolm Bowie (1991: 171-174) offers a complementary reading worth comparing to Bryson's. Bowie notes that Lacan neglects all the myriad details of Holbein's painting in order to lay stress on the death's-head. When we look at the anamorphosed figure, "the true deathliness of the image can be perceived only by sacrificing the rest of the painting's content" (173). The analyst depends on one detail to explain the concept of the "*objet a*," the perception of lack and truth of castration. This truth, he adds, can be universalized only within the context of the argument. Let us add that the "*objet a*" plays on its own *mirrored* perspective in speech, where the "*objet petit a*" becomes linked with desire, or appetite (from the Latin *petere*), in *a petit…* The subjacent wit in Lacan's formulation comprises, I shall argue, the underlying relation of Lacan with Holbein.

5 Woodward (1990 and 1991) contends that the deceptively simple system of a grid that assigns equal stress to all points of the area that it maps gives rise to the practice of conquest. He notes that a medieval idea of space, based on the relation of a center and a periphery that accords different levels of spatial importance, gives way to the abstract view of Ptolemy's *Geographia*, in which "space could be referenced to a geometrical net of lines of longitude and latitude and could thus everywhere be accorded the same importance" (1991:87). The shift was tantamount to an invention that led Fredric Jameson to see in the contemporary world order "geopolitical" conditions of totally gridded space (1992). Edgerton explains the expansive mechanism of the equipollent system on the basis of the logistics of the quincunx plan. At the center of a five-spot configuration (like that on a pair of dice), the self can extend from center to margin when it conquers a new area to the outside that becomes a new protective area, then a center, then a protective area, and so on, until all available space is controlled (Edgerton 1987:10–15).

6 Six alphabets, including that of the dance of death, are reprinted in Butsch 1878 [rprt.1969]: plates 62–67 and 69.

7 Gisèle Mathieu-Castellani rightly notes that in *Les*

Simulachres "*il s'agit moins ici de faire dialoguer texte et image que d'offrir une transposition en signes visuels des signes linguistiques: de même que le quatrain 'traduit' en langue vulgaire l'avertissement donné en latin par l'Ancien Testament, l'image 'traduirait' par la juxtaposition de ses signes un discours édifiant, plus éloquent que la parole*" (1988:45–46). The image accelerates the edifying effect of biblical speech; it condenses but also embodies, heralds, contains it.

8   Michel de Certeau has noted that the childish play of literalized forms—rebuses—is crucial for the creation of a space of subjective freedom that cannot be fixed or determined, "un lieu pour se perdre," in *La fable mystique* (1982:71–105): in Bosch "angels" are "angles." But Lacan is closer to Bataille than to Bosch. For Bataille the letter is an *angle* that opens the process of perception in a blinding, almost primal scene. At the beginning of *Madame Edwarda* we read, "Au coin de la rue Angoisse," a phrase that Lucette Finas studies extensively (1975:18–20). Angle/ Angel/Angst: **A** concretizes a primal venture into space in an almost *historiated* fashion. The incipit, "Au coin de la rue Angoisse," responds to the double view offered in the title above, "Madame Edwarda." Bataille and Lacan had extensive conceptual personal relations, as Jay (1993:248ff) implies.

9   Lacoue-Labarthe and Nancy (1973) have good reason to call into question Lacan's essentializing gestures in this essay. In the citation above we remark an unnamed but "essential" element in speech that Lacan says we *see* (*par quoi l'on voit...*), and the "essentially" localized manifestation of the signifier is marked at a point where speech and space seem to flow downward, together, toward the "lowercase" letter, in other words, the gridded table of boxes (*cases*) of letters in a printshop that puts the more frequently used type below the "uppercase" counterparts. The physical layout of the typographer's studio is reproduced in the drift of Lacan's observation.

10 See also Shirley (1983: entry 67, 74–75) on the history of the map, 355 x 545 mm. He reminds us that the map was folded into Grynaeus's text and that it accompanied the 1531 double cordiform map by Oronce Finé, which has none of the grisly decoration of the kind that Holbein excelled in figuring.

11 The scientific and symbolic import of this detail was not lost on the late J. Brian Harley. "The decorative features are attributed to Hans Holbein the Younger and his images tend to steal the show. Such pictorial elements in maps have been dismissed as whimsical decoration yet they had meaning and significance to sixteenth century men and women. At the north and south poles two cherubs are cranking the earth. Far from being fanciful this may express a pre-Copernican concept of the earth rotating on an axis" (1990:85).

12 We can remember how, in *Jokes and Their Relation to the Unconscious*, Freud tells "bad" jokes in order to produce hilariously serious analyses. The jokes are emblems subscribed by the explanatory legends. A relation of rivalry marks the seriousness and the jest of Freud's reconstruction of their logic.

13 This hypothesis would be fortified by what Chamberlin calls the "punning effect" (1913, vol. 1:202) of Holbein's devices. Holbein fashioned an image of a bear climbing a tree after honey for Matthias Bienenvater or Apiarus of Berne. For Christopher Froschover of Zürich he designed three devices with frogs set in a Swiss landscape.

14 So witty in fact that their presence in the painting makes risible the art historian's conjecture about why Holbein put them there. Dinteville, argues Chamberlin (1913, vol. 2: 50) was shown the proof sets of the dance-of-death alphabet, "and...he had been greatly impressed by them. He suffered from ill-health while in England, which may have had something to do with his choice of a device of so gloomy nature."

15 Early modern cartographers, argues Père Dainville (1970), often displayed their signature in hidden ways by putting their birthplace in the maps they drew. Here Holbein lets Dinteville's place of birth assume that role.

16 Lacan might be applying to Holbein what historically belongs to Descartes. The reason is taken up in my forthcoming *Self Made Map* (Minneapolis: University of Minnesota Press 1995), ch. 8.

17 Naomi Schor (1993: 138) shows that Sand's idealism unfolded from a strongly invested creative enterprise in the 1840s—she cites the preface to *La Mare au diable*—that was consoling, distracting, and regressive where the post-1848 position was mobilizing, hortatory, and progressive. Holbein does not figure in the picture.

18 Sand's picture of the plight of rural France may be inspired by Holbein's implied politics in this image of

the *Simulachres*. The woodcut was drawn in the early 1520s, "during the Peasants' War, years of misery and bloodshed throughout Switzerland" (Chamberlin 1913, vol. 1:207).

19 One of the more productive areas where perspective and language overlap is precisely that which identifies "point of view." Brunelleschi and Alberti codify viewing positions. Discourse theory inspired by Benveniste locates "subject positions" through instances of speech. That is why Hubert Damisch, speaking of Lacan's relation with the gaze in Holbein, asks if "the subject' is an effect of perspective as much as he or she is an effect of language. But from a perspective that is declared to be *artificial*—right where language is regularly put forward as 'natural'—and which would have appeared at a moment in history that would allow painting to reflect upon itself" (1987:147). Damisch shows that the very language used to locate viewing positions and subjectivity, hardly transparent, belongs to the same process that Lacan describes in his "experience" of Holbein's painting.

REFERENCES

Bakhtine, Mikkaïl. 1968. *Rabelais et le carnaval au Moyen Age et sous la Renaissance*. Paris: Gallimard.

Barthes, Roland. 1980. *La chambre claire*. Paris: Gallimard/Cahiers du Cinéma.

Bowie, Malcolm. 1991. *Lacan*. Cambridge, Mass.: Harvard University Press.

Brennan, Teresa. 1993a. *History After Lacan*. London: Routledge.

—. 1993b. "Age of Paranoia." In Verena Andermatt Conley, ed. *Rethinking Technologies*. Minneapolis: University of Minnesota Press, pp. 92–114.

Bryson, Norman. 1988. The Gaze in the Expanded Field." In Hal Foster, ed. *Vision and Visuality*. Seattle: Bay Press, pp. 87–114.

Butsch, Albert Fidelis. 1878 [rprt. 1969]. *Handbook of Renaissance Ornament*, with a new introduction and captions by Alfred Werner. New York: Dover Books.

Certeau, Michel de. 1982. *La fable mystique: XVIe-XVIIe siècle*. Paris: Gallimard.

Chamberlin, Arthur B. 1913. *Hans Holbein the Younger*. 2 vols. London: George Allen.

Dainville, Père François de. 1970. "How Did Oronce Finé Draw His Large Map of France?" *Imago mundi* 24: 49–55.

Damisch, Hubert. 1987. *L'origine de la perspective*. Paris: Flammarion.

Edgerton, Samuel Y., Jr. 1975. *The Renaissance Rediscovery of Linear Perspective*. New York: Basic Books.

—. 1987. "From Mental Matrix to 'Mappamundi' to Christian Empire: The Heritage of Ptolemaic Cartography in the Renaissance." In David Woodward, *Art and Cartography: Six Historical Essays*. Chicago: University of Chicago Press, 1987, pp. 10–50.

—. 1991. *The Heritage of Giotto's Geometry: Art and Science on the Eve of the Scientific Revolution*. Ithaca: Cornell University Press.

Finas, Lucette. 1975. La Crue: *une lecture de Georges Bataille, 'Madame Edwarda.'* Paris: Gallimard.

Goux, Jean-Joseph. 1985. "Descartes et la perspective." *L'esprit créateur* 25; 1:10–20.

Harley, J. Brian. 1990. *Maps and the Columbian Encounter*. Milwaukee: The Golda Meir Library.

Jameson, Fredric. 1992. *The Geopolitical Aesthetic: Cinema and Space in the World System*. Bloomington: Indiana University Press.

Jay, Martin. 1993. *Downcast Eyes: The Denigration of Vision in Twentieth-Century French Thought*. Berkeley: University of California Press.

Kuhn, David. 1967. *La poétique de François Villon*. Paris: Armand Colin.

Lacan, Jacques. 1966. *Ecrits*. Paris: Editions du Seuil.

—. 1973. *Le Séminaire XI: Les quatre concepts fondamentaux de la psychanalyse*. Paris: Editions du Seuil.

Lacoue-Labarthe, Philippe, and Nancy, Jean-Luc. 1973. *Le titre de la lettre*. Paris: Aubier-Flammarion.

Langer, Ullrich. 1990. *Divine and Poetic Freedom in the Renaissance*. Princeton: Princeton University Press.

Lecoq, Anne-Marie. 1987. *François Ier imaginaire*. Paris: Macula (Série Art et Histoire).

Mathieu-Castellani, Gisèle. 1988. *Emblémes de la mort: Le dialogue de l'image et du texte*. Paris: A.-G. Nizet.

Nordenskiöld, A.E. Rprt. 1973. *Facsimile Atlas to the Early History of Cartography*. New York: Dover Books.

Panofsky, Erwin. 1991. *Perspective as Symbolic Form*. Trans. Christopher S. Wood. New York: Zone Books.

Rosolato, Guy. 1993. *Pour une analyse exploratrice de la culture*. Paris: Presses Universitaires de France.

Sand, George. 1844 [rprt. 1964]. *La Mare au diable*. Paris: Garnier/Flammarion.

Schor, Naomi. 1993. *George Sand and Idealism*. New York:

Columbia University Press.

Shirley, Rodney W. 1983. *The Mapping of the World: Early Printed World Maps, 1472–1700.* London: The Holland Press.

Tory, Geofroy. 1529 [rprt. 1970]. *Champ fleury, au quel est contenu lart & science de la deue & vraye Proportion des Lettres Attiques* ... Paris: Geofroy Tory and Gilles Gourmont. Ed. and intro. by J. W. Jollife. The Hague: Mouton.

Woodward, David. 1990. "Roger Bacon's Terrestrial Coordinate System." *Annals of the Association of American Geographers* 80 (1) (March): 109–122.

—. 1991. "Maps and the Rationalization of Geographic Space." In J. H. Levenson, ed., *Circa 1492: Art in the Age of Exploration.* New Haven and London: Yale University Press; pp. 80–87.

4.1 Hans Holbein, "The Ambassadors," 1533, detail (London, National Gallery)

4.2 Hans Holbein, Historiated Alphabet, letter A, early 16th century

4.3 Hans Holbein, Historiated Alphabet, letter Z, early 16th century

4.4–7 Hans Holbein, illustrations in spandrels of Simon Grynaeus, *Novus Orbis* (Basel, 1532)

4.8 Hans Holbein, *Simulachres de la mort* (1538), "The Plowman," detail

5

The Visibility of Visuality

Peter de Bolla

It is common in the literature of visual theory to invoke the Enlightenment as some kind of ground upon which modern conceptions of the visual field are constructed. In part this invocation derives from a certain philosophical inheritance that we might describe in shorthand as the line of sight between Hegel and Lacan via Sartre. This inheritance has it that the philosophical project of the modern, that is, enlightenment, is intimately caught up with and deeply implicated in the conceptual field of the visual. Insofar as this idea goes, and like all broad characterizations of a difficult set of arguments it goes only a very small way, it is correct. However, what is glaringly missing from this telescoped account is a specifically nuanced *historical* perspective on Enlightenment modes and modalities of visuality. This absence is compounded by the fact that where attention has been drawn to the general area of the visual it has either surfaced in the philosophy and history of science, a discipline that has not sought to investigate the sociocultural noise that colors and distorts vision in its construction of visuality, or in the history of philosophical discussions of optics.[1] In both the history of science and philosophical treatments of the visual field, therefore, we find optics taking center stage, as one might argue it did for the Enlightenment itself.

My purpose, however, is to move away from optics toward the more amorphous cultural domain in order to focus on the visual field, or visuality. Throughout I shall take it as axiomatic that visuality encompasses social and cultural productions and practices as well as philosophical and technical descriptions of optics. This larger focus is particularly helpful in regard to the Enlightenment since visuality, for this period, is not only located in the virtual spaces created by cultural forms; it also tropologically determines the landscape upon which concepts are mapped. Vision is not only literally a topic of great concern to Enlightenment thought; it also furnishes, via an entire tropological field, some of the grounding figures of conceptualization in general. In this sense one might say that vision figures Enlightenment thought.[2]

Consequently visuality is both literally a topic under investigation during the Enlightenment and the name we might give to a figurative spacing that opens up, controls, or legislates the terrain upon which a large number of concepts are articulated. In this sense visuality is certainly not confined to the visible. These comments clearly point toward a very large topic for inquiry that could not conceivably be covered in the space of a chapter; I shall, therefore, limit my remarks to a very small corner of this larger field. Essentially I shall be attempting to suggest a way in which the work of historicizing visuality might begin, and I shall do this by approaching an archival account of the society of the spectacle.

In order to read that archive we shall need to address the specific frames we bring to bear upon the object investigated. In other words we cannot imagine that we see with disinterested eyes, nor indeed that the period in question was able to see "purely" through the lens of optical science. My archival account, therefore, shall be doubly subjected to "theoretical" framings: the first will take its cue from our own historical viewpoint, and the second will be derived from an eighteenth-century source.

In relation to the first frame, our own contemporary moment, we should acknowledge the debt we owe to the philosophical inheritance toward which I gestured in my opening; this philosophical discussion has been substantially attenuated by the work of psychoanalysis. It is, perhaps, in film theory that we currently find the most active engagement with concepts of visuality, and within that debate the work of Jacques Lacan has been extraordinarily influential.[3] I do not wish to rehearse some now well-worn arguments about the gaze and the subject found in Lacan's reformulations of Freud; to do so would be redundant in this collection. It is, however, important to acknowledge the persistence and penetration of the Lacanian account since we cannot turn a blind eye to a model of vision that has substantially determined how we see the interconnections between the subject and the visual field. In this sense we are unable to extricate ourselves from Lacan's gaze. Part of my purpose in this chapter will be to expose that gaze to a historicizing stare; in so doing I hope to insert a historical account within a theoretical one.

Consequently, while I shall endeavor to keep "history" separate from "theory" in order to stall the point at which Enlightenment modes of visuality are read through the lens of Lacanian psychoanalysis, such disintrications of history from theory are more likely to be announced than fully realized. Thus, though it may be tempting to read the Enlightenment as if it produced Lacanian theory *avant la lettre*, I shall struggle to hold the two frames apart in the hope that a more complex historicizing analytic will emerge.

LACAN AND THE GAZE

Lacan's interest in the visual and the gaze more specifically is, of course, tied up with a much larger and more complex topic: the formation of the subject. On a number of occasions this subject formation is explicitly referred to in visual terms, as in the Lacanian *locus classicus* of the mirror stage. But it is the use of the term "gaze" that I shall focus upon since this use will provide us with the articulation point between the present of analysis and my historical example; the purpose of so doing will be to bring some historical depth to the concept of the gaze. More specifically it is the inflections of gender, which are taken to be articulated in and through the concept of the gaze, that I shall concentrate upon.

In what might now be called the classic account the gaze is taken to objectify what it gazes upon, and as such it is understood in terms of the masculine objectification of women. This statement certainly puts the matter simply and crudely and distorts both the Lacanian model and those developed within film theory. Nevertheless it provides us with a point of departure since it signals the specific topic of concern in the following argument.[4] The most sustained Lacanian account of the gaze is to be found in *The Four Fundamental Concepts of Psychoanalysis*, where Lacan explicitly situates his own model of vision within the philosophical tradition inherited by Sartre. He writes: "The gaze, as conceived by Sartre, is the gaze by which I am surprised—surprised in so far as it changes all the perspectives, the lines of force, of my world, orders it, from the point of nothingness where I am, in a sort of radiated reticulation of organisms.... In so far as I am under the gaze, Sartre writes, I no longer see the eye that looks at me and, if I see the eye, the gaze disappears."[5] Lacan asks at this point, "Is this a correct phenomenological analysis?" and he answers "No." There then follows an extremely important moment in this chapter on the gaze in which the following is stated: "It is not true that, when I am under the gaze, when I solicit a gaze, when I obtain it, I do not see it as a gaze. Painters, above all, have grasped this gaze as such in the mask and I have only to remind you of Goya, for example, for you to realize this.

"The gaze sees itself.... The gaze I encounter...is not a seen gaze, but a gaze imagined by me in the field of the other" (p. 84). In my historical theoretical text, Adam Smith's *The Theory of Moral Sentiments*, we will encounter so strong a prefiguration of this analysis that questions of chronological priority will seem irresistible. Let us dwell a moment longer, however, with the Lacanian argument, in which the gaze is also imbricated within questions of voyeurism. As Lacan writes:

> A gaze surprises him in the function of voyeur, disturbs him, overwhelms him and reduces him to a feeling of shame. The gaze in question is certainly the presence of others as such. But does this mean that originally it is in the relation of subject to subject, in the function of the existence of others as looking at me, that we apprehend what the gaze really is? Is it not clear that the gaze intervenes here only in as much as it is not the annihilating subject, correlative of the world of objectivity, who feels himself surprised, but the subject sustaining himself in a function of desire? (pp. 84–85)

Here Lacan is at pains to disentangle the gaze from the economies of desire, to reimpose the boundary of interiority/exteriority in order spatially to orient the relations between the look and the gaze. This spatial construction is perhaps best exemplified in the three diagrams Lacan uses to illustrate the relationships between the subject, gaze, and look.[6]

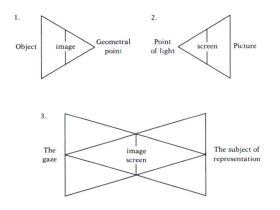

The first diagram has the look of familiarity about it; indeed, Leon Battista Alberti would have recognized it as an account of unilinear perspective. The "geometral point" corresponds to the place occupied by the artist who surveys the object to be depicted through the mediating frame of the image. In Alberti's time this mediating point would have been the transparent pane of glass through which the Renaissance artist saw the object and onto which, as the glass turned into canvas, he was to paint it. In this diagram the position of the eye is superimposed upon the position of the gaze: eye and gaze work in unison just as the Renaissance artist masters the world he surveys through the mechanical-conceptual apparatus of the camera obscura.[7]

Lacan, however, wishes to disrupt this rather cozy arrangement and to claim that the geometral point is only a "partial dimension in the field of the gaze" (p. 88). In fact Lacan understands this diagramatization of geometric perspective as primarily addressing space, not vision, and in support of this he cites the famous eighteenth-century debates concerning the abilities of a blind man correctly to read such spaces. The purpose of this attack is to deny the inherent Cartesianism in the model, that which precisely equates seeing with being. Lacan's rather neat destruction of this position is to show how, in unilinear perspective, the viewer, in his or her immersion in the image through the sightlines that converge on the vanishing point, is in effect "vanished away." The only way back from this point is through an inversion of the triangle, so that the viewer, who now finds him or herself in the position of the object, has to retrace the trajectory initially followed in order to occupy the position of mastery from which it departed. In this way the viewing subject becomes merely a function of the visual field.

Figure 5.2 represents the subject not as the master of the visual field but as the object of the gaze, as precisely the picture. The triangle has been inverted, and the means by which the subject (now objectified as that which is seen) enters the visual field is through the deliberately disembodied or inanimate "point of light." This inversion, in effect, strips intention out of the activity of looking. In this way the gaze is figured as irrecoverably external to the subject and the visual field is divested of its problematic of mastery; in its place the dominating viewer of the first diagram becomes the object in and of a spectacle.

In the midposition of Figure 5.2 we find the "screen," which, Lacan insists, is opaque. Consequently the subject who occupies the position of the picture can only do so by way of being projected onto the screen. In this sense the second diagram attempts to convey how a subject becomes a picture—as Lacan writes: "I must, to begin with, insist on the following: in the scopic field, the gaze is outside, I am looked at, that is to say, I am a picture" (p. 106). The third figure conflates the other two and makes the point even more strongly that it is only through what is called the "image" or the "screen" that subjectivity is constituted. Furthermore, the gaze is now explicitly in the position of the object looked at in Figure 5.1 so that the location for the activity of seeing is constantly shuttling back and forth between the thing made object in the visual field and the thing making it object. It should be clear by now that the subject is unable to occupy either of these positions with any stability. In this way the third figure pictures to us a schematization of the "spectacle of the world," and it is that world, appearing to us as spectacle, that provides the location for the subject-seeing, or subject-in-sight. As Lacan writes: "What determines me, at the most profound level, in the visible, is the gaze that is outside. It is through the gaze that I enter light and it is from the gaze that I receive its effects" (p. 106). Before exploring this entry into light, an entry into the domain of visuality, I shall return to my companion theoretical text, *The Theory of Moral Sentiments*, to situate Smith's account of spectatorial subjectivity within the visual culture of mid-eighteenth-century Britain.

THE VISUAL CULTURE OF ENLIGHTENMENT

If we are to take it as axiomatic that visuality is as much constructed in and through social, cultural, and discursive forms as those things that we might loosely and anachronistically take to be self-evidently visible, then we shall need to examine the nuances of the range of possible activities within the visual field that might have been available for any period. More specifically we need to investigate the differences between, say, looking or surveying, watching or spectating, that are articulated in Enlightenment discussions of viewing practice. This investigation is not only to point to the semantic differences that are delimited by these words in our lexicon and that are, therefore, to some extent coextensive with the nuances of these terms in our own period but also to a fully articulated and articulatable grammar of forms that constitute visuality in and for the Enlightenment. Individuals, insofar as they are constituted as subjects by this grammar of forms, take on specific roles such as "viewers" or "spectators," and these positionalities within the discursive dispersal of subjectivity are far from inert in relation to other definitional criteria surrounding the subject, such as class, social standing, and gender. A viewer in mid-eighteenth-century England had very precise contours: he or she was positioned by an activity, say looking, and was thereby situated in relation to a social and cultural topography that inflected specific social, economic, and gendered descriptions of the individual.

In point of fact looking represents just one option within the range of possible insertions into visuality; other activities within the domain of the scopic are delimited by terms such as "gazing" or "glancing." The period in question worked out an entire metaphorics of the eye in which these different activities were distinguished. For example, in the activity of viewing a landscape the eye might be "cast" to a particular point or "thrown" toward an object in the landscape known as an "eye-catcher." The eye might become "exhausted" or "sated"; sometimes it is described as being "hungry," at others "restless." Equally it might become fatigued as the eye becomes tired of too much visual stimulation. In all these cases eighteenth-century culture images to itself the organ of sight as both actively participating in the visual field and as its passive recorder. It is, then, not the subject who becomes sated but the organ of sight. I do not want to press this point in relation to the foregoing discussion of the Lacanian scheme, but it is worth noting since the culture we are now beginning to examine also figures subjectivity in complex ways.

Eighteenth-century modes of understanding this metaphorics of the eye reach toward the specifics involved in particular instances of our encounter with the visual field. Thus, for example, viewing the landscape park and viewing in the landscape park have a different set of governing frames to the inspection of pictures in a sale-room or gallery. These different locations and activities generate different modes and purposes for the eye and demand different somatic insertions within the spacings of the social and visual, or socioscopic. And further to qualify the circumstances, of course not all physical environments at all times demand and constitute precisely identical forms of viewing activity: not all gardens require the same modes of visual address and even one garden may demand different modes at different times or at different locations within it. Clearly what is needed here is a precise example, which I shall present in conclusion.

Visual culture for the period, as for our period, comprised a specifiable set of objects, activities, structures of consumption, and production of representations for which particular arguments needed to be made and on whose behalf particular policing activities needed to be set in motion. In making these arguments and policing this site of public production and display, a whole range of ideological commitments were either silently or openly articulated. We shall follow through a number of these arguments; in shorthand the division of opinion can be understood in ways that are familiar to our period in terms of the distinction between high and low, or popular, culture. For the period in question this distinction is particularly fraught since the concept of the cultural domain was only beginning to be hesitantly articulated at this time. Thus, where we might describe certain forms as "popular" (without perhaps fully understanding why we do so), such a demarcation would have been almost unthinkable for eighteenth-century commentators since what was at stake was precisely the formation of something that might in the first place be called "culture."

It is, then, more helpful to understand the division of opinion as falling between the requirement that one be educated in some shape or form in order to be able to "see" the works of culture and the notion that any response as long as it be in some sense "genuine" is as valid as any other. This kind of argument also has a familiar ring because it has dominated discussions of philosophical aesthetics ever since; it is the kind of argument one finds obsessively repeated in the face of nonrepresentational art in which the viewer has no ground of *vraisemblance* to stand upon in order to direct the eye. The point of division, then, occurs around an affective response, however this is made apparent, versus an educated and usually classifying gaze: the regime of the eye versus the regime of the picture.

In the case of the former the mid-decades of the eighteenth century witnessed an extraordinary experiment in grounding affective vision, or what might also be termed "sentimental vision." It is far from coincidental that this experiment coincides with the vast increase in volume of activity around the display, production, and marketing of paintings. But it would be wrong to assume that the socioscopic is focused exclusively upon high-art images, most especially painting, for the purview of sentimental vision is far broader than that. It includes, for example, the varieties of visual and visualizing activity found in surveying land, an activity that is itself divided into various techniques or technologies depending upon the specific functional requirements that motivate the survey. Landscape aesthetics, for example, in which a very carefully demarcated set of responses is outlined and regulated, determines one form of looking at the land, which is to be strenuously distinguished from those forms that motivate, for example, the agricultural survey. In both cases the visual is open to both regimes, the one leaning toward the affective registers of response, the other toward the categorizing impulses of taxonomy, but it is clear that function will determine the extent to which these different technologies of the look are activated.

Furthermore, there is considerably more at stake in the entry into visuality than just different modes of looking, for the activity of looking says something about the looker. It is precisely because of this that the experiment of sentimental vision holds out such interest, both for the period and for us, since it is based in a leveling and potentially democratic conceptual fold: all who have eyes to see are able to experience an affective response, to "feel," as an eighteenth-century theorist would have it. Throughout the mid-decades of the century, say between 1755 and the early 1780s, there were countless rehearsals of the arguments around this point. Thus, John Shebbeare, writing in 1755, makes the case for the eye: "…the true taste in gardens is formed on what we feel in ourselves, at the sight of different scenes in nature."[8]

The case for the picture, for the educated eye, is here put by Mathew Pilkington:

> As Painting is the representation of nature, every Spectator, whether judicious or otherwise, will derive a certain degree of pleasure, from seeing nature happily and beautifully imitated; but, where taste and judgment are combined in a spectator, who examines a design conceived by the genius of a Raphael, and touched into life by his hand; such a spectator feels a superior, an enthusiastic, a sublime pleasure, whilst he minutely traces the merits of the work; and the eye of such a connoisseur wanders from beauty to beauty, till he feels himself rising gradually from admiration to ecstasy.[9]

There are clear distinctions here between activities of slightly different sorts: looking in the garden is not identical to gazing at painted representations (although the latter may take place within the context of the former): in both cases it is the education of the eye that determines the different modes and modalities of looking, and such modalities are not exclusively focused upon the correct visual address to *objects* as such, since they are also deeply imbricated within images and representations of self. Consequently the incredible pressure around mid-century to work out, precisely to figure a way of representing, the composure and compass of the public sphere and to conceptualize this new cultural domain in terms of visuality, necessarily involved questions of propriety, of gender and class affiliation, which all bear upon subject definition. In brief the question that arises is, Who will be allowed into the domain of the visual, allowed in so that they might see the images in the gallery but also so that they might be seen looking at those representations?

Of course another possibility exists in relation to the fine arts, namely, that the arts themselves "educate" the viewer. At a time when increasing numbers of "common" people began to figure more forcibly within the public sphere, such arguments were inevitably made on behalf of certain ideological beliefs. Such beliefs might have it that everyone is capable of education, or alternatively the opposite view might be held, in which only those who already have entry tickets to the domain of visuality will be able to "see."

Here is the eighteenth-century argument made in a nonelite discursive realm in a primer on the arts intended for wide circulation:

> This is the Progress of Taste: By little and little the Public are caught by Examples. By seeing, they (even without taking notice of it) insensibly form themselves upon what they have seen: Great Artists produce in their Works the most elegant strokes of Nature: Those who have had some Education, immediately applaud them, even the common people are struck; *Interdum Vulgus rectum videt.* They apply the Model without thinking of it. Then by degrees retrench what is luxuriant in themselves, and add what is wanting. Their Manners, Discourse, and outward Appearance, all seem to be reforming, and this Reformation passes even into their Souls.[10]

This form of argument concerning the beneficial effects of "polite arts" is, of course, one of the ways in which the early modern period attempted to justify the expense of investing in non-productive luxuries and the pursuit of leisure-time activities. The argument runs thus: where good household management leads to economic benefits, so the support of the arts leads to a more humane society. As our writer explains: "… the Polite Man shall shine forth and shew himself by a lively and graceful Expression, equally remote from Rudeness and Affectation: two Vices as contrary to Taste in Society, as they are in the *Polite Arts*" (p. 5).

These and other advertisements for the beneficial effects of artistic production can be found throughout the Enlightenment. Joshua Reynolds was making such an argument, albeit in a rather elitist manner, in his *Discourses* when he proposed that painting should depict the general rather than the particular, the ideal rather than the specific, since these forms are relatively context-insensitive and therefore "educate" the viewer and improve society through time and across social boundaries. Reynolds was all for what John Stedman called "beauties of the understanding" and rather against the more affective, response "beauties of the eye": "those beauties which, by the means of vision, strike the sensory with little, perhaps without any reflection of the mind."[11]

For similar reasons the high cultural theory of the arts at this time legislated the hierarchy of representations. This hierarchy has traditionally been understood exclusively in terms of academic painting: the ordering of genres that insists on history painting as being the most elevated, precisely a beauty for the understanding. However, arguments concerning the genres constituted only one part of a general cultural eruption in which a range of objects and practices, of looking and production, burst upon the scene and jostled for attention in a variety of modes. This high cultural theory was closely linked to certain political and social goals, expressed most succinctly in the term "civic humanism," and its ambitions were clearly focused on the stratification of the visual domain into a series of hierarchized forms and practices requiring a range of skills and competences that one needed to acquire, either by dint of birth or through some kind of educative labor.

This high-cultural argument has been well documented and deeply researched so that now we are in a position to begin situating such arguments within a wider sphere.[12] More specifically we can begin to piece together the contestatory context in which these arguments were made, a context in which a professional or bourgeois culture competed with elite culture, sometimes as a parasite upon the body of the public and at other times as an alternative to it. The lines of battle can be seen quite clearly in relation to a common thread running through arguments within high culture about the hierarchy of genres. In these arguments portraiture was understood to have a lower position in the hierarchy than history painting.

A large number of strands make up this argument, which is certainly concerned with issues of nationalism and individualism as well as more technical debates about oil painting. Whatever the high-cultural argument asserted, it is nevertheless remained the case that mid-eighteenth-century Britain was overwhelmed with the production and circulation of portraits. Indeed, if one tabulates the number of successful submissions to the Royal Academy exhibitions throughout this period it becomes clear that even the Academy itself, prime mover in academic art theory and the hierarchy of the genres, was dependent upon the craze for and booming economy in portraits. In point of fact Sir Joshua Reynolds, the Academy's first president, exhibited vastly more portraits than any other genre throughout his tenure of office.

The fashion for portraits can be taken as emblematic for my argument since it demonstrates the heterogeneity of visual culture; it points up the question of how much the entry to visuality should cost. On the one hand, for example, painters who wished to make a living from painting might paint a likeness of a fashionable and important person without that person having sat for the portrait. If the painter was skillful enough the likeness would be applauded and custom would follow (indeed, the person represented might even commission a "real" portrait and sit for it). Here the value of the image lies precisely in its *vraisemblance*; but on the other hand, arguments about "true likeness" become redundant when one does not know the sitter. When this argument is extended over time and in relation to a national school of painting it becomes clear that portraiture is unlikely to maintain a high value, both in the sense of its position within the hierarchy and in straight economic terms of the price one might realize for the picture over time. Consequently, while the professional and aspiring middling sorts were advocating the commissioning and exchange of likenesses, high cultural theory was doing its best to trash what was by a very long way the predominant artistic form of the day.

The pleasure of portraiture is often thought to lie in the experience of recognition: we are thrilled by the art that renders a likeness. This thrill is clearly muted, if not eradicated, in the case of a representation of someone we have never seen, but it is equally intensified if the subject happens to be ourselves. It is this second case rather than the first that I shall dwell upon since the period we are investigating has an obsessive relationship to self-image. This obsession existed not merely in the literal case of portraits of oneself but also in the philosophical accounts of a well-regulated and mutually profitable society. The culture of visuality places a high premium on visibility.

In the case of the image we need to explore the specific culture of portrait production and consumption. Rouquet's commentary gives us some first impressions: he tells us, "[I]t is amazing how fond the English are of having their pictures drawn."[13] Such images came, of course, in a variety of forms: the high art social portrait by an academician was only one of the many possibilities. Others included miniature representations, silhouettes, or drawings in media other than oil. These less grand images would circulate almost like our own business cards, as Rouquet notes: "Portraiture is the kind of painting the most encouraged, and consequently the most followed in England: it is the polite custom, even for men, to present one another with their pictures" (p. 33).

The culture we are beginning to get in focus is suffused with the desire to see oneself and to exchange such self-images as a form of social practice: that is what being polite entails. In sitting for a portrait this fascination with seeing oneself is also evident since at least one handbook on painting in the early decades of the century suggests that portraits are most effectively accomplished by looking at the image in a mirror. Thomas Page instructs the painter: "… you must always have a Looking-Glass behind you, wherein at times you must look to behold your Work, for that will show you your faults; whether the masses of the Lights and Shadows, and the Bodies of the Colours be well distributed, and are all of one Piece."[14] This, an instruction for the painter, implicates the sitter to only a small degree in the reflective surfaces of the culture of visuality. Reynolds's practice, however, brings the sitter into the catoptric look very forcefully indeed. We learn from Charles Leslie's *Life* that Reynolds commonly set up his studio so that the sitter could see him-or herself coming into representation by the simple expedient of placing a mirror obliquely to the canvas.

Leslie is quoting Beattie, who sat for Reynolds on August 16, 1773: "I sat to him five hours, in which time he finished my head and sketched out the rest of my figure. The likeness is most striking, and the execution most masterly. The figure is as large as life. Though I sat five hours, I was not in the least fatigued, for, by placing a large mirror opposite to my face, Sir Joshua Reynolds put it in my power to see every stroke of his pencil; and I was greatly entertained to observe the progress of the work, and the easy and masterly manner of the artist...."[15]

Beattie, who claims this is an unusual practice, is corrected by Leslie, who notes: "In reality, Sir Joshua was painting from the reflection in the glass—his usual practice" (p. 33). This little anecdote points toward the fascination with coming into representation: seeing oneself made the object of the look.

Such objectification is accompanied by problematic aspects of being looked at, most obviously those concerned with the erotics of the situation. Self-regard is, perhaps, always caught up in an erotics of visualization, but in the case of having one's picture "taken" there are clear indicators of propriety. It was for this reason that women portraitists were strongly discouraged since it was believed that a woman painting a man would necessarily involve a scene of seduction. It is noteworthy that commentators on the practice of portraiture did not find the opposite situation, in which a man "takes" a likeness of a woman, equally problematic.

Similarly, it is clear from Leslie's *Life of Sir Joshua Reynolds* that portraits could often be realized with an audience of onlookers present there to witness the sitter's likeness appearing, as if by magic, in front of their eyes. The experience of sitting for a portrait, then, was one in which spectatorial activities infused the scene of representation, and such spectatorship might be autovoyeuristic as well as simply voyeuristic. Perhaps this invasion of what we would understand as a private space is more troubling to our own notions of propriety than it was to a culture in which spectating was an obsessive practice. Nevertheless, there are clearly problematic issues over the public nature of the space.

A visit to a portrait painter, depending of course upon one's particular station in life, would most likely be undertaken within the view of others. Studios were equipped with waiting rooms specifically to cater for the frequent arrival of clients who would pass the time by inspecting the wares displayed by the artist: those portraits he chose to advertise his skill and promote the idea that he was well connected. Thus, not only would one be able to note who had sat for this particular artist, one would also be seen by others in the "gallery" or waiting room who might themselves be contemplating having their portrait done. As Rouquet notes: "Every portrait painter in England has a room to shew his pictures, separate from that in which he works. People who have nothing to do, make it one of their morning amusements, to go and see these collections" (pp. 42–3).

As fashions came and went different artists would become more or less in demand and well-to-do sitters would make it their business to have a likeness taken by the current favorite portraitist. This practice might lead to problems for the artist, since his business would suddenly expand at such a rate that his pictures would need to be completed at great speed. The problem is described by Rouquet:

> A portrait painter in England makes his fortune in a very extraordinary manner. As soon as he has attained a certain degree of reputation, he hires a house fit for a person of distinction; then he assumes an air of importance and superiority over the rest of his profession.... His aim then is not so much to paint well, as to paint a great deal; his design is to be in vogue, one of those exclusive vogues which for a while shall throw into his hands all the principal portraits that are to be drawn in England. If he obtains this vogue, to make proper use of it, he is obliged to work extremely quick, consequently he draws a great deal worse, by having a great deal more business. Fashion, whose empire has long ago subverted

that of reason, requires that he should paint every face in the island, as it were, against their will, and that he should be obliged to paint much worse than he would really choose, even by those who employ him. (pp. 38–9)

If this is the unhappy lot of the portraitist, his sitter is not in much better shape since fashion demands that once one artist has slipped from favor another must replace him: hence the need to have one's portrait painted once again. Furthermore, the public nature of this coming into the visual is compounded by the fact that an ambitious artist would have been likely to submit his canvas for one of the many yearly exhibitions. Hence the prospect of being seen not only at the studio or in the process of having one's likeness taken but also on the walls of the exhibition room, where the public would be none too reluctant to judge the various performances (and by implication the sitters depicted).

The period is suffused with concerns about visibility; indeed, entry into this cultural domain can be described in terms of becoming a portrait: an image subject to the various exchanges surrounding the production and consumption of pictures. These images of *persons* are to some extent implicated within the closed discourse of the history of painting: portraiture has an internal history as well as relations to the other genres. But the more general embedding of self-image in a culture determined by the visibility and visualization of the subject requires more patient archival elaboration. It is with this aim that I turn to a "theoretical" account of the spacings of the socioscopic within eighteenth-century culture in order to approach this issue from a slightly different angle. Essentially what I will be doing is asking how far we can explore the visual culture of a past epoch through its own systematic and conscious accounts of the visual field.

ADAM SMITH: THE THEORY OF SPECTATORIAL SUBJECTIVITY

My text is Adam Smith's *The Theory of Moral Sentiments* (1759),[16] perhaps the most significant work of Scottish philosophy in the second half of the century. Throughout this exhaustive text of moral philosophy there runs a pretty continuous address to a concept that Smith labels the "impartial spectator." On account of this concept, there is a marked attention to matters concerning spectacle and spectatorship, terms to which we will need to add nuance in relation to the specifics of their use in Smith's text. The period in question was, of course, obsessed with questions concerning spectatorial comportment and behavior. This was a culture in which one of the most significant publications was entitled *The Spectator*, and in all manner of public events, from hangings to masked balls, were deeply implicated within the conceptual folds of the spectacle. Smith's text, then, is not so much emblematic as reflective, not merely responsive but also foundational.

Smith is primarily concerned with demonstrating how one might derive an ethics, that is, a mode of assessing and policing one's actions, from the simple observation that if all members of society acted solely upon the information they derive as individuals from their own experience, then the social would collapse as self-interest overrides all impulses toward benevolent action on behalf of others. Smith comes up with a solution to this problem through his appeal to the imaginative imputation of what another might feel, based on the evidence of our own experience. This, the doctrine of sympathy, is the motor that governs a just and ethically correct society.

This sympathetic imagination is not only focused on others who might lead lives more miserable than our own; in an extraordinary conceptual concatenation it is also focused upon the subject itself. So it is that the society of spectacle in which one sees others through the prism of sympathetic imagination is troped into a self-regarding spectator sport in the production of subjectivity itself. It is worthwhile following this argument in some detail, since it will illustrate the complexity of the visual field as it is addressed by Smith's ethics.

On the opening page of the treatise Smith explains the first tenet of the doctrine of sympathy: "By the imagination we place ourselves in his situation, we conceive ourselves enduring all the same torments, we enter as it were into his body, and become in some measure the same person with him, and thence form some idea of his sensations, and even feel something which, though weaker in degree, is not altogether unlike them" (p. 9). This passage describes the imaginative leap we make when confronted with others, which makes us resonate sympathetically to the plight of other individuals. Such sympathetic reactions are primarily governed by what we *see*. From the first, then, the visual is crucial in determining the entire system. Smith writes, "When we see a stroke aimed and just ready to fall upon the leg or arm of another person, we naturally shrink and draw back our own leg or our own arm; and when it does fall, we feel it in some measure, and are hurt by it as well as the sufferer. The mob, when they are gazing at a dancer on the slack rope, naturally writhe and twist and balance their own bodies, as they see him do, and as they feel that they themselves must do if in his situation" (p. 10). This observation is made on the second page of the treatise and is crucial in regard to almost all that follows, for what it makes absolutely clear is the reflective nature of this visual field: what one sees in the place of the other is translated by precise reflection into the body of the spectator. From this somatic reflection of the visual field in the body of the spectator it is a very small step to the ratiocinative or imaginative re-creation of the sensations and feelings experienced by the observed: "... the spectator must, first of all, endeavor, as much as he can, to put himself in the situation of the other, and to bring home to himself every little circumstance of distress which can possibly occur to the sufferer" (p. 21).

Smith makes it clear that the spectator will never quite manage to reproduce at the same intensity those feelings of the other since sympathetic sentiment is, in the last analysis, "imaginary" (p. 22). However, this difference leads the spectator to notice a tension within himself between the feelings he experiences in his own right and those he experiences through this imaginative projection onto the observed. It is this tension that leads the spectator to ponder not only what it might be like to be the afflicted person but also what it might be like to be spectated upon. In an extremely important sentence Smith writes; "As they are constantly considering what they themselves would feel, if they actually were the sufferers, so he is as constantly led to imagine in what manner he would be affected if he was only one of the spectators of his own situation" (p. 22). Here the catoptric nature of the society of spectacle begins to be fully and sophisticatedly articulated. Not only does the spectator in Adam Smith's theater of morality look upon others with imaginative sympathy; he also looks upon himself in the same manner. In this sense subjectivity is precisely not positioned in the eye of the beholder but, rather, in the exchanges that occur in the phantasmic projection of what it might feel like to be constituted as a subject by looking on the onlookers of our selves. The moral agent in Smith views himself in the light in which he is conscious that others will view him (p. 83); hence, we must "imagine ourselves not the actors, but the spectators of our own character and conduct" (p. 111). This extraordinary note continues: "[We must] consider how these would affect us when viewed from this new station, in which their excellencies and imperfections can alone be discovered. We must enter, in short, either into what are, or into what ought to be, or into what, if the whole circumstances of our conduct were known, we imagine would be the sentiments of others, before we can applaud or condemn it" (p. 111).

Agency here takes on a very indirect form, essentially being translated into spectatorial sympathy for ourselves. The full extent of this society of the spectacle is to turn even the subject as agent into the object of the gaze: we locate ourselves, or come to self-description, through the agency of a sympathetic fantasy projection in which we image to ourselves what we would look like were we the spectator looking upon us as we are looked upon. This reflection to the power of three is figured as a triangulation of the visual field, which might well be imaged in the form of Lacan's third diagram discussed earlier.

Smith, however, does not leave things here since he turns the figure one more time in his attempt to account for this overly voyeuristic scheme. It is in this respect that the infamous "impartial spectator" comes to the rescue. This idealized position, the spectator who is never locatable within a specific individual, within a real person, represents the best-case scenario: the spectator as the projection of every individual who aspires to the condition of the ethically sound. This idealized person must be internalized within the breast of every man who would be judged according to the precepts he holds dear. Smith writes,

> The man of real constancy and firmness…has never dared to forget for one moment the judgment which the impartial spectator would pass upon his sentiments and conduct. He has never dared to suffer the man within the breast to be absent one moment from his attention. With the eyes of this great inmate he has always been accustomed to regard whatever relates to himself. This habit has become perfectly familiar to him. He has been in the constant practice, and indeed, under the constant necessity, of modelling, or of endeavoring to model, not only his outward conduct and behavior, but, as much as he can, even his inward sentiments and feelings, according to those of this awful and respectable judge. He does not merely affect the sentiments of this impartial spectator. He really adopts them. He almost identifies himself with, he almost becomes himself that impartial spectator, and scarce even feels but as that great arbiter of his conduct directs him to feel. (pp. 146–7)

The result is a society in which one's sense of self and indeed one's actions are entirely regulated through the triangulation of the gaze: one looks at oneself as if one were a spectator for another. Above all else it is a society predicated upon the correct insertion of the subject into visuality: into the visual field constructed according to the phantasmic projection of an imaginary third person. Autovoyeurism might perhaps be what this insertion feels like, and it should be acknowledged here that given its sociocultural determinants, this mapping of visuality cannot remain inert in regard to markers of subjectivity such as economic status, class, or gender.

I want to pass on quickly now to an example, since what I have said so far remains pretty much at a theoretical level. If, as I have suggested, Smith articulates a position for spectatorship that not only relies upon the phantasmic projection of a third person who enables and enacts the visual, who makes visuality visible, but also in some curious manner erases the possibility of seeing with one's own eyes (a project, for example, explicitly launched in Hogarth's *Analysis of Beauty*, which constructs a model of visuality based upon the phantasmic projection of seeing from within the object out onto its surface—another form of the visual that also locates the gaze outside the body of the viewer)—if this is the position created by Smith, then what are its effects in the cultural realm?

Smith essentially claims that within the obsessively spectatorial culture of the Enlightenment the spectator is precisely constructed in and through fantasy. As such the position occupied by the real spectator is constantly produced as a site of contest: a contest in regard to one's social definition as either masculine or effeminate, ethically sanctioned or reprimanded, a man of retirement or a man of the world. We can see how these specifics of the site of contest are ranged by taking a very brief example in which the gender of the site of sight, the gender of the look, is clearly an issue.

THE VISIBILITY OF VISUALITY: VAUXHALL GARDENS

Vauxhall Gardens might be termed the *locus classicus* for a detailed investigation into the British eighteenth-century culture of the visibility of visuality. Here in these pleasure gardens the theory of spectatorial subjectivity was literally paraded in front of one's eyes; here one paid an entry fee in order to gain access to the spacings of a publicly visible culture of visuality.[17] It was more than fitting, then, that in a garden where above all else one went to look at others looking at oneself, to indulge in the delights of voyeurism through the eidotropic glance, the following contest around the gender of the look was staged.

My example illustrates the difficulty of unpacking something as complex as visuality when it is read historically, since the case I am going to present is not only folded into the contestatory spaces of the visual field and the ways that gender is constructed in such spaces, it is also deeply embedded within the larger sociocultural operations of gender itself. We cannot really speak of the visual without also speaking of the period's alignment of gender specificities. This is to signal that gender, for the period, is far from a binary division, the masculine and the feminine, but is constructed in a range of discourses that lay claim to determining status in regard to the question of sexuality and at the same time resist penetration by and register the impermeability of certain forms of the subject that encode specific gender assignations. I hope this range will become more clear in my example, an intricate account of an incident that took place in Vauxhall Gardens. The text was published in 1773 and is titled *The Vauxhall Affray: or, the Macaronies Defeated.*

The text is a collection of letters and reports of an incident that allegedly took place in the gardens in which a clergyman named Bate and an actress named Hartley were supposedly accosted by a group of macaronies, those strange effeminate creatures who were fashionable at the time. The so-called affray is quite explicitly the result of a contest over the gaze: Bate, the clergyman, claimed that he was made to feel so uncomfortable by the young men ogling the actress that he challenged one of them, a certain Fitz-Gerall. The ensuing argument was very clearly one over the spectatorial rights of the two men and, it should be made clear, was foregrounded by the specific location: Vauxhall Gardens, the place above all others in which the siting of the viewer was made so public, in which visuality was made so visible. The question in the dispute between the two men was, then, who should have power within the visual: the upstanding clergyman occupying the traditional position of the masculine spectator or the effeminate beau whose gender identity was less certain and viewing position less unambiguous.

We must note that the position of the spectatorial object, the woman Hartley hardly figures in the affray and that the politics of the gaze are contested by males occupying differing positions within the spectrum of eighteenth-century modes of masculinity. Bate, in his description, marshals cultural disapprobation in calling the macaronies, "these pretty beings" who stare "at her with that kind of *petit-maître* audacity, which no language, but the modern French, can possibly describe" (p. 11). Here Bate is attempting to disempower his rivals in the spectatorial contest: the beaux, while laying claim to the position of the spectator, are in fact a spectacle, objectified by Bate's gaze upon them as "pretty beings." Such objectification is intensified through the use of the term of abuse, "French," which for a certain part of this culture represents not only all that is other but all that is objectionable.

The question over the triangulation of the spectatorial position is explicitly raised by Bate in his comment that "to be a silent spectator of such insolence, would be tacitly to countenance it," that is, to occupy the position of the impartial spectator would leave the question of male gender undecided and the vectorial direction of the gaze ambiguous. Consequently Bate enters into the exchange of looks and therefore the contestatory spacings of visuality: "I became now the subject of their loud horse-laughs and wise remarks. Thus unpleasantly circumstanced, I thought it better to face these desperadoes, and therefore turned about and looked them, in my turn, full in the face; in consequence of which, some distortions of features, I believe, passed on both sides" (pp. 10–11).

What is happening here is a face-off in which each party attempts to master and control the site of spectatorial authority and in so doing make of the opponent not, as we saw in Adam Smith, the catoptric other who gives back self-image but the object of the look, the spectacle we witness. In this case the question of gender becomes extremely fraught since what these two differently inflected gendered men are fighting over is both the right to look at another object, the woman who occupies the picture plane upon which the spectator wishes to gaze, and the right to make a spectacle of oneself. This question is explicitly stated by Fitz-Gerall, who asks Bate "whether any man had not a right to look at a fine woman" (p. 13). Of course Bate believes the problem lies precisely in "any man," since some men occupy the powerful masculine position of the gaze whereas others do not and should not. Bate says in reply that he "despised the man who did not look at a fine woman" while going on to assert that Fitz-Gerall and his macaronies look at Hartley in the wrong way (p. 14). What we see going on here is a homosocial contest over the right to spectatorial authority.

The power relation does not flow only in one direction, however, since Bate, the "correct" male, admits the possibility that he might be seduced out of his upstanding masculinity when he claims that Fitz-Gerall's presence "of aerial divinity courted my thoughts from manhood, to a silent contemplation of the progressive beauties of the pygmy system" (p. 35). Here Bate comes close to expressing homophobia when faced with the demand that he articulate his own form of manhood, a feature of the encounter that is intensified by the inclusion of a poem in the text called *The Macaroniad*, which explicitly states that the macaroni occupies an ambiguous and disturbing mixed-gender position:

> But Macaronis are a sex
> Which do philosophers perplex;
> Tho' all the priests of VENUS' rites
> Agree they are Hermaphrodites. (p. 59)

Although this corroboration of Bate's "normalizing" masculinity and the objectification of the female by the gaze is pretty clear, an even more forceful policing of masculinity is performed by a so-called impartial spectator who writes a letter. In this contribution to the text Fitz-Gerall is advised "to appear *only* in petticoats at Vauxhall for the remainder of the season, as the most likely method of escaping the chastisement due for his late unmanly and senseless conduct" (pp. 71–72).

So it comes about that the position of the spectator whereby one form of the male gaze makes into another a spectacle is asserted as heterosexually normalized. The macaroni is removed from the possibility of acting as the other, the phantasmic projection of oneself as an onlooker, since he becomes objectified in the guise of an abnormal, effeminate male who nevertheless also strives to occupy the empowered position of the male gaze that objectifies the feminine. In the example, then, the gaze is not held to be monolithic, in one stable position, clearly defined and operating without causing disturbance within the visual field. On the contrary, it is shown to be mobile, a site of contest in which competing versions of masculinity attempt to render each other a spectacle to themselves. The moral of the story, then, is that it better to be a spectator than a spectacle.

This point is made explicit in another "letter to the editor" in which someone claiming to have overheard the conversation at the time of the fray sends in a report as follows:

Vauxhall Intelligence Extraordinary

Some part of the conversation between the rioters of this place being omitted in other papers, we insert it here for the entertainment of our readers.

Mr. Bate: Why do you, Sir, thrust yourself into this quarrel?

Mr. Fitz-Gerall: I would always be forward to assist my injured friend.

Mr. Bate: Forward enough—but would you defend him right or wrong? Has he not insulted a fine woman?

Mr. Fitz-Gerall: Insulted, Sir! I always thought a fine woman was only made to be looked at.

Mr. Bate: Just sentiments of a macaroni. You judge of the fair sex as you do of your own doubtful gender, which aims only to be looked at and admired.

Mr. Fitz-Gerall: I have as great a love for a fine woman as any man.

Mr. Bate: Psha! *Lepus tute es et pulpamentum quaeris?*

Mr. Fitz-Gerall: What do you say, Parson?

Mr. Bate: I cry you mercy, Sir, I am talking heathen Greek to you. In plain English I say, A macaroni you, and love a woman?

Mr. Fitz-Gerall: I love the ladies, for the ladies love me.

Mr. Bate: Yes, as their panteen, their play-thing, their harmless bauble, to treat as you do them, merely to look at: but pray, Sir, what have you to do in the present dispute?

Mr. Fitz-Gerall: To support my friend, and prove myself a man.

Mr. Bate: God help the friend who stands in need of such support; and as to your manhood, Sir, you had better secure yourself under your acknowledged *neutrality*, or you may feel the weight of my resentment

Mr. Fitz-Gerall: I see you are a bruiser, I shall answer you by my servant.

Mr. Bate: You speak like yourself, Sir; macaroni-like, you do everything by proxy; whether you quarrel, or make love, you answer proxy. (p. 100)

With my example, I have endeavored to demonstrate the extent to which gender and the gaze are both concepts of considerable elasticity. Unlike the contemporary theoretical account, which tends to impose a rigidly schematic version of the male gaze, the Enlightenment example demonstrates the complexity of the socioscopic. In *The Vauxhall Affray* this complexity is brought to light in a kind of contest staged between competing versions of masculinity and the gaze. Where Bate stands for a "normalizing" masculinity, his opponent Fitz-Gerall is painted as a self-regarding deviant, precisely the "pretty creature" whose "snow-white bosom [is] decorated with the miniature resemblance of his own sweet person" (p. 72). Though I have characterized these different positions as constituting some form of contest, it might also be relevant to note that a less conflictual possibility is imagined by the period in which something like a heteroptics of the visual field emerges. Perhaps it is this less conflictual form of our being in visuality that contemporary theory might profitably explore.

1 For discussion of the latter, see N. Daniels, *Thomas Reid's Inquiry: The Geometry of Visibles and the Case for Realism* (Palo Alto: Stanford University Press, 1974); E. C. Graham, *Optics and Vision: The Background of the Metaphysics of Berkeley* (London _____, 1929); John Yolton, *Perceptual Acquaintance from Descartes to Reid* (Minneapolis: University of Minnesota Press, 1984), and *Thinking Matter: Materialism in Eighteenth-Century Britain* (Minneapolis: University of Minnesota Press, 1983); Michael J. Morgan, *Molyneux's Question: Vision, Touch and the Philosophy of Perception* (Cambridge: Cambridge University Press 1977). For the former, see G. N. Cantor, *Optics After Newton: Theories of Light in Britain and Ireland, 1704–1840* (Manchester: Manchester University Press, 1983), and *The Discourse of Light from the Middle Ages to the Enlightenment* (Los Angeles, William Andrews Clark Memorial Library, 1985); N. Pastore, *Selective History of Theories of Visual Perception 1750–1950* (New York: Oxford University Press, 1971).

2 The ways in which this tropological activity colors the modern period have been investigated by Martin Jay in "Scopic Regimes of Modernity," in Hal Foster, ed., *Vision and Visuality* (Seattle: Bay Press, 1988).

3 Film theory is now a fully developed discipline with a voluminous bibliography; the classic account of the theoretical model of vision remains, however, Laura Mulvey, "Visual Pleasure and Narrative Cinema," in *Visual and Other Pleasures* (London: Macmillan, 1989). For the most useful recent contribution to this discussion, see Kaja Silverman, *Male Subjectivity at the Margins* (London: Routledge, 1992).

4 The Lacanian account has been subjected to feminist critique over the last ten or fifteen years, and this work has substantially attenuated the ways in which gender is taken to figure within the formation of the subject. The following discussion should be read within the context of this work. See Juliet Mitchell and Jacqueline Rose, eds., *Feminine Sexuality* (London: Macmillan, 1982); and for recent developments in a range of fields, Seyla Benhabib and Drucilla Cornell, eds., *Feminism as Critique* (Minneapolis: University of Minnesota Press, 1988).

5 Jacques Lacan, *The Four Fundamental Concepts of Psychoanalysis*, trans. Alan Sheridan (Harmondsworth: Penguin, 1977), p. 84. Later references to this work are cited in the text by page number.

6 These diagrams have become almost talismanic in the literature on the Lacanian model of the gaze. My own account is deeply indebted to those that precede it, most especially to the discussion in Silverman, *Male Subjectivity at the Margins*, pp. 145–153.

7 On the camera obscura as culturally embedded form for figuring vision, see Jonathan Crary, *Techniques of the Observer* (Cambridge, Mass.: MIT Press, 1990); and for a scrupulous account of the history of mechanical aids to visuality, Martin Kemp, *The Science of Art* (New Haven: Yale University Press, 1990).

8 John Shebbeare, *Letters on the English Nation* (London, 1755), p. 27.

9 Mathew Pilkington, *The Gentleman's and Connoisseur's Dictionary of Painters* (London, 1770), p. viii.

10 Rouquet, *The Polite Arts, or, a Dissertation on Poetry, Painting, Musick, Architecture and Eloquence* (London, 1749), p. 4.

11 John Stedman, *Laelius and Hotensia: or, Thoughts on the Nature and Objects of Taste and Genius* (London, 1782), p. 32.

12 The most important account of the civic humanist theory of the fine arts is to be found in John Barrell, *The Political Theory of Painting* (New Haven: Yale University Press, 1986). Since its publication a number of further books have contributed to the debate initiated by Barrell; see in particular David Solkin, *Painting for Money* (New Haven: Yale University Press, 1994); Marcia Pointon, *Hanging the Head* (New Haven: Yale University Press, 1994); and John Barrell, *Painting and the Politics of Culture* (Oxford: Oxford University Press, 1992).

13 Rouquet, *The Polite Arts*. Later references to this work are cited in the text by page number.

14 Thomas Page, Jr., *The Art of Painting* (Norwich, 1720), p. 81.

15 Charles Leslie, *Life and Times of Sir Joshua Reynolds: with notices of some of his contemporaries* 2 vol. (London, 1865) vol. 2, p. 32. Later references to this work are cited in the text by page number.

16 The edition referred to is edited by D. D. Raphael and A. L. Macfie (Oxford, 1976). For an exemplary discussion of the range of issues raised by Smith's text, see the introduction to this edition. Later references to this work are cited in the text by page number.

17 For discussion of Vauxhall, see: T. J. Edelstein, ed.,
Vauxhall Gardens (New Haven: Yale Center for British
Art, 1983); David Coke, *The Muse's Bower: Vauxhall
Gardens 1728-1786* (Sudbury, 1978); Brian Allen,
Francis Hayman (New Haven: Yale University Press,
1987); David Solkin, *Painting for Money* (New Haven:
Yale University Press, 1992); and Kristina Straub,
Sexual Suspects (Princeton: Princeton University
Press, 1992).

Gillian Beer

When the psychologist and experimental scientist George Henry Lewes wrote his six "Studies in Animal Life" for the *Cornhill Magazine* in 1860,[1] he stipulated that they be prefaced with an epigraph from Wordsworth's poem "*The Excursion*":

> Authentic tidings of invisible things;
> Of ebb and flow, and ever-during power,
> And central peace subsisting at the heart
> Of endless agitation.

In the later nineteenth century almost every one of the words in that passage underwent transvaluation. The "ebb and flow, and ever-during power" became not tidal only but a metaphor for a closed system within which the amount of energy remained constant (the first law of thermodynamics). New homologies were discerned between sound and sight, particularly through Hermann von Helmholtz's innovative studies of physical optics and acoustics and through their popularization by John Tyndall in the major general magazines, in public demonstrations, and in his published lectures.[2] Above all, the "central peace subsisting at the heart of endless agitation" ceased to be a benign sustaining power and, instead, became the ultimate form of cosmic death when, according to the second law of thermodynamics, entropy reaches its maximum and no energy remains available. "Things" themselves proved to be modes of motion rather than stable entities. Instead of being described as material particles, light, like heat and sound, was newly understood as a mode of motion: as the astrophysicist George Airy wrote, "We shall suppose that light is the undulation of a medium called *ether* which pervades all transparent bodies."[3] Unbounded, irrecoverable, the performance of energies lay beyond the reach of eyesight, and even perhaps beyond the reach of any signification outside mathematics. Vision was, in a quite new way, subordinate to the invisible.

Alfred Russel Wallace, codiscoverer with Darwin of the principle of natural selection, put it positively in his *fin-de-siècle* work *The Wonderful Century*: "This great principle enables us to realize the absolute interdependence of all the forces of nature.... All work, all motion, every manifestation of power we see around us, are alike the effects of heat or other radiant forces allied to it."[4] There is, he declares, "no origination of force upon the earth." Work, energy, lapsing, and equilibration were all equally imagined as expressions of universal wave activity, only fleetingly visible.

The *invisible* thus became a site of debate and perturbation for later-nineteenth-century people. Tussles developed for the control of meaning relating to that which is invisible: tussles between scientists and spiritualists, materialists and Christians. Among my examples here are little-known writers; it is a mistake to imagine that only those whose work is still best known to us responded to what was newly thought, as if by some special privilege. Instead, provocative readings and perceptions emerged from a whole variety of positions. The authenticity of the eye's insight was put in question; the synaesthetic chiming of the senses, particularly hearing and sight, came to have a greater valency within and beyond scientific enquiry. The eye itself, in Helmholtz's work, proved to be an imperfect instrument incapable of stable resolution. Far from dominating explanation or experience in this new mind-set, sight must welter in a world strung through with energy that declares itself equally as heat, light, sound. At this period, also, the sun's energy was understood to be unrenewable, slackening implacably toward the heat-death of the universe.[5]

The invisible, instead of being placidly held just beyond the scope of sight, was newly understood as an energetic system out of which fitfully emerges that which is visible.[6] Among scientists the arguments principally concerned the nature of the invisible medium for transmitted energy that they called ether: Was it viscous, vibratory, gravitational, elastic, kinetic, electromagnetic? Whatever it was, it was taken to be all-pervading, invisible, and inarguably *there*, materially so. In his account of James Clerk Maxwell for the *Dictionary of National Biography*, R. T. Glazebrook wrote in 1894: "In light waves periodic changes in the ether are taking place.... The laws of these vibrations, when they are completely known, will give us the secret of the ether."[7]

Ether was the key secret of the universe remaining to be unlocked, but it was also a secret that paid scant regard to the human. Light, sound, and heat were all, variously, modes of motion; most of their activity took place beyond the reach of human sensory capacity as "ether vibration." The "invisible" was becoming increasingly secularized; it seemed to be a domain now capable of being described predominantly in scientific terms. Were these "authentic tidings"?

The unease occasioned by the new physical theories of the invisible contrasts tellingly with the optimism that Barbara Stafford evokes in her description of Enlightenment responses to the microscope. She presents a sanguine and poetic account of the noninvasive uncovering of the body's interior enabled by the development of microscopes during the late eighteenth century:

> Detailed images conveyed information and brought to the surface, as it were, the mysterious structures of life floating somewhere below the skin. Instruments sent a flood of lightning-swift nonverbal and graphic messages from an unknown and beautiful dimension. The extension of vision permitted a new form of travel. Opaque depths were opened up, becoming transparent without the infliction of violence. The veil of the invisible was gently and noninvasively lifted.[8]

This is a highly topographical version of the invisible: sea and land are evoked at once, and the whole depends upon *resolution*. Stable entities, "structures of life," though mysterious, become visible. The invisible is both what lies beneath the skin in a phenomenal sea and yet also a covering, a "veil" that may be withdrawn. Stafford's description here, despite its invocation of the oceanic, is quite unlike the invisible processes that concern me in this argument.

Important work has recently been accomplished, for example, by Evelyn Fox Keller and Ludmilla Jordanova on sight and seeing in medical and scientific discourse from the Enlightenment through the nineteenth century.[9] They have both emphasized the imagery of secret interiorities, female forms. That particular notion of invisibility relies upon the idea of concealed and darkened interiors actively broached from without by the investigative scientist. As Keller puts it in her essay "Making Gender Visible in the Pursuit of Nature's Secrets":

> The ferreting out of nature's secrets, understood as the illumination of a female interior, or the tearing of nature's veil, may be seen as expressing one of the most unembarrassedly stereotypic impulses of the scientific project. In this interpretation, the task of scientific enlightenment—the illumination of the reality behind appearances—is an inversion of surface and interior, an interchange between visible and invisible, that effectively routs the last vestiges of archaic subterranean female power.[10]

My concern is with a different imagining of the invisible: not the dissective opening up of that which is enclosed but rather a permeating and propulsive energy, at once powerful and wasting. My later example of Stewart and Tait shows the degree of aggressive resistance roused by the implications of the laws of thermodynamics, especially the second law, as it fell foul of social and gendered expectations.

The new "authentic tidings" told against any anthropocentric or transcendental organization such as that proposed by Carlyle in the 1830s. Carlyle had offered the invisible as an emblem of the engrossment of all meaning in the human: "Man...though based, to all seeming, on the small Visible, does nevertheless extend down into the infinite deeps of the Invisible, of which Invisible, indeed, his Life is properly the bodying forth."[11] Humankind—perhaps more precisely, as he puts it here, Man—permeates the "infinite deeps" as well as incarnating the invisible. But the converse was not yet part of the imagination: that the invisible permeates the human frame, that the human is unbounded because pulsed through by process. The invisible world had been, for many, easily accepted as a state below or (more often) a state above, a transcendent space inhabited by angels and godhead—even a state *around*.

That condition is wonderfully described in John Henry Newman's sermon "The Invisible World," written before 1843. He prefaces it with a passage from Corinthians II (4, 18): "While he look not at the things which are seen, but at the things that are not seen: for the things which are seen are temporal; but the things which are not seen are eternal." Newman asserts that despite the capaciousness of

> this universal world which we see, there is another world, quite as far-reaching, quite as close to us, and more wonderful; another world all round us, though we see it not, and more wonderful than the world we see, for this reason if for no other, that we do not see it. All around us are numberless objects, coming and going, watching, working or waiting, which we see not: this is that other world which eyes reach not unto, but faith only.[12]

Until that last phrase the language is poised between that of science and that of hope: "The world of spirits, then, though unseen, is present; present, not future, not distant" (p. 257).

Such an understanding of the world seemed to make room for a spiritualist interpretation in which emanations take on physical form and lost presences may be materially evoked.[13] And the arrival of thermodynamics and "the ether" gave a quite new "scientific" valency to such possibilities. In Robert Browning's poem *Mr. Sludge, "The Medium"* his fraudulent spiritualist medium, Mr. Sludge, puts the traditional quasi-material view well.

> The First Fact
> We're taught is, there's a world beside this world,
> With spirits, not mankind for tenantry;
> That much within that world once sojourned here,
> That all upon this world will visit there.[14]

Sludge argues that such beliefs are primary, internalized: "See now, we start with the miraculous."

> First comes the Bible's speech; then, history
> With the supernatural element,—you know—
> All that we sucked in with our mothers' milk,
> Grew up with, got inside of us at last,
> Till it's found bone of bone and flesh and flesh.
> See now, we start with the miraculous. (p. 193)

After the two laws of thermodynamics entered public awareness, however, the invisible seemed to make us simply receptors of its traffic. In the tradition of many mystics, the invisible could be accepted as a condition inexpressible, yet one that buoyed up human dignity. It figured an altitude above reason, a depth beneath reason, a reach beyond reason, where human and divine might merge. But by the 1850s, the invisible world might seem to be out of human control, the hermeneutics of religious reading no longer quite apt. Only the emanations from the "spirit world" might, through mediums, briefly be made the servants of human wishes and curiosity. Making things visible, making them emerge, became (among other things) a means of regaining control.

John Ruskin in *Ethics of the Dust* sardonically resisted the new forms of explanation in physics by counterpoising the physical body of a young girl dancing. He in turn was rebuked by the *Westminster Review* when the book appeared in 1866 for indecently opposing scientific authority:

> This is the manner in which he thinks it decent to oppose certain well-ascertained conclusions of modern science: "Lecturer.—Do you think you don't know whether you are alive or not? (Isabel skips to the end of the room and back). Yes, Isabel, that's all very fine, and you and I may call that being; but a modern philosopher calls it being 'in a mode of motion.' It requires a certain quantity of heat to take you to the sideboard, and exactly the same quantity to bring you back again—that's all." (p. 46) Paley has said that you can't refute a sneer. Luckily, however, a sneer refutes itself. But we will not bid Mr. Ruskin look to Paley, but rather to Butler, who in his famous tenth sermon says "it is as easy to shut the eyes of the mind as those of the head."[15]

To bring Ruskin to heel, the reviewer neatly turns to Bishop Butler, whose work on analogy continued to underpin natural theology. Natural theology supposed a godhead expressed in the activities of the material world rather than by revelation, so Butler's analogy between the "eyes of the mind" and "those of the head" trumped Ruskin's objections to the reductionism of thermodynamics.

Increasingly the invisible came to declare itself as a condition within which we move, and *of* which we are, lateral, extensive, out of human control; worse, not amenable to analysis yet replete with phenomena. The invisible might prove to be a controlling medium, not a place to be explored; a condition of our existence, not a new country to be colonized. Paradoxically, this realization dawned alongside the great advances in microscopes, telescopes, and optics in the mid-nineteenth century.

Even as the domain of sight advanced by means of such instruments, the evidence was mounting that the eye was an uncertain instrument and men of science insecure observers. Moreover, the implications of wave theory undermined male as much as female autonomy. Sometimes the two contrasted ideas, piercing and emanating, associated with the invisible and its disclosure were caught together. Often gender ascriptions and discriminations were expunged and wave theory set all humankind adrift, blinded and eyeless. Male and female were no longer fixed limits. New physical theories ("energetics," "wave theory") meant, the great physicist James Clerk Maxwell mused in 1874, that "we are once more on a pathless sea, starless, windless, and poleless."[16]

This invocation of the sea is not contingent but intrinsic to the new understandings of a universe extensive, propulsive, in which the agency and medium was an invisible luminiferous ether. The work that Maxwell and Helmholtz were doing disturbed all oppositions of inside/outside, invisible/visible. Instead of disclosure or exposure—the hauling of the hidden into the light—all life becomes a medium, a discharge, or a pathway. The visible forms that energy takes are evanescent and contingent. Evolution and physics both emphasized life forms as transitional and transformative, without stay or constancy, discomfiting indeed. And the imagery of waves and the oceanic, universalized as part of scientific discourse, also became a medium for exploring sexuality and gender in the writing of men and women alike, for example, in the work of writers such as Edward Carpenter or Mathilde Blind. Blind's poem *The Ascent of Man* reimagines the beginning of the universe and opens thus:

> Struck out of dim fluctuant forms and shock of electrical vapor,
> Repelled and attracted the atoms flashed mingling in union primeval,
> And over the face of the waters far heaving in limitless twilight
> Auroral pulsations thrilled faintly, and, striking the blank heaving surface,

The measureless speed of their motion now leaped into light on the waters.[17]

Instead of an older triumphalist drama of enlightenment there were waves: waves of light, sound, heat. The explorations in physical optics, acoustics, and—fundamentally—thermodynamics emphasized permeation and transmission. Instead of the scientist forensically exploring a hidden space, a shared system flowed through humankind and other forms, living and inert alike. As its heat flowed, energy became less and less available for conversion into work until a state of universe-death is reached.

May Kendall caught the implications in her comic poem of exasperated despair, *Ether Insatiable*. Here Energy is initially personified as female and ether as neutral and all powerful, but by the poem's end gender has been surpassed by universal defeat: "And no one will win—but the ether, / That fills circumambient space!"[18] The poem recounts the falling back of human endeavor, the dispersion of energy into an implacable ether that is figured as irresponsive and mindless appetite. Even the smallest affect contributes not to human progress but to human evanescence: "There is not a hushed malediction /There is not a smile or a sigh /But aids in dispersing, by friction, / The cosmical heat in the sky."

The whole poem runs:

Now Energy's bound to diminish—
    The harder she struggles and moils,
The faster she speeds to the finish,
    The end of her infinite toils.
A million of planets beneath her
    Strong hands she may mould or efface—
'Tis all to the good of the ether,
    That fills circumambient space!

All's quietly caught up and muffled
    By a strange and intangible foe,
The ether serene and unruffled,
    The ether we see not nor know.
Life, radiance, in torrents dispelling,
    The universe spins to its goal;
And radiance and life find one dwelling—
    This ether's the tomb of the whole.

There is not a hushed malediction,
    There is not a smile or a sigh,
But aids in dispersing, by friction,
    The cosmical heat in the sky;
And whether a star falls or whether
    A heart breaks—for stars and for men
Their labour is all for the ether,
    That renders back nothing again.

And we, howsoever we hated
    And feared, or made love, or believed,
For all the opinions we stated,

> The woes and the wars we achieved,
> We, too, shall lie idle together,
>   In very uncritical case—
> And no one will win—but the ether,
>   That fills circumambient space.

Here the ether is an obliterative medium, scarcely to be distinguished from death, save that this death is not individual but universal, without recourse to any further signification. The pounce and bounce of the poem's rhyme scheme, the jaunty spring of the meter, figure a resistance to entropy even while the poem's semantics describe an inevitable running down.

IMPERFECT VISION, PERSISTENT SOUND

The eye had traditionally been represented as the ultimate argument for a designed universe, and the microscope and telescope seemed only to extend its authority. An organ of such perfection, it was asserted, could not have been produced by chance. Writing in the 1830s in one of the Bridgewater Treatises setting out to demonstrate God's immanence in the natural world, Charles Bell concentrated his argument for design on the hand because he saw the eye as the already taken-for-granted example, non-negotiable. Indeed, when Charles Darwin began his researches he accepted the perfection of the eye and saw that as a stumbling block for his theories of adaptation and selection.

Had Darwin known, Helmholtz had already in his 1855 treatise "Accommodation" made it clear that the eye was by no means a perfect instrument. Eyes have, as his biographer Leo Koenigsberger summarized the argument, "a slight but perceptible defect of centering which produced the so-called astigmatism of the eye: the effect of which is that we cannot clearly see horizontal and vertical lines at the same distance simultaneously."[19] In a letter written at the time Helmholtz is more forthright: "The human eye is not even properly centered, the magnitude of the corneal eccentricity appears to be quite irregular and adventitious" (p. 137). It was to be fifteen years before Darwin knew Helmholtz's findings, which actually predate *The Origin of Species* (1859). In the final edition of *The Origin of Species* Darwin inserted a paragraph in which, with great relief and delight, he adduced Helmholtz's view.

> Helmholtz, whose judgment no one will dispute, after describing in the strongest terms the wonderful powers of the human eye adds these remarkable words: 'That which we have discovered in the way of inexactness and imperfection in the optical machine and in the image of the retina, is as nothing in comparison with the incongruities which we have just come across in the domain of the sensations. One might say that nature has taken delight in accumulating contradictions in order to remove all foundation from the theory of a pre-existing harmony between the external and internal worlds.'[20]

That opinion authoritatively chimed in with Darwin's fundamental argument that natural selection is part of a process of adaptation, not of design, and that one should therefore expect to find imperfections, not absolute precision, in even the most complex organs. But this agreement was one of the rare accords between evolution and physics at the time.

Helmholtz's downgrading of the eye had further consequences, since the nature of the imperfections that he pointed out were that they made some forms of image resolution impossible. Much earlier work on microscopes and telescopes assumed that as we lower or raise the threshold of perception we gain access to forms essentially similar to those already known, smaller or farther off, maybe, but not unlike in kind. As a corollary of that view, current forms of knowledge could be expanded but were not radically re-formed by such instruments. As Rosalind Krauss notes, however, the implication of Helmholtz's evidence concerning visual perception was that resolution was inherently unreliable: "The physiological screen through which light passes to the human brain is not transparent like a window pane; it is like a filter, involved in a set of specific distortions."[21] In the first of his essays on light John Tyndall made the point vividly: "A long list of indictments might indeed be brought against the eye—its opacity, its want of symmetry, its lack of achromatism, its absolute blindness, in part. All these taken together caused Helmholtz to say that, if any optician sent him an instrument so full of defects, he would be justified in sending it back with the severest censure."[22]

Moreover, not only the distortion but the extreme tenuity of our senses was brought home as the subsonic, ultrasonic, and subsensible (in Tyndall's term) began to surround and imbue the human. Daguerreotypes (the earliest photographs) made visible the white light of the sun. In 1853 Helmholtz changed the term "invisible rays" to "ultraviolet rays" when he found that if paper were soaked in quinine the human eye "could detect all the refragible rays of this region which were able to pass through the prisms."[23] In the 1890s, as Wallace noted in *The Wonderful Century*, came "that peculiar form of radiation termed the X, or Rontgen Rays which extends our powers of vision in a direction and to an extent the limits of which cannot yet be guessed."[24] Vision was extending its bounds, but the effect was to suggest how much lay beyond its powers and its focus, how fleeting its intervention.

It is in this setting that Walter Pater's dictum that "all arts aspire to the condition of music" can be better understood. Ideas of the invisible world as a hidden, cloistered interiority or as a radiant future both came into question. There was, however, one means of retrieving high meaning for the invisible: in Helmholtz's view the ear was a much finer and more competent organ than the eye. Sound began to assume the status as ideal function that sight had earlier held. In the conclusion to *The Renaissance* (1873) Pater acknowledges the new understanding of the body: "Our physical life is a perpetual motion of them—the passage of the blood, the waste and repairing of the lenses of the eye, the modification of the tissues of the brain under every ray of light and sound—processes which science reduces to simpler and more elementary forces."[25] In *Plato and Platonism* Pater argues the history of philosophy with a strong sense of its relevance to the contemporary later-nineteenth-century debates concerning chaos, lapse, and waste of energy as the fundamental condition; Heraclitus, he says, sought the other side of the argument and so, prospectively and in doubt (here, "if there be such"), does Pater. The resolving metaphor that is to mediate between waste and significance is that of composed music: "to reduce that world of chaotic mutation to *cosmos*, to the unity of a reasonable order, by the search for and the notation, if there be such, of an antiphonal rhythm, or logic, which, proceeding uniformly from movement to movement, as in some intricate musical theme, might link together in one of those contending, infinitely diverse impulses."[26] Pater's dissolving of the boundaries between rhythm and logic is a desperate restorative measure. Maxwell preferred the term *agitation* to *rhythm* and firmly resisted Herbert Spencer's attempt to substitute rhythm in his description of thermodynamics.

Nevertheless, the ear became the chosen arbiter of refined discriminations. It deflected the obliterative sameness feared in ether and its undulations. Attempts were also persistently made to find an equivalence between the visible and the auditory. In the pages of *Nature* a sustained debate took place over several years during the 1870s about the degree to which the octave and the spectrum are "naturally" homologous. The counterargument presented was that out of infinite fine gradations of pitch and of color seven hues and notes have been elected and named. The apparent homology is, therefore, a metaphor only, a way of asserting pattern. That pattern is based on the human preference for analogy, not the order of the universe.

Sound waves and light waves seemed to hold out the promise of congruity, a traffic across the border of visible and invisible. The work of Lord John Rayleigh and of Helmholtz in acoustics could, on occasion, produce a synaesthetic novelty. Maxwell, in his essay "The Telephone," lushly described Sedley Taylor's newly named and invented "phoneidoscope," which used sound vibrations to produce colors on a thin film: "The wail of the siren draws musician and mathematician together down into the depths of their sensational being, and where the gorgeous hues of the phoneidoscope are seen to seethe and twine and coil."[27] Music became visible. Rare, however, was either perfection or accord in the new relations of the visible and the invisible in science. And that disturbance became part of a more diffused cultural uneasiness about the continuity of identity and about the nature of the future.

The new representations of the invisible needed metrics more than images, mathematics as much as discourse. Agnes Mary Frances Duclaux (Mary Robinson) (born 1857) attempted in her poem *The Idea*[28] to retrieve the idea of an unseen other world for a religious language, inflected through these new concerns—a kind of ether as godhead, number as meaning, sound as invisible deity.

> Beneath this world of stars and flowers
> That rolls in visible deity,
> I dream another world is ours
> And is the soul of all we see.
>
> It hath no form, it hath no spirit;
> It is perchance the Eternal Mind;
> Beyond the sense that we inherit
> I feel it dim and undefined.
>
> How far below the depth of being,
> How wide beyond the starry bound
> It rolls unconscious and unseeing,
> And is as Number or as Sound.
>
> And through the vast fantastic visions
> Of all this actual universe,
> It moves unswerved by our decisions,
> And is the play that we rehearse.

Duclaux's determinism is expressed in the tight and unexpected final rhyme of "universe" and "rehearse." The spare precision of this language is very different from the oceanic roll of many of the other attempts to plumb the invisible at that time: "And is as Number or as Sound." The poem is sustained by prior certainties, but even those certainties are now informed by language and speculations drawn from wave theory.

George Eliot and Thomas Hardy, notable agnostics, turned away from the orthodox idea of eternal life as light to find ways of thinking about eternity through *sound*. George Eliot, humanist and postreligious, wrote a secular prayer that had great currency among her contemporaries and for some time after her death. It begins thus:

> O, may I join the choir invisible
> Of those immortal dead who live again
> In minds made better by their presence.

Immortality and resurrection are ethical, not transcendental, concepts here. Her concluding idea of heaven is of continued presence as *diffusion*. Her hope is to

> Be the sweet presence of a good diffused,
> And in diffusion ever more intense.
> So shall I join the choir invisible
> Whose music is the gladness of the world.[29]

Sound is the redeemed alternative to the visible here; a harmonious acoustic eternity is invoked. George Eliot's tentative meliorism has to authenticate itself in scientifically acceptable expression: she does it by fusing the old choirs of angels with the new Helmholtzian language of sound waves. The turn toward sound chimes in with a fresh imagining of what endures: not the permanent or substantial but pulsation and sound wave.

In his poem *In the Museum* Hardy contrasts the fossil of an extinct bird with its song. The fossil is "the mould" in both senses: it preserves the bird's form like a mould but presents form also as detritus and decay, "mould." The bird's species is invisible now, gone before man came, but the song continues, not only—as poets have long declared—because other birds of the same kind sing the same song. Now acoustics and wave theory allow Hardy a further leap: the song literally never ends and neither does that of the woman singing last night. Both continue to pulse as sound waves through the universe, making a part of that diapaison that he reaches in the magnificent final line: "In the full-fugued song of the universe unending." *Unending* is not only temporal but topographical: the universe is without bounds, filled with air waves laden with sounds inaudible to us but physically there, overlapping and propulsive, "full-fugued."

> I
> Here's the mound of a musical bird long passed from light,
> Which over the earth before man came was winging;
> There's a contralto voice I heard last night,
> That lodges in me still with its sweet singing.
>
> II
> Such a dream is Time that the coo of this ancient bird
> Has perished not, but is bent, or will be blending
> Mid visionless wilds of space with the voice that I heard,
> In the full-fugued song of the universe unending.[30]

Hardy, through song, can sustain the universe as "unending" while the intensity of his metaphor is informed by current wave theory and acoustics.

The physicists Balfour Stewart and Peter Tait, respected theorists (Tait was Maxwell's principal scientific correspondent and coauthor with Arthur Thomson (Lord Kelvin) of *Treatise on Natural Philosophy*, 1867), grappled with the problem of reconciling scientific and Christian belief by extending the boundaries of argument—as well as space. They sought to find a way beyond the inevitably deathly outcome of final physical equilibration within a closed system. The visible universe, they argue, is indeed transitory: "If we suppose the material universe to be composed of a series of vortex-rings developed from an invisible universe which is not a perfect fluid, it will be ephemeral, just as the smoke-ring which we develop from air, or that which we develop from water, is ephemeral."[31] "The available energy of the visible universe will ultimately be appropriated by the invisible." But all is not lost: creation, they argue, "belongs to eternity and development to time." The solution they offer is that "the visible system is not the whole universe, but only, it may be, a very small part of it; and that there must be an invisible order of things, which will remain and possess energy when the present system has passed away."

Their reasoning is that "if we regard the dissipation of energy which is constantly going on, we are at first sight forcibly struck with the apparently wasteful character of the arrangements of the visible universe." This point is the nub of the matter: Stewart and Tait use ethical concepts—an appreciation of frugality as opposed to "waste"—to clinch their argument. Somewhere in the furthest extent of creation energy is recycled, not depleted. The idea has its attractions to an ecological age too. It could be argued that this position has foresight, prospectively imagining, in other terms, at least the discovery of radioactivity early in the twentieth century. Stewart and Tait give lucid accounts of the current state of physical knowledge and acknowledge the inevitable decline of the visible universe. But for them the universe is a matter of finding a preferred argument, a preferred set of standards that will allow the physical world to measure up to the expectations of the work ethic and muscular Christianity: "The dissipation of energy is a great fact in a moral as well as in a physical sense. In those good old times *men* fought with *men*,—irrepressible energy, rather than any sordid passion or uncontrolled vice, constantly pulling the trigger!" In an uncontrolled swerve in their argument from the dissipation of energy to rape, they express outrage at men who now "vent their despicable passions in murderous assaults upon women and children." Then, in a sinister paean of praise to the efficacy of the invisible power of electricity, they complacently prophecy the punishment that will become possible, leaving no visible trace. The protean powers of electricity are described without irony:

> It is probable that before many years have passed, electricity, which by some mysterious means enables our nerves to call our muscles into play, which enables us to converse with one another at distances of thousands of miles, which alike plates the teaspoon and illuminates the lighthouse, will be called upon by an enlightened legislature to produce absolutely indescribable torture (unaccompanied by wound or even bruise), thrilling through every fibre of the frame of such miscreants.[32]

Throughout *The Unseen Universe* these rapid and uncritical transitions are performed in the argument, and argument becomes a matter of will: "We cannot be satisfied with a make-believe universe, or one consisting only of dead matter, but prefer a living intelligent universe, in other words, one full conditioned. Finally, our argument has led us to regard the production of the visible universe as brought about by an intelligent agency residing in the unseen." Only God, that is, "the Creator—the Absolute One," and he therefore is above the universe and the conditioned.

This disturbing work went rapidly through a number of editions. It gives one adverse examples of the ways assumptions about gender entered what might on the face of it look like gender-free arguments. Here, a particular construction of masculinity becomes the arbiter of arguments about the capacities of the universe.

In contrast, for many artists and scientists at the time the oceanic becomes the unstable, visible metaphor for the fundamental condition of all existence, a condition that itself is and must remain *invisible*.

Walt Whitman had established a possible language and rhythmic pulse for such description. He did so with a sensory vocabulary that drew exhaustively on vision, but the iterativeness of the poem's form suggested not sight but movement, waves surging and lapsing: his poem *Salut au Monde* poses the subjective, obsessionally reflexive, question: "What do you see, Walt Whitman?" It gives eighty-three answers, each beginning "I see." Sea and see mingle in the spume of endless repetition, but the oceanic also becomes a means of escaping the separation of observer and observed.

Gerard Manley Hopkins and Edward Carpenter both drew on Whitman's resource of sight sprung on rhythmic impulsion and repetition. Strikingly, all these writers shared homoerotic sexuality, despite the diversity of their lives. The language of the first law of thermodynamics (the amount of energy in a closed system remains constant, though its manifestations may alter) allowed for a transgendered poetry of sustained transformations in which, though dissipated, nothing is lost, and the energy of the ocean remains constant though its waves vanish.

Edward Carpenter's poem "By the Shore" opens with a night scene in which the poet progressively becomes suffused by wave and ocean and identity dissolves into the body of water:

All night by the shore.
    The obscure water, the long white lines of advancing foam, the rustle and thud, the
panting sea-breaths, the pungent sea-smell,
The great slow air moving from the distant horizon,
    the immense mystery of space, and the soft canopy of the clouds!

The swooning thuds go on—the drowse of ocean goes on:
The long inbreaths—the short sharp outbreaths—the silence between.

I am a bit of the shore: the waves feed upon me, they come pasturing over me;
I am glad, O waves, that you come pasturing over me.[33]

Carpenter's poem, mimicking the ocean's beat, continues for several pages. It ends but does not conclude.

The examples I have adduced range from the work of innovative scientists at the forefront of the new physics to those who half-knew or even discountenanced what their fresh theories proposed. Clearly, they were not all affected alike. In many cases indications from scientific ideas melded with other life materials. But as I have also shown, life materials haunted scientific inquiry. Helmholtz described the relief that it gave him to sit on a clifftop and watch the waves of the ocean, relief from the constant effort of intellectual imagining of invisible wave activity in other forms. Precisely because the oceanic had been a recurrent form for thinking through life processes from Heraclitus and Lucretius on, it became a possible medium for new feeling now that it was also caught in current scientific explanation. It could suggest both the intimately physical experience of the body and its bounds, alongside a new understanding of boundlessness and the passage of invisible energies.

With the entry of "energetics" and wave theory into general currency came the question of how to give authentic expression to permanently and profoundly unseen processes. Vision was certainly not granted any easy authority one hundred years ago. Surprise is sometimes expressed that Freud in his early career was so much affected by the work of Helmholtz. Seen in the context of the affects I have described, Freud's response becomes evidence of his capacity to catch the reverberations that sound most intimately in many lives of his time.

6.1 Claude Monet, "Trains at the Lazare Station," detail of smoke and steam (Fogg Art Museum)

6.2 Georges Michel, "The Storm" ca 1820–30, detail, Musée des Beaux-Arts, Strasbourg

1 Published in book form as *Studies in Animal Life* (London: Smith, Elder, 1862). See Rosemary Ashton, *George Henry Lewes: A Life* (Oxford: Clarendon Press, 1991), p. 223.

2 John Tyndall, *Fragments of Science: A Series of Detached Essays, Addresses, and Reviews*, 2 vols., 10th ed. (London: Longmans, Green, 1899).

3 George Airy, *On the Undulatory Theory of Optics: Designed for the Use of Students in the University*, new ed. (London and Cambridge: Macmillan, 1866), p. 19, revised from a first edition of 1831. See also his *On Sound and Atmospheric Vibrations, with the Mathematical Elements of Music* (London: Macmillan, 1868).

4 Alfred Russel Wallace, *The Wonderful Century: Its Successes and Failures* (London: Swan Sonnenschien, 1898), pp. 28–30.

5 I have published several essays that relate to this argument: see "The Death of the Sun: Victorian Solar Physics and Solar Myth," in Barry Bullen, ed., *The Sun Is God: Painting, Literature, and Mythology in the Nineteenth Century* (Oxford: Clarendon Press, 1989); "Helmholtz, Tyndall, Gerard Manley Hopkins: Leaps of the Prepared Imagination," *Comparative Criticism*, vol. 13 (Cambridge: Cambridge University Press, 1991); "Wave Theory and the Rise of Literary Modernism," in George Levine, ed., *Realism and Representation: Essays on the Problem of Realism in Relation to Science, Literature, and Culture* (Madison: University of Wisconsin Press, 1993). See also Daniel Pick, *Faces of Degeneration: A European Disorder c. 1848–c. 1918* (Cambridge: Cambridge University Press, 1989); Peter Dale, *In Pursuit of a Scientific Culture: Science, Art, and Society in the Victorian Age* (Madison: University of Wisconsin Press, 1989); Peter Harman, *Nineteenth-Century Physics* (Cambridge: Cambridge University Press, 1982); Geoffrey Cantor and Michael Hodge, eds., *Conceptions of Ether: Studies in the History of Ether Theories* (Cambridge: Cambridge University Press, 1981).

6 It had taken quite a considerable time for Thomas Young's undulatory theory of light to establish itself, partly because his ideas, already put forward at the turn of the nineteenth century, were oppressively mocked for years in the *Edinburgh Review* by Henry Brougham, who was later Lord Chancellor of England. So dominant were the humanities in the middle and upper classes that it was hard for a scientist to have his theories accepted as substantial without backing from the journals. Young's discoveries had to be remade by Fresnel in France and Helmholtz in Germany.

7 Sidney Lee, ed., *Dictionary of National Biography*, (London: Smith, Elder, 1894, p. 120.

8 Barbara Stafford, *Body Criticism: Imaging the Unseen in Enlightenment Art and Medicine* (Cambridge, Mass.: MIT Press, 1991), p. 343.

9 Ludmilla Jordanova, *Sexual Visions: Images of Gender in Science and Medicine Between the Eighteenth and Twentieth Century* (Hemel Hempstead: Harvester, 1989); Evelyn Fox Keller, *Reflections on Gender and Science* (New Haven: Yale University Press, 1985).

10 Evelyn Fox Keller, "Making Gender Visible in the Pursuit of Nature's Secrets," in Teresa de Lauretis, ed., *Feminist Studies/Critical Studies* (1986), p. 69.

11 Thomas Carlyle, *Sartor Resartus*, book 3, ch. 3 (London: Chapman and Hall, n.d.), p. 133.

12 John Henry Newman, "The Invisible World," p. 251.

13 See my "Wave Theory and the Rise of Literary Modernism" for discussion of the materialist John Tyndall's encounter with a spiritualist medium and their accommodation.

14 Robert Browning, *Mr. Sludge, "The Medium," The Poetical Works of Robert Browning*, vol. 6 (London: Smith, Elder, 1870) pp. 162–218.

15 *Westminster Review*, Belles Letters, 29 (April 1866): 595–596.

16 Unpublished letter to Tait, November, 1974, Cambridge University Library; quoted with the library's kind permission.

17 Mathilde Blind, *The Ascent of Man*, intro. Alfred Russel Wallace (London: Fisher Unwin, 1899). First published 1889.

18 May Kendall, "Ether Insatiable," in Alfred H. Miles, ed., *The Poets and the Poetry of the Century*, vol. *Humour, Society, and Occasional Verse* (London: Hutchinson, 1898), p. 624. Originally published in Kendall's *Songs from Dreamland* (1894).

19 Leo Koenigsberger, *Hermann von Helmholtz*, trans. Frances Welby (Oxford: Clarendon Press, 1906) p. 137.

20 Morse Peckham, ed., *The Origin of Species by Charles Darwin: A Variorum Text* (Philadelphia: University of Pennsylvania Press, 1959), pp. 373–437.

21 Rosalind E. Krauss, *The Originality of the Avant-Garde and Other Modernist Myths* (Cambridge, Mass.: MIT

Press, 1985), p. 15.

22 John Tyndall, *Six Lectures on Light: Delivered in America in 1872–1873*, (London: Longmans, Green, 1875), 2d ed. p. 8.

23 Koenigsberger, *Hermann von Helmholtz*, p. 133.

24 Wallace, *The Wonderful Century*, p. 39.

25 Walter Pater, *Works*, vol.   (Oxford: Oxford University Press, 1967), p. 233.

26 Ibid., vol.   , pp. 17–18.

27 W. D. Niven, ed., *The Scientific Papers of James Clerk Maxwell*, vol. 2 (Cambridge: Cambridge University Press, 1890), p. 754.

28 Agnes Duclaux (Agnes Mary Frances Robinson) in *The Oxford Book of Mystical Verse* (Oxford: Oxford University Press, 1917), p. 401.

29 George Eliot, *Collected Poems*, ed. Lucien Jenkins (London: Skoob Books, 1989), pp. 49–50.

30 James Gibson, ed., *The Variorum Edition of the Complete Poems of Thomas Hardy*, (London: Macmillan, 1979), p. 430.

31 Balfour Stewart and Peter G. Tait, *The Unseen Universe or Physical Speculations on a Future State*, 4th ed. revised and enlarged (London: Macmillan, 1876), pp. 156–157, 143–144.

32 This version of the passage is taken from the second edition, pp. 107, 169–170.

33 Edward Carpenter, *Towards Democracy* (London: George Allen, 1912, p. 192. The poem was first published in 1881–1882. See also "The Ocean of Sex," p. 383.

Contemporary
Perspectives

A new or renewed focus on questions of vision seems to be a significant feature of the development over the past ten years or so of the field variously called "theory" or "cultural studies." The immediate causes of this focus appear to be multiple, but it seems hard not to instance at least the ongoing tendency of theory to understand itself as a critique of representation; the increasing interest among literary scholars in film study; and a growing awareness within the discipline of art history of developments in adjacent fields. Typically, this interest in the visual has taken the form of a "critique of vision"—a systematic suspicion of the apparent transparency and naturalness of vision. Among the various works that inform this critique one might note such influential works as Laura Mulvey's "Visual Pleasure and Narrative Cinema," Michel Foucault's *Discipline and Punish*, and the various books and essays in which Norman Bryson attempts to dismantle "the natural attitude" toward art history.[1]

There are a lot of questions one can put regarding this development—questions about the sense of the field in which it appears to emerge, the particular cast of the critical project, or the adequacy of the term "critique of vision" to cover the various activities apparently conducted in its name. For the most part this chapter is given over to an exploration of two French discussions of the "gaze" that have exerted a considerable shaping influence on the current discussions, so it may be useful to say at the outset that the tour is conducted with a view toward opening or reopening some of these larger questions.[2] One consequence of this is that the essay will turn, in a manner that may strike some readers as abrupt, from questions about vision to questions of theory *tout court*. The essay's title thus means to signal in advance a relation between its own divided interests and the division of the gaze from which it sets out—as if no theory of vision were adequately elaborated unless taken to the point at which it renders explicit its vision of theory.[3]

Certainly one of the strongest statements of the current critique of vision is to be found in the very first sentence of Fredric Jameson's *Signatures of the Visible*. This sentence reads: "The visual is *essentially* pornographic, which is to say that it has its end in rapt, mindless fascination; thinking about its attributes becomes an adjunct to that, if it is unwilling to betray its object.... Pornographic films are thus only the potentiation of films in general, which ask us to stare at the world as though it were a naked body." Against this hold of vision, Jameson advances a proposition both clear and familiar: only good, solid, essentially political history can rescue us from this fascination and its mindlessness (only this will cure us of the curse of the Westin Bonaventure).[4]

It is important to recognize this view as essentially Sartrean. Here, for example, is one of the central examples from Jean-Paul Sartre's discussion of the "look" in *Being and Nothingness*:

> Let us imagine that moved by jealousy, curiosity, or vice I have just glued my ear to the door and looked through a keyhole. I am alone and on the level of a non-thetic self-consciousness. This means first of all that there is no self to inhabit my conscious-

ness, nothing therefore to which I can refer my acts in order to qualify them. They are in no way known; I am my acts and hence they carry in themselves their whole justification. I am a pure consciousness of things, and things, caught up in the circuit of my selfness, offer to me their potentialities as the proof of...my own possibilities.

That's the first moment of the narrative: rapt, fascinating, mindless, and as purely free as anything in Sartre. "But all of a sudden I hear footsteps in the hall. Someone is looking at me! What does this mean? It means that I am suddenly affected in my being and that essential modifications appear in my structure."[5]

The name Sartre gives these "essential modifications" is "shame," and shame, he says, "is shame of self; it is the recognition of the fact that I am indeed that object which the Other is looking at and judging. I can be ashamed only as my freedom escapes me in order to become a given object." Still later, Sartre says, "in order for me to be what I am, it suffices merely that the Other look at me," or again, "My original fall is the existence of the Other. Shame—like pride—is the apprehension of myself as a nature although that very nature escapes me and is unknowable as such. Strictly speaking, it is not that I perceive myself losing my freedom in order to become a thing, but my nature is—over there, outside my lived freedom—as a given attribute of this being which I am for the Other."[6]

He who looks is free; and he (or she, because Sartre's narrative implicitly places a woman beyond the keyhole even as it is a woman who provides the first example of the objectifying force of the look[7]) who is looked upon falls into nature, mere being, shame and mortification (to be what you are is, for Sartre, finally to be dead).

I have quoted Sartre at some length partly because I will later turn to another narrative that is constructed in clear awareness of and opposition to Sartre's and partly because there is a lot going on in these passages. Beyond what is obviously being said about the objectifying force of the Look, there is a certain amount of important Sartrean machinery on display: for example, the marked contrast between my inside, where I am free and of a piece with my acts, and my outside, where I am seen and my freedom stolen; and then there is the oddness of the whole scenario—three persons lined up, each enclosing another in its cone of vision in such a way that only one ever figures as a person—first Sartre in his freedom and then the Other in his. Between object and person, between "I" and "him" there is no second person, or, perhaps more accurately, every approach to "you" reduces, like a complex fraction, into a simpler product of "I" and "him" or "he" and "me." There is an implicit theology here (and that no doubt is why the "original fall" enters into the account): the Other with a large "O" is he who sees without being seen and his is the only real first person, before which all others are merely others with a small "o." And, of course, one does not want to miss the work of the images themselves: if we see these people enclosed with one another's cones of vision it is at least in part because vision has been given to us as an opening out from a point-source—my keyhole, his eyes—and the door through which Sartre peers locates him as forcefully outside his object's lived freedom as his own body locates the Other outside his.

This story is a deeply familiar one in contemporary theory. We know it from a now strongly established line of feminist criticism that has gained its fullest theoretical articulation in film study and, more recently, in art history: the male gaze is that through which the feminine is made object and stripped of its freedom. And we know it through Michel Foucault's work on the panopticon and its various architectural and scientifico-technical offspring: my submission is secured through the imposition of visibility on me. And we can probably continue to recognize it, despite the shift in register, in Louis Althusser's notion of interpellation: my naming calls me into visibility and so, in his double sense, subjects me, rendering me a subject. "Recognition" is appropriation: when you call me worker, then I am a worker; when you call me nigger, then I am black.[8]

But here we are beginning to tip into a different narrative about vision, one in which visibility is no longer a brute condition but a consequence of something else, of our possession of or by language. This difference between interpellation and the imposition of vision will, however, not cut terribly deep until and unless the basic interpersonal logic of the initial scenario is changed in some deeper way. Any critique of vision predicated on the Sartrean scenario will never be more than a critique of recognition in general. It seems to me that there are strong and wide currents in contemporary theory that follow this course. The general and distinctly non-trivial work of these currents is the undoing of stereotypes—that is, blocking or at least placing in question a broad range of contemporary recognitions, typically by asking who is being recognized and who is granting or imposing that recognition. If this line is, at least in terms of its French lineage, Sartrean, it is plausible to suggest that its academic fortunes in America are linked as well to the afterlife of what used to be called the New Left, particularly to the Marcusean critique of repressive tolerance with its argument that recognition can constitute a form of subjection. There are also some serious troubles that come with pursuing this line—most notably the political difficulties that accompany any radical orientation to identity and the epistemological difficulties that follow from any effort to absolutely separate (real) identity and (imposed) recognition.[9]

Sartre's name is not often invoked in contemporary theoretical discussions of vision. The name one most often hears is that of the psychoanalyst Jacques Lacan. But Lacan's stories about vision are very different from the one we've just reviewed and, in fact, open a very different theoretical prospect. Of the two stories I mean to treat, one is quite well known (which will not keep me from reviewing it here). The other, although some attention has been paid to it, has not typically been taken up in the context of vision. The first of these—a story about the young Jacques Lacan trying to become a man of the people—is told in a context that makes it, in part, a counternarrative to Sartre's.[10] The second is interestingly seen in such a context but is presented primarily as a puzzle about time and logic as they appear in psychoanalysis; if one wants to give it a larger philosophical context, the best candidate probably would be something like Hegel's way of trying to tie time and logic together—which might have the virtue of reminding us that in Hegel the early incomplete dialectic of failed recognition, the dialectic of master and slave, is completed later, in more complex circumstances, in a moment of mutual recognition.

To the first story.[11] Young Jacques is afloat with a group of Breton fishermen. They are making their more or less difficult living, and he, presumably, is "identifying" with them. He may even be working, but it's not his living—it's his summer. One of them points to a sardine can glinting on the waves and says, "You see that? Well, it doesn't see you!" Presumably the other fishermen have a good laugh, and Lacan has to decide—the joke demands of him something like a decision, but it also seems that if he actually has to make a "decision," he will, so to speak, miss the boat—how to participate in that laughter (or how to withdraw from it). As in Sartre's story, a certain upsurge of vision brings a certain distance or alienation in its wake. But if Lacan has been deprived of anything, it is not his freedom—just a fiction of solidarity that can be reaffirmed if he finds the right way to join in the laughter it calls forth. It's perhaps hard to describe what would be "the right laughter" here. Not laughing surely renders the fiction untenable, but too quick or too easy laughter would ring hollow, undermining the very community it means to affirm or reconstruct. What's wanted is perhaps a laughter that admits what has been undone while affirming a shared general awareness of the undoing or undone-ness of any presumed community; it would also be a laughter that in some sense affirms both the right of the fisherman to identify Lacan and the justice of that identification—even as it also moves to contest or transform or undo it.

But the moral that most directly interests Lacan is the visual one. Lacan, the fisherman, and the sardine can form a trio counterposed to Sartre's. The looks and recognitions that flash among them are triangular, and if there is any one agent whose vision embraces the others, that agent is not remotely human. And even here we risk going too far: if there is anything like agency to be associated with the flashing sardine can, it is not its own but the sun's (the story has then Bataillean roots of some sort).[12] It is, in general, a story about being seen, about visibility apart from human seeing of the Sartrean kind.

The second story is about three prisoners who are called into the warden's office. The warden then says:

> For reasons I don't have to go into now, I've got to free one of you. In order to decide which one, I've set a sort of test for you to take, if you agree.
>
> There are three of you. Here are five disks differing only in color: three are white, and two black. Without letting you know which one, I am going to place one of these disks on each of you, between your shoulder blades where you cannot see it directly—nor indirectly since there are no mirrors here.
>
> Then you will have all the time you want to examine your companions and the disks each is wearing—but of course you will not be allowed to speak to one another. Besides your own interest will prohibit you from doing so: the first one able to deduce his own color will gain the liberty I can dispose of.
>
> However, it's necessary that your conclusion be grounded in logic, not mere probability. To this end, we ask that when one of you has reached a conclusion, he walk through that door where, separated from the others, he will be judged on his response.[13]

The warden then puts a white disk on each of his prisoners. Can they solve their problem? How?

The initial solution is this: after examining one another for a time, all three go toward the door. Each reasons as follows: "I can see that the other two are white. If I were black, each of the others would be saying of himself, 'If I were black, the other would have seen the two black disks and left already. Since he hasn't, I can't be black.' Since both of them would have followed the same chain of reasoning, they would then have left together, each knowing himself to be white. But they haven't done that, so all three of us must be wearing white, so I'll leave."

For those who enjoy such puzzles, this is all very elegant. But Lacan suggests that it's not quite adequate. Given the role each assigns in his chain of reasoning to movement on the part of the other two, the moment they all move to the door together is a moment of crisis, since it also realizes that movement whose absence is crucial to the deduction. So they will all three stop together—before seeing that this very hesitation is itself a confirmation of their individual deductions. And then they will all, finally, proceed out together.

Lacan's primary interest in this puzzle is in questions about the role of time in psychoanalysis—particularly in the relations among times he distinguishes as proper to "recognition," "understanding," and "concluding."[14] But it is, in part, a visual puzzle, and one whose solution consists in refusing—or, in this case, being defeated by—the first evidences of the visual in favor of the evidences of one's visibility. And there, unlike in Sartre's story, giving oneself over to visibility and its coding is the hesitant means to freedom. The mutual and indirect recognition the prisoners attain depends absolutely on the triangularity of the situation: whereas in their deductions they take themselves as twos, the thread on which their lives and freedom hang is made of each prisoner's ability to take those pairs as existing always in view of a third.

One could of course add to these stories Lacan's most famous story—the one he tells in and around Poe's "Purloined Letter"[15]—which is also in some measure a story about vision, the visible and the invisible, and the inadequacy of dual relations to their articulation. Here the point would be, most simply, that the story depends on the recognition that there is nothing behind the visible (that, for example, the Symbolic is not *behind* the Imaginary, that these registers are imbricated otherwise, on or as a single surface). All three of these stories come to the same set of points: that vision and visibility are asymmetrical—that is, if it is always someone who sees, it is not always by someone that one is seen or to someone that one is exposed—and that this asymmetry is bound up with our ability to imagine our selves and the relations amongst ourselves as fully social.[16] Taken together these points mean that the real terms of our sociability are grounded in the inhuman: we have three persons because there is something at work in our mutual facing of one another that is not simply ourselves, that plays "he or she" to our "I" and "you" and that plays "it" to "he" and "she" in just the same way. This last point brings us to the same fact of a gendering of vision that comes more directly, if less comprehensibly, on the Sartrean route.[17]

It is because there is this inhuman element at work in our sociability that one cannot imagine or theorize that fact without some appeal to, for example, dead fathers—and it is because of this also that the "psyche" of "psychoanalysis" is perhaps best translated as "soul" (rather than, say, "mind" or "personality"). Certainly one of the things that interest me deeply is the way in which Lacan's general schemas here all force a distinction of some sort between recognition and acknowledgment. It is recognition that mortifies in Sartre and those who follow his lead—just as for Hegel it is Christianity that can, in the end, deliver us from the mortification of imposed misrecognition into the region of mutual recognition. But Lacan's nondialectical grasp of these matters can find its only end not in recognition but in acknowledgement (that is, for example, the force his laughter with the fishermen should carry if he is to carry on with them).

If we want, now, to be relentlessly explicit about Lacan's tale of a tub it seems to me that we can say either that Lacan and Petit Jean represent the *infans* and its mirror image as they discover one another by grace of the caregiver whose unheard voice is that of the Father or that they stand to each other as Mother and child before the voice of the Father. The first way of filling out the allegory stresses the unacknowledged Symbolic substructure of the mirror's scene of recognition; the second stresses the Oedipal demand for acknowledgment of that structure. That the sardine can is explicitly not human is a way of registering that the Father, as Father, is dead (speaks for and from language and not as a subject employing it). The sun that is marginally present in the narrative only as that which the sardine can reflects would then be well enough understood as something like the brute fact of reproduction insofar as it exists, unremarked and unremarkable, in some world other than ours—as the mere general condition for the continuation of a species by the production of new individuals. Our reality has always already passed this moment (this is the great lesson Lacan draws from Lévi-Strauss's *Elementary Structures of Kinship*, allowing him to pin Freud's family drama to the fact of language). We may, just as Lacan and Petit Jean do, actually stand in the light of this sun—owe our being to it—but our access to it comes only by virtue of its refraction through signification, displacing us in relation to it.[18] The sardine can is the material remarking of the sun, as language is the material remarking of our unaccountable contingency; as such, it is the condition under which we become visible to—and so divided from or in—ourselves. In this sense the sardine can marks the difference between Paternity—a particular node in a system of exchanges that articulaes filiation and alliance—and what one might call "siring," a biological function not so marked (this repeats in relation to vision a more general argument I've tried to make about how Lacan's three registers work: from the moment the real gives itself as remarkable—becomes, then, the Real—we have access to it only through the play of Imaginary and Symbolic it sets in motion[19]).

This would also suggest that the laugh I offer as Lacan's best response should be understood as an accession to castration as the condition of explicit entry into a social (rather than species) existence. It is, I think, a version of Bataille's laugh (and so presumably related to Foucault's as well). The comedy is jus that, standing in the light, we remain, like Lacan and Petit Jean, invisible to one another, merely lucid one might say, until that lucidity is remarked and restricted, and with that our intimacy with one another appears as lost (this is Bataille's urgent comic vision of sacrifice and the sun, the impossibility of the general and the inadequacy of the restricted[20]). All of this is perhaps worth saying just because it can show something about how the Bataille-based exchange between Blanchot and Nancy on community can find one important expression, as it does in *The Inoperative Community*, in a thought of "exposure," a word not limited to questions of the visual and the visible but also not fully separable from them.[21]

This account places something of a premium on a contrast between "recognition" and "acknowledgment" which perhaps stands in need of some glossing. I take acknowledgment to be irreducibly an act—happening not in the visual instant of recognition[22] but necessarily in time and as a relation of at least two moments. It takes up what has been offered, it hesitates, it corrects an earlier response: in all its forms it carries a certain belatedness or dependency at its core. This rhythm derives from the way in which that which is acknowledged is always something other than the subject and not finally subsumable under the subject's preexisting repertoires—but also something from which the subject cannot simply turn away or simply disentangle itself. As Stanley Cavell notes, a failure of acknowledgment is something for which one is responsible in ways one is not for a failure of recognition.[23]

It seems to me that this contrast between recognition and acknowledgment provides a useful way to frame the other text to which Lacan's most sustained meditation on vision overtly responds—Maurice Merleau-Ponty's *The Visible and the Invisible*.[24] The text of "Seminar XI" makes it clear that Lacan's remarks are occasioned by the posthumous publication of *The Visible and the Invisible* and that at the outset he intended little more than a brief digression. Reading the published text, one can easily follow Lacan as he moves from *The Visible and the Invisible* back to *The Phenomenology of Perception* and then forward again to the late essays of *Signs, Sense and Nonsense,* and *The Primacy of Perception*—so it is worth asking what there is in Merleau-Ponty's work generally, and his late work especially, that so draws Lacan on.[25]

The Visible and the Invisible is far from a finished text; in general it licenses us less to speak of Merleau-Ponty's "theory of vision" than of his struggle toward such a theory and toward the terms in which such a theory could be expressed. These two issues are clearly closely intertwined for Merleau-Ponty. It seems at least roughly right to say that his methodological orientation toward something he calls "*hyperreflexion*" cannot be thought through except by his thinking through the apparent visuality embedded in words like "reflection" and "self-reflection"—so that Merleau-Ponty's repeated worrying over the phenomenology of, for example, his touching one finger with another is continuous with his struggle to bring vision to words. And lurking in the background of this struggle, as in all of Merleau-Ponty's late work, is his awareness of the challenges posed to his phenomenological approach by both psychoanalysis and the contemporary turn toward linguistic models. This awareness is no doubt most explicit in the passage in which he works both to acknowledge the force of the Lacanian proposition that "the unconscious is structured like a language" and to blunt its force by drawing a sharp distinction between "ready-made language, the secondary and empirical operation of translation, of coding and decoding, the artificial languages, the technical relation between a sound and a meaning which are joined only by express convention" and "the speaking work, the assuming of the conventions of his native language as something natural by him who lives that language"—a distinction Lacan, in 1964, would surely reject.[26]

At the heart of what Merleau-Ponty wants to say about vision there are the following thoughts:

- Vision happens in the world, as one of its facts. We do not simply see the world, it also shows itself to us. We are, in these terms, the place through which the world comes to visibility, and our seeing of it is therefore not simply our own. Vision is a chiasmus in the world, a site of its interlacing in and through itself.

- This chiasmus cannot be articulated in purely visual terms. We are the place the world sees or shows itself because we are of the world, continuous with it.

- What needs then to be thought through is the way in which our belonging to the world is manifested as our visual separation from it, our having it as objects within a horizon from which we are significantly but not absolutely distant.[27] Vision is the place where our continuity with the world conceals itself, the place where we mistake our contact for distance, imagining that seeing is a substitute for, rather than a mode of, touching—and it is this anesthesia, this senselessness, at the heart of transparency that demands our acknowledgment and pushes our dealings with the visual beyond recognition.

Merleau-Ponty thus repeatedly circles back to the figure of the painter—Cézanne, above all—whose canvases offer up to us the continuity of seeing and touching. In doing so he implicitly links his work with the complex meditations on vision that inform the writings of such early-modern art historians as Alois Riegl and Heinrich Wölfflin—meditations that distinguish within the visual between the haptic and the optic and that attempt to understand this internal opposition as centrally informing our notions both of the work of art and of its historicity, apparently separate topics that can be subsumed under the single question of the appearing of the work of art.[28]

Lacan takes over a good bit of this approach. He too poses vision as essentially chiasmatic,[29] although what Merleau-Ponty calls "Flesh" Lacan takes as the Symbolic; what Merleau-Ponty phrases as continuity Lacan rephrases as displacement;[30] and what Merleau-Ponty explores as an essentially asocial encounter of self and world Lacan rewrites in fully social terms. This is and is not a sea change: what remains constant is the sense that visibility itself is enigmatic, that the task at hand is not that of getting behind it but of staying within its duplicity.[31] As Lacan puts it, "The picture does not compete with appearance, it competes with what Plato designates for us beyond appearance as being the idea. It is because the picture is the appearance that says it is that which gives appearance that Plato attacks painting as if it were an activity competing with his own."[32]

This passage is perhaps a good enough hook on which to hang the most palpable contrast between Sartre on the one hand and Lacan and Merleau-Ponty on the other as theorists of vision—which is, quite simply, that Sartre can say what he has to say about vision without reference to painting. This is something that neither Lacan nor Merleau-Ponty can do: we can say for both of them either that painting obliges us to acknowledge that which the visual both overlooks and depends upon, or that human seeing (the seeing of speaking, embodied, and desiring beings) will always find itself in a world in which there will be paintings. That these paintings may then function at times in the ways that so concern Sartre, Jameson, Bryson, and others may still be true, but this function would be a modification of or defense against the inner complexity of the visual and not an account of it.[33]

This sense of an abiding problem within, or even as, the very visibility of the visible is not peculiar to Lacan and Merleau-Ponty. It deeply informs the writing of Jean-François Lyotard (most notably in *Discours, Figure*, which finds its starting point in Merleau-Ponty, but also in the transformed problematic of the sublime and the unpresentable that organizes *The Inhuman*) and can be registered as well, albeit more obliquely, in the work of Maurice Blanchot (*La Folie du jour*) and Jacques Derrida.[34] In the cases of Blanchot and Derrida, any direct debt to Merleau-Ponty seems less important than a common derivation from Martin Heidegger, whose question, "How is there something rather than nothing?" expressly aims to shift our attention from questions of what is behind what (as, say, Ideas might seem to behind appearances) to questions about what it is for something to appear.

One of Heidegger's favorite ways of putting this notion is in terms of things coming into light, entering or withdrawing from a "clearing" (*Lichtung*), and this image can serve as a useful guide to another significant context for Lacan's excursus on vision. Here one would want to speak, beyond any explicit authorization in Lacan's text, of Goethe's *Theory of Colour*.

There are, I think, two ways to imagine the relation between Lacan and Goethe. The first is to say that Lacan inherits a certain rhetoric of light embedded in post-Goethean German philosophy and works to recover it as theory within the register of psychoanalysis. The second is to say that Goethe and Lacan share a sense, implicit for Goethe and more nearly explicit for Lacan, of the visual field as a field transfigured by language.

In thinking about a certain inheritance of Goethe, it would be important that Hegel followed Goethe on light and that he ordered his use of visual metaphor to that theory in such a way that those metaphors became centrally informative of much post-Hegelian German philosophy.[35] Heidegger's *Lichtung* is not Newtonian, not an empty space traversed by lines of light, but a welling up of light in an interplay with darkness that is generative of a multicolored world of things, and Lacan, no doubt with a push from Bataille, is also fundamentally oriented to this space or place of light (light is something we enter or that enters us, not something that shines upon us).[36] This is the point of Lacan's strictures on Descartes, Diderot, and "geometral perspective"—all of which are, in his view as in Goethe's—"simply the mapping of space, not sight."[37]

At the level of what one might imagine as a shared intuition into the rhetoricity of vision—what I have been describing as its division from itself, the insistence of a certain heterogeneity at the heart of its transparency—I would point to Lacan and Goethe's joint insistence that the field of vision is above all a play of light and opacity arising from bodies and images in displacement. This applies whether we think of how Lacan is and is not in the picture in his parable of the sardine can or of his remarks about the screen or stain or mask, or turn to Goethe's extraordinary assertion that "to produce colour, an object must be so displaced that the light edges be apparently carried over the dark surface, the dark edges over a light surface, the figure over its boundary, the boundary over the figure."[38] It is the complex relation of figure and boundary Goethe tries to illuminate here that perhaps permits our speaking of the rhetoricity of vision—and it will be of some importance to be clear about the difference between this way of posing the linguistic constitution of vision and any more directly semiotic approach to it.

These remarks are, of course, speculative at best and would need to be considerably fleshed out, preferably in both historical and theoretical terms, to be fully persuasive, but they do, I think, help open out the sense of Lacan's passage from "The Split Between the Eye and the Gaze" through "Anamorphosis" and "The Line and Light" to "What Is a Picture?" The experience of a picture is, above all, an experience of light in its materiality and in its radical difference from the lines by which we can, blindly, claim to map a space imagined to exist apart from us and to which we are not essentially exposed.[39]

One general outcome here may be the recognition that Lacan's theory is deeply responsive to the various modes of self-division in the visual that are repeatedly registered both in the history of art and in art history's attempts to understand its object—not only Wölfflin and Riegl or Goethe against Newton but also all those contests of line and color, painting and sculpture, North and South—so many complex instances of vision's incessant and constitutive turn against itself. This turn continues to shape, as it must, the most powerful of contemporary art criticism and art history—for example, Rosalind Krauss's complex negotiations with sculpture and photography, Lacan and Lyotard, surrealism and Greenbergian modernism.[40]

If we see this work as participating in a certain critique of vision, it will not be Sartre's and Jameson's, and it will not take the shape of a critique of representation. It will have the shape of (and my phrasing here is, in the context of current art criticism, tendentious but I hope nonetheless justified) "radical self-criticism," where self-criticism does not name a reductive movement toward an essence but the very structure of the thing in question.[41]

One last point can turn us toward some thoughts about how we, "theorists," now stand toward or find ourselves within "the gaze" and how we have come to that position. And that is that Goethe, Heidegger, Lacan, and Merleau-Ponty as well as others I've mentioned (Blanchot, Derrida, Lyotard) all take it that there is a direct connection between what they want to say about vision and the question of its saying or writing. That is, they argue that the writing that would show what is to be seen about vision cannot advance itself as either transparent or reflective in the usual way. They have an interest in opacity. To put it slightly differently: they are obliged to cash in the ancient chip that ties "theory" to spectatorship.[42]

It remains then to ask why, if Sartre and Lacan are as different as I have claimed them to be, contemporary theory so insistently conflates them, so repeatedly reproduces Sartre under the name of Lacan.

Presumably one could offer, as my marginal remark about Nietzsche suggests (see note 42), an answer at the scale of Western thought itself. And one can also offer, as Joan Copjec brilliantly does in "The Orthopsychic Subject," an answer scaled to the particular twists and turns of the complex relations among Althusser, Bachelard, Foucault, Lacan, and others.[43] What I will offer are a few unjustified and suspicious remarks about the reception and contemporary situation of French theory in the United States.

In general, Lacan has been over-read as the theorist of "the mirror stage." More particularly, there has been a strong desire to see the four seminar sessions devoted to vision as expanding upon or elucidating the earlier work. In a sense they do so—but not by further exploring the logic of the Imaginary. Instead, they offer an account of the Symbolic underpinnings of the visual Imaginary— not what the mirror seems to show but the seams that do not show stains or inscriptions that are the invisible condition of its apparently transparent reflectivity (for example, the father's words as he holds his child up to the mirror: "See, Chris, that's you").

But we are, evidently, interested in the Imaginary, in the mirror; we cling to it—as we cling to other moments of theory: for example, Foucault's *Discipline and Punish*, which is repeatedly read as if it contained a theory of vision. It does not. What it does contain is an account of the emergence of a practice of vision that finds its fulfillment in, among other things, the contemporary social sciences, of which it is an explicit critique, and Sartre's theory of vision, of which it would seem to be an implicit critique. Foucault himself holds, at least on the evidence of that text, no "theory of vision."

That we want him to is perhaps a measure or symptom of our own attachment to theory. It is as if we have staked some significant part of our grasp of theory's work in the figure of the prison-house, or in the twin figures of prison and mirror insofar as they jointly fill out a sense of the way language, at least as it has been explored in the tendencies we now call "theory," seems to steal us away from the world or enclose us in ourselves. We were, for example, prepared to take the prison to be a figure for the news and consequence of theory well before Foucault came to examine its history; when he did so, we were surprisingly ready to take his history for theory, discarding along the way the more complex and much more overtly Heideggerean Foucault of *The Order of Things* in favor of this new crypto-Sartrean.[44] "Theory" and the means and objects of its critiques become oddly conflated here—as if the prisoner were to imagine he would be free if only he could watch himself more closely than even the jailer can (and isn't this just what the prisoner, on Foucault's account, will inevitably come to believe?).

The obvious conclusion here is that our insistence on theory and our attachment to these tropes of isolation and separation go hand in hand—even and perhaps most especially where we take the task of theory to be to break out of the isolation. Theory so construed—the theory we seem to want—would operate in the same field and according to essentially the same logic as the social sciences themselves; its deepest stakes would continue to be in surveillance and punishment, the composition of forces, normalization, and examination. And our attachment to these things would be, as Foucault argues, the very form of our contemporary attachment to ourselves, our willingness to remain transfixed before the mirror, absurdly willing it to deliver us to our naked selves (this would be the pornography of the theoretical gaze).

The interest that drives the repeated transformation of Lacan back into Sartre and that insists upon Lacan as above all the theorist of the Imaginary is then not separable from a certain interest in or ambition for "theory"—that theory should at once capture its object and leave it free, render it visible and leave it in its proper privacy. What, one might say, "theory" above all wants is not to be touched by its object—as if a permanent and unmeasurable distance were to be secretly maintained as the condition of what we nonetheless claim as theory's approach to its object.

It is possible that in Merleau-Ponty and Lacan, as in Derrida and Lyotard, all of this is being configured otherwise—neither prison nor mirror, not theory but displacement. This would be the sense of their writerly practices.[45] But if it is so, then the work of that writing would be a work not of subjects but of objects, passing over themselves and one another.

I have insisted here and there both on the signal importance of a reference to painting in both Merleau-Ponty and Lacan and on a certain relation between their discussions and those that animate the origins of modern art history. I have done so because I take the special insistence on a certain objectivity (a certain having or touching of an object) at work in the former and the movement at once within and without disciplinary boundaries implicit in the latter's refusal of any simple self-containment of the visual, to be important parameters for an exercise of theory that does not allow itself the imagination of a subject before whose gaze there might or might not be a world. Instead, such an exercise of theory is committed to understanding how it is that subjects find themselves appropriated to—touched by—what one might call the look of things.[46]

On this view, we are asked to grasp our apparent theoretical or visual appropriation of and distance from objects as a peculiar modification of a prior attachment to them or of their prior attachment to us. This particular modification may not be entirely or always desirable—especially since it is a modification, like Euripides' modification of his attachment to his predecessors, which does not break that attachment but does succeed in rendering it invisible and unthinkable, and which does so in and as its very claim to lucidity. That this is always possible is one lesson, and that it is therefore always actual is another. That we remain, as a consequence of this very duplicity, pledged to the impossible articulation of the world is the third. None of these lessons would be "meta-theoretical"—they do not take the form of a reflection on theory—which is why there is no end to their saying or the occasions of their saying. They are objective—by which I mean that they are a consequence of the fact that we can find ourselves in no other place or way than in our exposure to what is, in or beyond us, other.

1   See Laura Mulvey, "Visual Pleasure and Narrative
    Cinema" in *Visual and Other Pleasures* (Bloomington:
    Indiana University Press, 1989); Michel Foucault,
    Surveiller et punir: Naissance de la prison (Paris:
    Gallimard, 1975); and Norman Bryson, *Vision and
    Painting: The Logic of the Gaze* (New Haven: Yale
    University Press, 1983). A later summary statement of
    Bryson's position, "Semiology and Visual
    Interpretation," can be found in Norman Bryson,
    Michael Holly, and Keith Moxey, eds., *Visual Theory:
    Painting and Interpretation* (New York: HarperCollins,
    1988), pp. 61–73, along with my "Reflections on
    Bryson," pp. 74–78.

2   At the time this chapter was written I was unable to
    draw upon either Rosalind Krauss's *The Optical
    Unconscious* (Cambridge: The MIT Press, 1993) or
    Martin Jay's Downcast Eyes: *The Denigration of Vision
    in Twentieth-Century French Thought* (Berkeley:
    University of California Press, 1993), both of which I
    take to be central to the renewed focus on questions
    of vision. Elements of both works have been available
    for some time, either in published form or as public
    lectures, and have had considerable influence on the
    way some issues are posed in this essay, so I should
    perhaps note that I am in general drawn to Krauss's
    way of exploring vision (although we also place our
    emphases in significantly different places and, at least
    at times, draw significantly diverse consequences
    because of that). Because *The Optical Unconscious* is
    animated primarily by questions arising from Clement
    Greenberg's emphasis on modernist "opticality," the
    interested reader may also want to consult Krauss's
    "Cindy Sherman: Untitled" (in *Cindy Sherman:
    1975–1993* [New York: Rizzoli, 1993]) where she more
    directly engages issues arising from Mulvey's account
    of vision—especially section 3 ("Gleams and
    Reflections"), which takes up much of the Lacan
    material I also discuss. By contrast, Jay and I seem to
    be at some odds, both about the interpretation of
    Lacan and about the actual role of vision in recent
    French thought. I would hope that the differences on
    narrowly Lacanian issues will be apparent to any
    reader of both texts, but it is perhaps worth being
    explicit that much of what Jay takes to be denigration
    of vision I am much more inclined to read as (an
    admittedly complex) valorization of it.

        I should also note in this context Margaret
    Iversen's even more recent essay, "What is a

Photograph?" (*Art History* XVII,2 [September 1994]:
451–464) which argues—entirely persuasively to my
mind—that Roland Barthe's *Camera Lucida* is best
understood as a direct derivation from Lacan's work
on vision, and explores much of the same Lacanian
material I engage here. In a footnote to her closely
related review of Jay's book (*The Art Bulletin* LXXVI, 4
[December 1994]: 730–732), Iversen makes explicit
the difference between our two readings. The final
revisions to this essay have thus attempted to be as
explicit as possible about how I take the specifically
psychoanalytic allegory of Lacan's central scenario.

3   A further, related thought, less argued than enacted,
    is that the current prominence of the problematic of
    vision is itself the product of a special moment of
    disciplinary division and interference as "theory"
    passes from the fields in which it was first elaborated
    into art history and art criticism. It is the implied
    relation of this interdisciplinary situation to Goethe's
    theory of color discussed below that underlies my
    title's juxtaposition of color and theory.

4   From a little lower on the same page: "This book will
    argue the proposition that the only way to think the
    visual, to get a handle on increasing, tendential, all-
    pervasive visuality, as such, is to grasp its historical
    coming into being." Fredric Jameson, *Signatures of the
    Visible* (New York: Routledge, 1992), p.1.

5   Jean-Paul Sartre, *Being and Nothingness*, trans. Hazal
    Barnes (New York: The Citadel Press, 1968),
    pp. 235–236.

6   Ibid., pp. 237–239.

7   Sartre's discussion of the look opens with the
    following sentences: "This woman whom I see coming
    toward me, this man who is passing by in the street,
    this beggar whom I hear calling before my window, all
    are for me objects—of this there is no doubt. Thus it
    is true that at least one of the modalities of the
    Other's presence before me is object-ness." Ibid.,
    pp. 228–229.

8   It is perhaps worth remarking that the passage from
    visual submission to linguistic interpellation invites
    one to think about a further contrast between the
    Althusserian view of language as naming (and so
    subjecting) and J.L. Austin's arguments for the ethical
    centrality of the performative dimensions of language.
    Although such a comparison would obviously move
    beyond the visual terrain staked out by this chapter, I
    believe it would uncover a parallel range of issues.

9 See, for example, Craig Owens, *Beyond Recognition: Representation, Power, and Culture* (Berkeley: University of California Press, 1992) and my review of it in *Art and America* (July 1993).

10 See Jacques Lacan, *The Four Fundamental Concepts of Psychoanalysis*, trans. Alan Sheridan (New York: W. W. Norton & Co., 1978), p. 84, where the rejection of Sartre's phenomenological description is explicit and unambiguous: "Is this a correct phenomenological analysis? No. It is not true that, when I am under the gaze, when I solicit a gaze, when I obtain it, I do not see it as a gaze." The grounds for this rejection are important to my argument: "Painters, above all, have grasped this gaze as such."

11 See ibid., pp. 95ff.

12 This open's another path toward understanding Lacan's orientation toward questions of community and solidarity rather than Sartrean freedom. Parveen Adams's chapter in the present volume, "Father, Can't You See I'm Filming?" brings out clearly this central emphasis on intimacy and sacrifice.

13 Jacques Lacan, "Le temps logique et l'assertion de certitude anticipée: Un nouveau sophisme," in Lacan, *Ecrits* (Paris: Seuil, 1968), pp. 197–198.

14 Note that "recognition" is at best a transient and preliminary moment in the dialectic.

15 Jacques Lacan, "Le séminaire sur 'La Lettre volée'" in *Ecrits*, pp. 11–61.

16 The social consequences of this thought are perhaps most fully played out, beyond Lacan, in Jean-Luc Nancy's central emphasis on "exposure" as the medium of community. See Jean-Luc Nancy, *The Inoperative Community*, trans. Peter Connor et al. (Minneapolis: University of Minnesota Press, 1991).

17 Were one to push further into this insofar as it pertains directly to psychoanalysis one would examine the fit between Sartre's theory of the Look and his rejection of the Unconscious. One might also want to take note of remarks like the following (from a review of Bernard Williams's *Shame and Necessity*): "With shame, the internalized other is a watcher (thus, primitively, it is shameful to be seen naked, but not to be naked); with guilt, the internalized other can be imagined as a voice, speaking as victim or judge." Richard Jenkyns, "How Homeric Are We?" *New York Times Book Review*, April 25, 1993, 3.

18 This suggests a way of reading Lacan's play with Venn diagrams in *Encore* as also an exercise in the Gothean

optics I turn to below, the circles in it now appearing as the work of a figure carried over its boundary—a thought I like insofar it extends the suggestion I've made elsewhere ("In the Light of the Other," *Whitewalls* 23 [Fall 1989]: 10–31) that Lacan's diagrams frequently engage a desire to account for their own visibility and so can often be treated as elements in a visual and not simply schematic practice. (This last distinction takes it, in keeping with the overall argument of this chapter, that opacity is a defining dimension of the visual over and against the [intended] transparency of the schematic.)

19 On this, see my description of the postscript to "The Seminar on 'The Purloined Letter'" in "Psychoanalysis and the Place of Jouissance," *Critical Inquiry* (December 1986): 349–370.

20 See the discussion of the "Four Discourses" as I take Lacan to present them in *Encore*, in "Psychoanalysis and the Place of Jouissance."

21 Between the Lacanian theory of vision (or visibility) and that discussion, there is, of course, the argument, conducted one way by Philippe Lacoue-Labarthe and Jean-Luc Nancy in *The Title of the Letter: A Reading of Lacan*, trans. François Raffoul and David Pettigrew (Albany: State University of New York Press, 1992) and another way by Derrida in "Le Facteur de la Vérité" (in Jacques Derrida, *The Postcard: From Socrates to Freud and Beyond*, trans. Alan Bass [Chicago: University of Chicago Press, 1987]), over how exactly one is to count or admit one's inability to count the number of agents in this scene. One way to work through that puzzle might be to review the argument over "The Seminar on 'The Purloined Letter'" with an eye to these issues.

22 On the critique of visual instantaneity, see Rosalind Krauss, "The Blink of an Eye," in David Carrol, ed., *States of Theory* (New York: Columbia University Press, 1990), pp. 175–199, and "The Story of the Eye," *New Literary History* 21,2 (Winter 1990): 283–298.

23 Stanley Cavell, *Must We Mean What We Say?* (Cambridge: Cambridge University Press, 1976), p. 264.

24 Maurice Merleau-Ponty, *The Visible and the Invisible*, trans. Alphonso Lingis (Evanston, Illinois: Northwestern University Press, 1968).

25 This is not Lacan's only published engagement with the work of Merleau-Ponty; I will touch briefly below on his 1961 homage "Maurice Merleau-Ponty" in *Les*

Temps Modernes 184–185 (October 1961): 245–254.

26 Merleau-Ponty, *Visible and Invisible*, p. 126. It is, I think, less clear that Lacan would reject this position or reject it as vigorously in the early 1950s.

27 This is a distinctly visual version of what Heidegger had put more generally as a matter of "de-severance" and spatiality in *Being and Time*, §23ff. For Sartre, this spatial distance-and-bridging becomes the absolute distance between Being and Nothingness— so that, as Mark Magleby has pointed out to me, in Sartre's text objects within the narrator's visual field are repeatedly presented in measurable relation to each other whereas the narrator's distance from or proximity to the object in this field remains unmeasurable.

28 See Marshall Brown, "The Classical is the Baroque: On the principles of Wölfflin's Art History," *Critical History* 9 (December 1982): 379–404, Margaret Iverson, *Alois Riegl: Art History and Theory* (Cambridge: The MIT Press, 1993), and Stephen Melville, "The Temptation of New Perspectives," *October* 52 (Spring 1990): 3–15.

29 The "double dihedron" introduced in chapters 8 and 9 of *Four Concepts* is nothing other than a figure of chiasmus. I have tried elsewhere (see "In the Light of the Other") to sketch out something of its complexity as a visual figure.

30 Notice especially here how Lacan passes from Merleau-Ponty on the painter's hand and eye to the thought that a bird would paint by dropping its feathers, a snake by casting off its scales, and a tree by letting fall its leaves (*Four Concepts*, p. 114).

31 This has meant that a certain tradition of art history in France, oriented to both Merleau-Ponty and Lacan, has repeatedly moved to take up the problem of painting in terms not of a surface and what lies or seems to lie behind it but of a surface and an obverse that is its necessary and irreducible concomitant. See, for example, Yves-Alain Bois, "Painting as Model" in his *Painting as Model* (Cambridge, Mass.: MIT Press, 1990); Hubert Damisch, *Fenêtre jaune cadmium, ou les dessous de la peinture* (Paris: Seuil, 1984); and Georges Didi-Huberman, *La peinture incarnée* (Paris: Minuit, 1985). Jacques Taminaux's "The Thinker and the Painter," in M. C. Dillon, ed., *Merleau-Ponty Vivant* (Albany: State University of New York Press, 1991), pp. 195–212, explores the foundations for this view in Merleau-Ponty.

32 Lacan, *Four Concepts*, p. 112.

33 I would not want to leave the impression that Lacan and Merleau-Ponty have the same theory of vision; the various rephrasings and displacements I've tried to briefly chart have deep and serious consequences. Lacan's 1961 essay on Merleau-Ponty lays these differences out clearly—Merleau-Ponty remains fixed on "presence," misses the insistence of the Symbolic within the Imaginary and of the signifier within the body, and so on. At the same time, this essay clearly lays out a preliminary version of the rapprochement that informs the discussion in *Four Concepts*. Lacan is fully justified in his response to the question that concludes the section on vision: "Miller: This leads me to ask you if *Le Visible et l'invisible* has led you to change anything in the article that you published on Merleau-Ponty in a number of *Les Temps Modernes*? Lacan: Absolutely nothing" (p. 119).

34 I hesitate to include Gilles Deleuze within this broad generalization simply because I have not read enough of him. Certainly *The Fold: Leibniz and the Baroque*, trans. Tom Conley (Minneapolis: University of Minnesota Press, 1993) seems to work in the same region.

35 To take but one example, the critique of knowledge pictured as "a more or less passive medium through which the light of truth reaches us" in §73 of the *Phenomenology of Spirit* is not comprehensible on Newtonian theory but has to be made out by reference to Hegel's *Philosophy of Nature* and its reference back to Goethe.

36 The essay on Merleau-Ponty for *Les Temps Modernes* is, if anything, even more explicit about a shared recognition of the materiality of light: Comment s'égaler à la pesée [pensée?] subtile qui se poursuit ici d'un éros de l'oeil, d'une corporalité de la lumière où ne s'evoquent plus que nostalgiquement leur théologique primauté?" (p.253).

37 And this should make us wary of Lacan's willingness to diagram his theory in apparently Newtonian or Cartesian terms. See my "In Light of the Other."

38 Johann Wolfgang von Goethe, *Theory of Colours*, trans. Charles Eastlake (Cambridge, Mass.: MIT Press, 1970), §208.

39 It is around this formulation that one can draw together Lacan's interest in *The Visible and the Invisible* and his appeal to Roger Caillois's "Mimicry and Legendary Psychaesthesia" (translated in *October*

31 [Spring 1984]: 17–32). Rosalind Krauss has picked up particularly strong on the side of Lacan's meditation in a series of essays, including "Corpus Delicti," *October* 33 (Summer 1985): 31–72.

40 If Krauss is in some ways exemplary here, she is also not the only player in the field. In addition to the various works in which Hubert Damisch, Georges Didi-Huberman, and others approach the question of painting and its obverse, one would also have to mention the work of Michael Fried, whose focus on dialectic of absorption and theatricality in modern paintings finds its own historical and theoretical way through the complex twining of Merleau-Ponty and Lacan and whose exchange with Linda Nochlin over Courbet's paintings of women offers a striking picture of the stakes in the current theoretical division of the gaze. See Sarah Faunce and Linda Nochlin, eds., *Courbet Reconsidered* (Brooklyn: The Brooklyn Museum, 1988); and Michael Fried, *Courbet's Realism* (Chicago: University of Chicago Press, 1990).

41 The tendentiousness lies in the widespread identification of the phrase "radical self-criticism" with the work of Clement Greenberg and Michael Fried, so my appeal to that phrase here marks, among other things, the passage from the critique of vision as it has been elaborated primarily in literary criticism and film study to the very different critique emerging in art history and criticism as a response to that field's own strong problematic of modernism.

42 This is a way of saying that they are playing at the table Nietzsche set in *The Birth of Tragedy*. In a sense one has said everything that needs to be said about Socrates and the project he set in motion in saying that he alone joined the Athenian audience as spectator—until he found in Euripides a writer of plays for which participation simply meant spectatorship.

43 See Joan Copjec, "The Orthopsychic Subject: Film Theory and the Reception of Lacan." *October* 49 (Summer 1989): 53–71.

44 This is, of course, an interpretation of the impact of Jameson's writings—from *Marxism and Form* (1971) through *The Prison House of Language* (1972) and on up to *Signatures of the Visible*—on the current understanding of theory in the United States. It can also serve as a way of understanding the importance of the encounter with Jameson's work for a critical itinerary like that of Craig Owens in the visual arts.

45 It is just here that one may begin to think about the differences between Krauss's *The Optical Unconscious* and Jay's *Downcast Eyes* not simply in theoretical terms, but in terms of the ways those theoretical differences carry with them radically different stances toward the writing of history—that is, radically different understandings of one's attachment to the past and therefore also of the appropriate way that relation is to be registered in its writing. Jay offers a somewhat uneasy defense of his "look from above" as integral to "seeing" the past in the closing pages of the introduction to *Downcast Eyes*, and a fuller defense of the position of the "synoptic intellectual historian" in "Two Cheers for Paraphrase" in his *Fin-de-Siècle Socialism and Other Essays* (New York: Routledge, 1988).

46 Such appropriation to the look of things" might equally well be called "depropriation," and it is indeed in something like these terms that Rosalind Krauss and others have written about the work of Cindy Sherman in contrast with those accounts that attempt to assimilate Sherman's work to the problematic of "the male gaze." One might also note in this context Philippe Lacoue-Labarthe's account, in *Portrait de l'artist en général* (Paris: Christian Bourgeois, 1979), of the Swiss artist Urs Luthi's "depropriations." One way to put the general thrust of the present essay is to say that it takes vision to be unthinkable outside of the movement by which "appropriation" and "depropriation" are bound to one another.

8

Imaginary Identity: Space, Gender, Nation

Helga Geyer-Ryan

In this chapter I want to explore, under the current impact of warfare and racism at the heart of Europe, the possible affinity between structures of political identity and the vision of boundaries. Violence against ethnic, political, and national otherness has today reached a scale in Europe that nobody would have thought possible before 1989. The recent political changes, the increased resistance to immigration, the economic recession in the West, and the equally disastrous constructions of capitalist economies in the East have thrown the identities of many people into crisis.

The disintegration of old identities unleashes unforeseen forces of destruction. They reveal the violence with which in 1945 political identities were forged out of the debris of World War II into the shape necessary for the new communist states successfully to secure social cohesion. Today's eruption of violence again bears witness to the painful reconstruction of identities out of the fragments of shattered life histories.

There seems to be a zero-sum game of difference under way: at the very moment that the clear-cut demarcation between the liberal West and the communist East has crumbled, new frontiers have to be established against the threat of political borderline cases. These new borders are grafted onto the pre-1945 lines of ethnic or national identities, as in the cases of the former Yugoslavia and Soviet Union or of Germany in its effort to resist immigration from the East. The wider repercussions can be observed in the increase of ethnophobic idiosyncrasies in other European countries such as France, Great Britain, Russia, Austria or Rumania, and even the Netherlands.

The physical atrocities of warfare and the resurgence of neofascistic activities bear witness to the truth of a point made by Walter Benjamin in his 1921 essay "Critique of Violence."[1] To principle, Benjamin observes, the drawing of borderlines, whether literal or figurative—though they may be as plain to read as scars on a body—is a ritual designed not so much to secure one's possessions by constituting a new law as to mark the exhibition and foundation of power, represented as law. So the erupting violence of recent remarcations of more archaic borders is a gesture that repeats the force with which those borders were once established, a force that is inscribed in every laying down of limits. These limits and that force are at the root of the formation of national identities.

In the following pages I want to look at the connection between borders, power, identity, and the imaginary and their inscription in the field of vision. I want to show why discourses of politics and economics, as constructions in the field of language, when operating on their own fall well short of explaining, much less changing, these practices of violence.

In his seminal study *Orientalism*, Edward Said analyzes the effects on the image of the self caused by a mental set he calls "imaginary geography." According to Said, "imaginary geography" plays a crucial part in the construction of the so-called Orient as the historical and cultural other of Western identity. The East-West divide is a truly symbolic borderline because there is no fixed geographic point from which it could operate. Instead, it is a spatial metaphor for the relationship between the self and the other, which can be actualized at any point of identified interest in the First World. "It can be argued that Islam (in the shape of the Muslim populations of North Africa, Turkey and the Indian sub-continent) is now the primary form in which the Third World presents itself to Europe, and that the North-South divide, in the European context, has been largely inscribed onto a pre-existing Christian-Muslim division."[2]

The East-West borderline has its roots in the first texts of our cultural heritage, starting with Homer and the Greek dramatists. The later conflict between Christianity and Islam was inscribed on the opposition between ancient Greece and Asia, and it was reinforced by the traumatic experiences of the Crusades and the invasions of the Huns and Turks. The political East-West tensions after World War II have dramatically deepened the symbolic trench, a territorial splitting that today, right in the heart of the new Europe, is still corrupting even national politics: witness the strange aversion of West Germans to come face to face with their new East German compatriots.

Said's enterprise is to reconstruct historically the various cultural discourses that give narrative body to the politics of imaginary geography in the Western symbolic order. In isolating a spatial formation at the heart of cultural narrations of historical and political identity, Said ventures in an important and innovative direction. But he does not investigate the foundations of space as an imaginary formation.

Why is it that underneath the communicative capacities of discourses, knowledge, symbolic exchange, and differentiation—beneath, in other words, the structures of time—there seems to persist the bedrock of space and vision (*geo*graphy, *imagi*nation), registers that are, if not independent of time, at least resistant to its sway? But let me turn first to another cultural discourse, where vision also plays a central part: that of art history. What would generally be regarded as the most important representation in the history of Western art—important because of its widespread dissemination and reproduction, cherished for its symbolic function and its affective value? The portrayal I have in mind is so central to our civilization that we no longer perceive it: it is the image of Mary holding the baby Christ in her arms.

Consider the composition and spatial arrangement of this pivotal scenario. Apart from being the semantic cornerstone of our Christian heritage the signifier, the formal execution of the mother-child relationship, exerts a powerful influence on our unconscious perception. It is an exact reproduction of the mirror stage as described by Lacan. We see a baby aged between six and eighteen months on his mother's arm. It looks straight at the viewer, who stands in the position of the mirror. The mother's look is directed either toward the baby or straight into the "mirror." In both cases her look confirms the mirror's function of providing the baby with a premature image of his own corporeal unity and autonomy. In most pictures the baby is gesticulating, the logic of which becomes clear when we read his gesture as the delighted recognition of his own reflection and the kinetic exploration of the space between mother, child and mirror image. It is the moment when the child for the first time takes the place of a subject opposite an object.

The mirror stage, providing the baby with the illusion of fullness and presence by imaging the self as a unified body, still belongs to the preoedipal phase. It is the transitory condition for the entry into the oedipal phase and the symbolic order, which are integral to the laws of patriarchy. The narratives of the symbolic order, always structured in time and therefore tilted toward difference and death, offer the child sexual, cultural, historical, and political identifications. These narratives will eventually be anchored more or less rigidly in positions of identity, propelled by the unifying impact of the mirror image.

But this ideal ego, pretending to be autonomous and coherent in the pseudosecurity of its space and under the gaze of maternal love, is beset with difficulties. Identity, being constructed by way of a mirror image, always coexists with its alienation from that image of the self as other. The basic unreliability of identity crops up as emotional ambiguity toward any other, a constant oscillation between affirmative identification and hostile repulsion.

The passage through the mirror stage and the ensuing oedipal phase that stabilizes the infant in what D. W. Winnicott calls "a true self" are dependent not only on the interpretive ordering of experiences in the symbolic order but also on the more archaic mother-child relationship of the preoedipal phase. This phase is shot through with aggressive introjection and repulsion, only mollified by the indirect influence of the father of prehistory as an instance of divergence between mother and child.[3] The so-called true self is not more accomplished than the false self (according to Melanie Klein we are all cured psychotics). But it has access to a more flexible identity because of less traumatic experiences with the preoedipal mother, a more successful internalization of the good object, and the softening of mirror stage effects like rigidity or loss of self as a result of immersion in the diversity of the symbolic order. What light can the mirror stage—the centrality of which in our culture is captured in the tableau of the Virgin and Child—throw on the question of space as an imaginary formation?

As a result of massive migrations in our contemporary world, the symbolic orders, incorporating the social and sexual contracts that distribute positions of identity, have been thrown into crisis. The victims are not only those who are forced into exile and emigration, though they bear the cruelest burden, but those who are confronted with immigration and who experience the arbitrariness and relativity of the symbolic order through their encounter with the other.

There is a difference in the case of tourism and communicative technologies where through the exchange of money and goods the symbolic orders of both cultures are preserved. Because there is no hierarchy through power and domination, there is no loss, only seduction.

However, in the case of emigration and immigration, the shock of the other can produce regressions into structures of the mirror stage or even further back into psychotic dispositions. Thus, since the collapse of the communist symbolic order, extreme cases of xenophobia have emerged in Germany; in other European countries the rhetoric of racism has also accompanied the new nationalisms, which are implicitly antifeminist as well. The same phenomena erupted in France when it was suddenly faced with massive immigration from the Maghrebine countries.

The calls for national purity reflect the reemergence of an archaic stage in the psychobiography of the subject, a stage even prior to the mirror stage. A semantics of purity indicates the virulence of the abject, an effect of the utter fragility of the subject position. The abject signals the rejection of the overpowering body of the mother at a time when the baby is not yet able to form an object. In xenophobia, the phobic object stands in for the fear of the reemergence of an existential void that had been camouflaged by the security of the mirror image and the laws of the symbolic order.

The anxieties of absence, loss, and castration that lie at the root of xenophobia are triggered by the collapse of the fantasy of the whole, unified, undamaged body in a space that is conceived of, metaphorically and metonymically, as the body's extension or double. The importance of this spatial doubling of the body as its own support can be grasped in Gaston Bachelard's *The Poetics of Space*. Bachelard attributes the affective value lining the use-value of a house to the unconscious memory of the mother's womb and body and the bodily imaginations of the infant. He even sees the body as a field of engravings resulting from the subject's tactile and kinetic experiences with the house. "Beyond memories, our first home is physically inscribed into ourselves. It consists of a cluster of organic habits. We are the engrams of the functions of habitation in that first house and all the other houses are only variations of one basic theme. The word 'habit' is very often used in order to signify that passionate relationship between our body which doesn't forget and that unforgettable house."[4]

In "The City and the Imaginary" Donatella Mazzoleni analyzes more explicitly than Bachelard both the house and the city as the body's doubles. Against the cultural preference for temporal structures such as narrative or *différance,* she insists on the priority of space in shaping the perception of our bodies.

> But the lived experience of non-verbal, pre-logical space is only partly translatable into language or narratable in a story. In it we find the spatialization of primary pulsations—Eros and Thanatos—that cannot be contained by the web of any structure or story. The articulation of these impulses are always twofold: there is a need to return to a space which is a container of life, which can metabolize death itself (living)—then there is the need to symbolize, to deflect outwards the death instinct (constructing). We could perhaps say that constructing, in so far as it is a symbolizing activity, arises from the dwelling of the instincts because of that 'primary paranoia' which attempts to redeem the overwhelming relationship with one's own overshadowing mother figure. Semiology is not sufficient for our interpretation. What is needed is a 'geotica' and an 'anthropanalysis' of the psychic structures deeply rooted in our cultures: thus an archetypology of the imaginary.[5]

Likewise a nation, perceived not so much as a historical but rather as a geographical unit, in other words as a space, a body with clearly marked contours on a map, a quasi-organic compound of geopolitical details, seems to be imbued with the same imaginary power Bachelard or Mazzoleni detect in the house or the city. Thus, in the following quotation the term "city" might readily be replaced by the term "nation":

> The city is also the body's double. Like the house, it is also, in some way, a lived space, anthropomorphic. We can speak of a city as long as the totality of those who produce and live a collective construction constitute a collective anthropoid body, which maintains in some way an identity as a 'subject'. The city is therefore a site of *identification.* Thus the city has a somatic individuality and a membrane, which may be palpable, and which both surround and limit its somatic individuality.[6]

One thinks immediately of the Great Wall of China or of the Berlin Wall, which was national as well, and we remember that the first refugees in our written tradition (women, by the way) asked for shelter not in another nation but in another city, the ancient polis.

If we conclude that after the house and the city, the nation might be the body-ego's third double, then we can recognize the prelogical, prelinguistic conditions of xenophobia. The influx of strangers is experienced as an assault on and a violent penetration of that unified but always fragile and precarious body-self, a process that gives rise to the fragmentation and collapse of the imaginary autonomous ego.

Only with reference to such a primeval need for space can the outstanding success of Edgar Reitz's film *Heimat* in Germany be understood. *Heimat* provided the postwar German imagination with an extensive topology of the house, the town, and the county, thereby marginalizing the compromised nation as an infected double of the body politic. The film does not endorse xenophobia in the form of anti-Americanism as much as some critics have argued; rather it equates the United States with the metropolis, a formation whose rank growth can no longer be contained within the perceptual apparatus designed by the unifying and demarcating mirror stage.

Against such a theoretical background, the logic of the ghetto or the restriction to the harbor area of foreign travelers in ancient Greek cities can be seen as the means of locating, isolating, and visualizing[7] an otherwise amorphous enemy—amorphous because, outside the delusions of the imaginary, there is no enemy distinguishable from one's own body.

The legacy of the mirror stage threatens the subject with two extremes, which will influence every relationship between subject and other: the vanishing of the subject as a consequence of the subject's identification with the other or the aggressive rigidity of the subject as a resistance to the overpowering other. The prerequisite for a stable subject position after the mirror stage and the oedipal phase is a prior positive loving relationship between a baby and a nonpossessive mother.[8] Only such a relationship can provide the balance, the flexibility of identity necessary to avoid the prison of a mortifying body armor at one extreme and the loss of self in psychotic disintegration at the other.

Equally important in this respect is the subject's access to symbolization, where anxieties can be externalized and new identities internalized. Already as early as the time of the mirror stage, the "symbolic underpinnings of the visual imaginary"[9] might help to prevent the later dominance of the violent "pornographic gaze"[10] of male chauvinism—chauvinism in this case literally understood as xenophobia.[11]

If the psychobiographies of girls and boys show differences produced by different positions toward castration, oedipal rivalry, or the pornographic gaze, then it may be sexual difference that gives rise to the different reactions of men and women in their encounter with strangers. Of course, according to the law of the *folie à deux* a man and a woman could react with exactly the same paranoid aggression as described by Victor Burgin in his essay "Paranoiac Space."[12] But aggression—murderous aggression against the supposed invader of the pure body politic—is first and foremost a male reaction.

The rivalry of the oedipal phase and the so-called heroic virtues of the male in the symbolic order enhance the aggressive position of the preoedipal phase and the fortifying effect of the mirror stage to the point of rigidity. Furthermore, the stronger repression of the incest wish in the male and the consequently more strenuous denial of his own body, both of which are necessary for the preservation of the patriarchal order, make a man's access to his unconscious far more difficult than a woman's. Yet without an admission of this fundamentally alien sphere of the self there can be no acknowledgment of the stranger as a member of one's own kind.

Julia Kristeva reminds us in her study *Etrangers à nous-mêmes*[13] that from the very beginning of our subjectivity and individuality, which are based on our splitting into unconscious and consciousness, we are always already strangers to ourselves. Only the lifelong, cathartic experience and reliving of that division through art or other imaginative practices can prevent or mitigate the petrifaction of the imaginary self. In visual terms, what is required against the domination of the reifying gaze is the construction of a whole register of different ways of looking, an approach that could give rise, in analogy to Bakhtin's theory of polyphony, to a theory of polyscopy.[14] In spatial terms, this construction means developing a capacity for mobility, transitory states, nomadism, and voyaging; the occupation of places in different narratives or the renaming of old places and spaces would likewise be involved in rituals of mobility.

For women this construction might look quite different, and neither Kristeva nor Mazzoleni nor Burgin nor Bachelard deals with the possible consequences of sexual difference. In a patriarchal society women are in fact doubly strangers: first in their relation to their own unconscious and second in their function as the margin, the other, the body, the unconscious, the fetish of men. Not only are women's bodies literally less unified and fortified than men's under the permanent threat of male physical violence, of forced intrusion and penetration, but they are also more prone to loss of ego in processes of fusion or identification in amatory states or when the unconscious surfaces.

Such a disposition should make it easier for women to confront the stranger without immediate hostility. But, unless their ego is buttressed, they could be in danger of losing their sense of their bodies' limits, and the reappearance of the existential void could throw into relief anorexic disturbances, depression, melancholia, or suicidal attacks.

So, what women might need in order to encounter strangers in a nontraumatic way might be not so much rituals of mobility as conditions that would stabilize their bodies in their environment, enabling them to take up a place beyond men's spatial and interpretive control. In *Hiroshima mon Amour, L'amant*, and *Le ravissement de Lol V. Stein* Marguerite Duras has written compellingly of the fascination that the *xenos* holds for women, but she also shows the high price that must be paid in mental stability.

Similar observations can be made regarding the relationships between women and cities in the event of mental crises. A number of celebrated male writers have described their experiences of being marooned in a strange city. These experiences can be compared metaphorically with the crisis of the body and the reappearance of the unconscious in the effect of the uncanny. Walter Benjamin, in his account of a first stroll in an unknown city[15], Sigmund Freud in his wanderings in an unfamiliar Italian town,[16] and André Breton in his defamiliarization of Paris under the psychic influence of Nadja[17]—all three undergo an imaginary estrangement of space that they describe in terms of seduction, depersonalization, and feelings of the uncanny. However, in their cases, the assault of the "other scene" is finally pacified by the reintegrating forces of the ego and the rationality of the street map. Only Nadja goes on living an imaginary, magic relationship with Paris, which infuses Breton's rationality with liberating flashes of the unconscious. But when she is left by Breton, who retreats safely into the "pure" love of another woman, it is Nadja who ends up in a madhouse.

In Sylvia Plath's *The Bell Jar*, the mental crisis of Esther Greenwood makes itself felt for the first time in the bizarre alienation of New York, which is transformed into an environment of abomination. Likewise, Christa Wolf registers her loss of political identity, the result of her having discovered that she was being observed by the secret service, as a disintegration of her symbiotic attitude to Berlin. Her home becomes literally "*unheimlich*."[18]

Only on condition that the differences between the sexes are taken into account can women be told that really "Heimat is a mirage, a delusion." Reitz says, "Heimat is such that if one would go closer and closer to it, one would discover that at the moment of arrival it has gone, it has dissolved into nothingness."[19] And therefore we never arrive again once we have left.[20]

Heimat might be a delusion; it might even become a dangerous one. Yet, as I hope my argument has shown, it is a necessary delusion. It is as necessary as our inheritance of imaginary unity is unavoidable. But we must be aware of it, and it must not be too rigid. Bachelard sees the dangers of immobility symbolized in what he calls the "final house." This house would be the house of death, he says, symmetrical with our birthplace or the house of our parents. Instead he praises the dream house, the eternal house of the future, a place, but a place always in the making. The dream house has the openness of the other place, which takes into account the otherness of ourselves. When the good mother is internalized along with the house, the city, the nation, Europe, and all the other places of identity so that they can be left behind in reality, only then can the bliss of otherness—its life-enhancing *promesse de bonheur*—be given a proper place, a true home of one's own.

1 Walter Benjamin, "Kritik der Gewalt," in Benjamin, *Gesammelte Schriften*, vol. 2, eds. Rolf Tiedemann and Hermann Schweppenhäuser (Frankfurt/M.: Suhrkamp, 1977, pp. 179–203. English version, "Critique of Violence," in *One-Way Street and Other Writings*, trans. Edmund Jephcott and Kingsley Shorter (London: New Left Books, 1979), pp. 132–154.

2 Edward Said, *Orientalism* (London: Routledge & Kegan Paul, 1978), p. 97.

3 Julia Kristeva has theorized Freud's notion of the preoedipal and nonsexed "father of personal prehistory." According to her it is the maternal voice that gives the child its first identification with the earliest third party—the father of personal prehistory. "The loving mother, different from the caring or clinging mother, is someone who has an object of desire, beyond that she has an other with relation to whom the child will serve as a go-between. She will love her child with respect to that other, and it is through a discourse aimed at that Third party that the child will be set up as 'loved' for the mother…. Without a Third party, the bodily exchange [is not maternal fondness but] abjection or devouring." Julia Kristeva, *Powers of Horror: An Essay on Abjection*, trans. Leon S. Roudiez (New York: Columbia University Press, 1982), p. 34.

4 Gaston Bachelard, *The Poetics of Space*, trans. Maria Jolas (Boston: Beacon Press, 1960), pp. 14–15).

5 Donatella Mazzoleni, "The City and the Imaginary," in *New Formations* 12 (1990): 91–104, esp. pp. 92–93.

6 Ibid., p. 97.

7 See also Simon Goldhill's essay "Refracting Classical Vision: Changing Cultures of Viewing," chapter 2 in this volume, where he speaks about the use of the scopic powers of public life in the polis of Athens to mold the identities of her inhabitants.

8 See for instance D. W. Winnicott, *Playing and Reality* (London and New York: Tavistock/Routledge, 1991 [1971]), pp. 97, 103, 107. See also my note 3.

9 See chapter 7 in this volume by Stephen Melville, "Division of the Gaze, or, Remarks on the Color and Tenor of Contemporary 'Theory.'"

10 See chapter 14 in this volume by Parveen Adams, "Father, Can't You See I'm Filming?"

11 See Susanne Kappler, *The Pornography of Representation* (Cambridge: Polity Press, 1986), esp. chapters 1–4 and 11.

12 Victor Burgin, "Paranoiac Space," in *New Formations* 12 (1990): 61–76.

13 Julia Kristeva, *Etrangers à nous-mêmes* (Paris: Gallimard, 1988).

14 See also Martin Jay, *Downcast Eyes: The Denigration of Vision in Twentieth-Century French Thought* (Berkeley: University of California Press, 1993), p. 592.

15 Benjamin, "Moskau," in *Gesammelte Schriften*, vol. IV, (1972), pp. 318–319.

16 Sigmund Freud, "Das Unheimliche," in *Studienausgabe*, vol. IV (Frankfurt/M.: Fischer Verlag, 1970). pp. 241–274, esp. pp. 259–260.

17 André Breton, *Nadja* (1928) (Paris: Gallimard, 1964).

18 Christa Wolf, *Was bleibt* (Frankfurt/M.: Luchterhand Literaturverlag, 1990).

19 David Morley and Kevin Robbins, "No Place Like *Heimat*: Images of Home(land) in European Culture," in *New Formations* 12 (1990): 1–23, esp. p. 19.

20 Even Odysseus, according to Horkheimer and Adorno, Derrida, and Lévinas the epitome of homecoming, never really comes home properly. See my essay "From the Dialectic of Force to the *Dialectic of Enlightenment*: Re-reading the *Odyssey*," in Helga Geyer-Ryan, *Fables of Desire: Studies in the Ethics of Art and Gender* (Cambridge: Polity Press, 1994), pp. 220–246.

9

Illuminating Passion: Irigaray's Transfiguration of Night

Cathryn Vasseleu

In his study of modernity and vision, *Downcast Eyes: The Denigration of Vision in Twentieth-Century French Thought,*[1] Martin Jay argues that Luce Irigaray is an antivisual theorist. Jay bases his assessment of Irigaray's position on her account of the ocularcentrism of Western philosophy, selecting her work as the most polemical of the many contributors to the post-1968 feminist debate in France who have drawn associations between ocularcentrism and masculine identity.[2] However, Jay's discussion omits aspects of Irigaray's interest in the representability of feminine subjectivity and eroticism that have not been considered by theorists of vision in general. Rather than confining her project to an elaboration of the implication of metaphors of light in the representation of a masculine identity, I will argue that Irigaray also adopts and develops a genealogical approach to the material conditions of that which comes to light. Though Irigaray's project in *Speculum*[3] is to retrace the movement by which a maternal genealogy is lost in the dissemination of light, she also has an ongoing interest in redefining a love of light that is dependent on its embodied, material conditions and, above all, its sexuate beginnings. This theme can be traced in a series of provocative alliances that Irigaray makes with various philosophers, particularly in *An Ethics of Sexual Difference.*[4] In this chapter I will discuss the way in which Irigaray takes up the theme in relation to Emmanuel Lévinas's depiction of the feminine in his "Phenomenology of Eros."[5]

LUCE IRIGARAY
AN ANTIVISUAL THEORIST?

Irigaray and Derrida are grouped together in Jay's chapter on deconstruction and vision, in which he considers the two philosophers' analyses of vision in the context of their readings of ocularcentrism. Derrida's work is interpreted not as a denigration of vision but as a deconstructive position: "It would be imprecise to call the suspicious approach Derrida does take to the primacy of vision in Western culture a straightforward 'critique' of ocularcentrism." On the other hand, Jay indicates that the general trajectory of his discussion of Irigaray will be the revelation of her "radicalization of the antivisual components in deconstruction" rather than the deconstruction of ocularcentrism.

There is no denying that much of Irigaray's criticism is directed toward the privileging of the visual in Western culture, which she argues is tied to the perpetuation of a monological masculine subjectivity. She has been criticized for making generalizations based on her own globalizing reach or for her assumption of a prevailing phallocentric signifying economy.[6] There is a danger of interpreting comments by Irigaray, such as the following, as unvarying pronouncements of women's relationship to vision: "Investment in the look is not as privileged in women as in men. More than any other sense, the eye objectifies and it masters. It sets at a distance, and maintains a distance. In our culture the predominance of the look over smell, taste, touch and hearing has brought about an impoverishment of bodily relations."[7] However, there is more to Irigaray's theorization of the visual than a consideration of the privileging of the gaze in a phallocentric economy will allow. Irigaray also pursues the trail of an unaccountable materiality that is systematically eliminated in the adoption of a metaphysics of presence. She extends this assessment of the workings of heliocentrism to Derrida's naming of woman as writing or *différance*. Just as the sun is metaphorically incorporated into philosophy, woman as trope of *différance* incorporates femininity while excluding any claim to a feminine identity by women: "...ever more hemmed in, cathected by tropes, how could she articulate any sound from beneath this cheap chivalric finery?"[8] The trope of woman is an endless deferral of identity, independent of any material referent. As Jay quotes Irigaray, in the idealist rationality of heliocentrism woman cannot refer to any women in particular. Woman is "never anything but the still undifferentiated opaqueness of sensible matter, the store (of) substance for the sublation of self, or being as what is, or what he [sic] is (or was), here and now."[9]

Irigaray is more ambivalent about vision and Derrida is more in sympathy with Irigaray's refusal to embrace the other of metaphysics than is allowed in Jay's comparison of the two philosophers, set up as it is in terms of Derrida's ambivalence toward vision and Irigaray's antivisual stance. Jay discusses Rodolphe Gasché's Derridean foregrounding of the materiality of signifying practices and the proposition that perfect specularity can never be entertained.[10] Jay concludes that although Derrida is hostile to any traditional privileging of the eye. On the other hand, Jay limits his consideration of Irigaray's rewriting of the assumption of undifferentiated matter to its negative implications for vision.

Like Derrida,[11] Irigaray regards light as the founding metaphor of metaphysics. In "Plato's *Hystera*,"[12] which is devoted to a discussion of the first part of Book Seven of Plato's *Republic*, Irigaray considers Plato's organization of light and space in terms of the photologic of heliotropes. However, rather than emphasizing the dependence of metaphysics on metaphors of light, Irigaray directs her attention to the gender of philosophy, which, as Derrida proposes, sees itself in terms of metaphors of light. In Irigaray's naming of Western philosophy as photology, the weight of her argument does not fall on the elaboration of light as the founding metaphor of metaphysics. Her argument is instead directed toward the figuration of a complicity between photology and phallocentrism. She argues that the complicity with phallocentrism is equally apparent in phonocentrism. Insofar as philosophy speaks of itself as a "love" of a wisdom that is equated with light, it reduces eroticism to a love that photology is singularly able to reveal. Irigaray's consistent argument is that such a love is both inadequate to the representation of women's desire and to any sexuate intercourse/expression.

Irigaray's analysis of photology is of a metaphoricity that ensures that any engendering of maternal origin is never to come to light. Irigaray emphasizes that feminine participation in representation is subsumed within an exclusively patrilineal economy, where it remains supplementary to a fantasy of masculine autogenesis. The exclusion is achieved in the differentiation between form and matter, in which matter remains the site of an unthematizable materiality. Though masculine identity is formulated in opposition to matter, the feminine as matter cannot be thought. As Judith Butler explains, "For Irigaray, the 'feminine' which cannot be said to be anything, to participate in ontology at all, is—and here grammar fails us—set under erasure as the impossible necessity that enables any ontology."[13]

In place of this erasure of the participation of matter, Irigaray develops her well-known concept of a sexualized morphology, or a notion of the sexed body.[14] Her aim is to reopen the constitution of matter that has been directed toward the establishment of an isomorphism between an imaginary masculine body and systems of representation.[15] In Irigaray's words, photology stands as an unsexed "heliogamy," or a system of ex-static relationships that is "disastrous for the still organic membrane of the eye: living tissue, unfit to receive the glare of such a fiery star."[16] There is nothing erotic, yet alone materially conceived about the fixed light of the Platonic sun. Considered in this context, Irigaray's concern regarding vision includes an eroticizing of the source of light—a theme that I will take up in the following section.

In terms of his intention to provide an overview, Jay's description of Irigaray as an antivisual theorist is more than justifiable. His analysis reiterates a prevailing assumption in detail. However, his analysis is also indicative of the absence of any significant differences of interpretation of Irigaray's stance in relation to vision. An irony of Jay's inclusion of Irigaray as one of the antivisual theorists, against whom he argues in favor of an ineradicable passion for the freedom of vision, is that no opening remains for considering the extent to which Irigaray addresses illumination as an ineradicable passion.

FECUNDITY AND ILLUMINATION

As I will outline in this section, Irigaray's account of illumination represents a unique challenge to the light of heliocentrism. In some respects her approach to vision is aligned with Emmanuel Lévinas, who along with his colleagues Maurice Blanchot and Georges Bataille can be loosely described as a philosopher who is preoccupied with conceiving of a communion that occurs without the mediation of light. For Lévinas, light is the medium of the phenomenal world, which appears as a distantiated object inhabitable by and belonging to the seer. However, in order to thematize existence, Lévinas argues that it is not sufficient to account for the contents of consciousness. It is also necessary to consider the disappearance of the phenomenal world into that which is refractory to representation, or the sense of an unthematizable materiality that still endures in the absence of light. Lévinas refers to this as a "night" in which a sense of impersonal being is experienced as the anonymous restlessness of "there is."[17] The feminine belongs to the same order of existence—the feminine is a non-negatable presence that persists in the absence of light.

Lévinas's analysis of the feminine in "Phenomenology of Eros" as a carnality that both transcends and is inadequate to signification completes his phenomenology of night.[18] Lévinas conceives of feminine identity as an enduring mystery whose exorbitant carnality becomes an overwhelming obsession in the erotic encounter. As a singularity that is both inadequate to and surpasses expressivity, eroticism exposes carnality as the evasion of significance. The body loses any identifiable status in erotic nudity and is exposed as an ungraspable, unsignifiable materiality.

Lévinas argues that there is a fundamental dispossession or exteriority of origin underlining the totality of the visual. This dispossession, refractory to manifestation, is of the order of differentiation rather than illumination.[19] Lévinas distinguishes between the qualitative presence of the visual, as a totality limited by its dependence on an indefinable materiality, and proximity, as the infinity of unthematizable disjunction. It is by means of the latter that Lévinas conceives of an originary, transcendent other in ethical rather than ontological terms. However, when Lévinas embraces the absence of the feminine in the caress, he does so in visual terms. In Lévinas's characterization the carnal, the feminine, withdraws from the harshness of the light. The caress is an obsession with an evasion of presence that persists in the absence of light:

> The caress is a mode of the subject's being, where the subject who is in contact with another goes beyond this contact. Contact as sensation is part of the world of light. But what is caressed is not touched, properly speaking. It is not the softness or warmth of the hand given in contact that the caress seeks. The seeking of the caress constitutes its essence by the fact that the caress does not know what it seeks. This "not knowing," this fundamental disorder, is the essential...always other, always inaccessible, and always still to come. The caress is the anticipation of this pure future [*avenir*], without content. It is made up of this increase of hunger, of ever richer promises, opening new perspectives onto the ungraspable. It feeds on countless hungers.[20]

Lévinas characterizes the resistance of the feminine to incorporation as a self-effacement that eludes the grasp. In going beyond the sensation of contact, the caress is a losing sight of touch rather than a perpetuation of the tactile.[21] I would suggest that the action of the caress is conceived by Lévinas as the obverse of *groping*, or the hand's blind venturing in its attempt to alter and bring the elemental to light.[22] This is not an encounter whose indefinability is an opening to a transcendent other.[23] The caress is a disorder of light. To the extent that Lévinas considers eroticism within a phenomenological paradigm, the caress is a breaking up of sensibility rather than a bringing of the ethical and the feminine together on the plane of eros.[24]

Irigaray's disagreement with Lévinas begins with his limitation of the feminine to an interlude in light. To Lévinas, the feminine is a passive undoing of a virile aspiration in relation to light, and he concentrates on the withdrawal of the feminine in his phenomenology of the caress. Eroticism is a movement away from light, beyond contact, a dissolution of identity into an unsignifiable carnality. By contrast, Irigaray regards the caress as an incomparable sense of incarnation, as a gesture prolonging its incompletion. Rather than merely a diffusion of formal identity that is sought out in the elusiveness of touch, Irigaray conceives of the caress as a participation in the alterability or transmutability of flesh. This conception is not set against Lévinas's text but instead extends the significance of the caress in a way that he does not consider.

Irigaray begins her reading of Lévinas's "Phenomenology of Eros" with her own description of erotic pleasure, which she describes as a pleasure taken by sensuality in its beginning. This notion is not an archaeological or a "new-age" conception of eroticism, nor is it a rediscovery or reenactment of an original birth. Erotic pleasure is an imaginary beginning, a birth after and before the present, which will never have taken place. It is an opening only to a perpetuation of that opening. Voluptuousness undoes all schemas, all thematization of the world; it is a beginning without memory, a beginning that knows no other. In contrast to conscious motivation, erotic pleasure is an acceptance of that which gives of itself, of that which is of no account. It has no basis in the subject that sees things but is a state of immersion, a being lost in the "sensual pleasure of birth into a world where the look itself remains tactile—open to the light."[25]

A well-known feature of Irigaray's work is her association of eroticism with the encounter of wonder. In her reading of Descartes's *Meditations*, Irigaray draws on Descartes's reading of wonder as the first of the passions:

> Wonder is not an enveloping. It corresponds to time, to spacetime before and after that which can delimit, go round, encircle. It constitutes an *opening* prior to and following that which surrounds, enlaces. It is the passion of that which is already born and not yet re-enveloped in love. Of that which is touched and moves toward and within the attraction, without nostalgia for the first dwelling. Outside of repetition. It is the passion of the first encounter. And of perpetual rebirth? An affect that would subsist among all forms of others irreducible each to the other. The passion that inaugurates love and art. And thought.[26]

Irigaray refers to the touching in wonder as the touch of the caress. The caress is not so much a touch as it is the gesture of touch, an alternation between movement and posture, simultaneously dissolving and constituting itself without memory or distinction. This gesture is a never-to-be-grasped touching, an attraction without consummation, always on the threshold of appetite, not yet anticipating or yearning for an other. The caress affirms and protects its infinite otherness in the prolongation of a birth that will never come to pass. Untouched by mastery, it is before and beyond any subject or setting. Life, made familiar in its consumption and habitation, is suspended and reopened in the gesture of the caress.

For Irigaray, the caress is the most elementary gesture of fecundity. She links this gesture, attentive to the regeneration and renewal of life, with a love that is given over to the source of light. The source of light, as far as Irigaray is concerned, is the fecundity of matter—a night in whose elemental indivisibility there is a future "where things have not yet taken their places but remain possible."[27] The movement of illumination is what precedes any ordering of and incorporation into a world prior to any vision. Conceived of in terms of the caress, light is the first discovery, the first (re) enfolding of flesh, the materialization of the body, the birth into a world. Illumination is the passage necessary to the creation of form—the possibility of morphogenesis, the body that is never coincident with itself.

Rather than theorizing matter as the abyss of light, for Irigaray illumination is a never-to-be-grasped beginning, a beginning without which there can be no emergence of life out of chaos and formlessness. Illumination is "that less-than-nothing which is not nothing—light."[28] Irigaray conceives of illumination as a passion, as a first and inexhaustible love.[29] Illumination is an encounter of wonder, an encounter born of a carnality that cannot be apprehended. This wonder is a source of animation—a movement in one's being, not of any lasting impression. It is an opening up to light that brings nothing into relief, conveys no sense of things, is unfixable and unopposable. It is an opening of affection.

There are several aspects of Irigaray's account of illumination that I would like to expand upon here, although I will confine my comments to describing rather than critically discussing. First, in figuring the source of illumination in terms of the caress, Irigaray makes a break with the system of ex-static relationships of Platonic light. Lévinas characterizes the withdrawal of the feminine other as a phenomenologically defined failing, and the trajectory of his ethics can be described as a dream of passing beyond light. In his phenomenology of night, Lévinas turns from the sun in search of a nocturnal, powerless source of light. Derrida described Lévinas's conception of erotic light as "a community of non-presence, and therefore of non-phenomenality. Not a community without light...but a community anterior to Platonic light. A light before neutral light, before the truth which arrives as a third party, the truth 'which we look toward together....'"[30]

Lévinas describes voluptuousness as a movement away from the light. Irigaray takes this movement further. Voluptuousness is an abandonment of the familiar, a staking of life in the insecurity of each moment. It is a re-turning, a state of movement, a corporeality oscillating between matter and light. I would describe her project as a genealogy of photosensitivity[31] rather than a photology that illuminates reason or nature or god. Far from simply being a movement into night, this is a passion for an unopposable, unknowable, unfixable light. Wonder is not only an astonishment by light but a perpetual movement, an opening up to light within the immobilization of sight. The sheer novelty of light and not the clarity of knowledge is what animates the thoughts of the philosophers. For Descartes it is a passion for a light that, free of an object, rejuvenates the brain.[32] For Nietzsche, it is the lightness of losing one's gravity in a contact with newness—in a spark that annihilates thought.[33]

Irigaray's conception of erotic light is a dream not of passing beyond light but of a sexual community within the light. Her conception of a light before Platonic light takes her not into the night of nonphenomenality but to a philosophy of the elemental, a philosophy before and after Platonic light.[34] For Irigaray, the caress is "an ecstasy that remains *in-stant,*" or a returning with/in the self.[35] A factor in Irigaray's formulation that works against the trajectory of Lévinas's ethics is that erotic light is unsurpassable, unopposable. It is a beginning that is materially conceived. There is no means of transcending this erotic beginning, which is a transcendence in itself. In remaining on the threshold of the instance, it will never have come to pass.

A second aspect of Irigaray's formulation of illumination is its departure from the modern heliocentrism of atomic light. Atomic physics is generally credited with uncovering the sun residing at the core of every atom of matter. According to Irigaray, woman remains on the side of the electron in this paradigm as a negativity that circulates toward but never returns to herself as a locus of development of a positive form.[36] Capitalizing on the unprecedented potential for the destruction of matter contained within this atomic schema, Irigaray argues, to the contrary, that a culture of sexual difference requires that negative and positive poles be present in each sex: "What is missing is the double pole of attraction and support, which excludes disintegration or rejection, attraction and decomposition, but which instead ensures the separation that articulates every encounter and makes possible speech, promises, alliances."[37]

Irigaray theorizes the exorbitant ultramateriality in which lovers are absorbed as a heterogeneous affection that cannot be defined in terms of self-same. Eroticism is the passion of the first encounter: "of that which is touched and moves toward and within the attraction, without nostalgia for the first dwelling."[38] The dissipation of form into carnality is an erotically constituted opening, which is irreducible to memory, consummation, or distinction. In Irigaray's hands, instead of transcending and falling short of representation, the equivocacy of matter is a dynamic opening.[39] Irigaray theorizes this opening as the *mucous*. The mucous is a labile, positive reserve that in remaining interior is never experienced as either an idea or a thing. It is an interior unopposable to any other, an interval of freedom and attraction that is refractory to concepts of containment and dissipation, penetration and recollection, visibility and form.

To describe the indeterminacy of the mucous as unrepresentable would be to miss the point. The mucous is a continuation of the body beyond the threshold of flesh and its erasing in an indistinguishable contiguity and porosity of interiority and skin. This opening is refractory to control or closure. It is the body as threshold or passage, where no distinction between interior or exterior world, or the body as object or subject, can be sustained. The graspability of the phenomenal body is suspended in the prolongation of a carnality that dissolves and constitutes itself without trace.[40]

The atomic notion of the disclosure of presence is based on the transformation of matter into light.[41] Against a heliocentric model of light's engendering, in which any joining or passage between matter and light in illumination is effaced, Irigaray conceives of the origin of light as a sexual beginning. This is not a biological or precultural beginning but a mobile differentiation or spacing—a giving up of all that is familiar, a being given over to a nonincorporable elemental indeterminacy. The sexual encounter is not, as Lévinas theorizes, a lapse in presence but an opening that cannot be assumed without schemas or telos or anticipation of presence. It is an erotically constituted conjunction, an immemorial lability of flesh that resembles no other. Irigaray reverses the order of fecundity and conception, claiming that fecundity is an opening without which there can be no conception.

A third aspect of Irigaray's account of illumination is that her emphasis on light's erotic beginnings forces a reconsideration of a feminine commitment to light as a medium of expression. Lévinas reiterates that the mastery of light is not a feminine vocation. Aligned on the side of the self in its carnality, rather than a subjectivity in its own right, the feminine represents the limits of subjectivity in the body's materiality. Lévinas theorizes eroticism as a passion for an other whose materiality is inadequate to and transcends meaningful exchange. Within this schema the feminine embodies a descent into carnality and, accompanying this, a loss of visibility.

Irigaray argues that Lévinas's theorization of eroticism confines the feminine to a nonexistent dwelling in an unlit and infantile place. Whereas the caress is the threshold of man's fecundity, it relegates the woman lover to an extravagant carnality that will never dwell in the light of day. For Irigaray, lovers negotiate the chiasm that together they become, entrusting in their exchange of love that they will each be delivered separately into the world "...surpassing the corruption of what has already been seen. Return to a certain night whence the lovers can arise differently illuminated and enlightened. They give themselves to each other and give up what has already been made. Of themselves and of reason. Opening to an innocence that runs the risk of folding back on itself in defense of the past. In this gesture each one runs the risk of annihilating, killing, or resuscitating."[42] For Irigaray, the abandonment of the loving gesture is not simply a quitting of the status of existent but, for a woman lover as much as a man, the most absolute trust in the transcendence of flesh in an unthematizable sensible transcendental. The fecundity of erotic love exists in the creation of inter-mediaries that allow movements within/between one state and another.

The depth of night to which Lévinas refers in his phenomenology of erotic love is described by Irigaray as a place to which not only a man but also a woman lover returns, to which she allows herself to sink, given over to the source of a light in which she too can be reborn. Lévinas limits his experience of erotic love to the phenomenology of the caress. In her study of Lévinas and also in her theorizing of the elemental, Irigaray invokes the unthematizability of orgasmic flesh: "luminous night, touched with a quickening whose denseness never appears in the light. Neither permanent-ly fixed, nor shifting and fickle. Nothing solid survives, yet that thickness responding to its own rhythms is not nothing. Quickening in movements both expected and unexpected. Your space, your time are unable to grasp their regularity or contain their foldings and unfoldings. The force unleashed has an intensity which cannot be anywhere measured, nor contained."[43] Here, Irigaray proposes a carnality whose lability is devoid of the separation of night and light. The primordiali-ty of this depth must be distinguished from the concept of depth as "bathos" that refers to a geo-metrical depth of already formed material things. Irigaray conceives of depth as a medium, as an immersion whose density is not nothing, without which it is not possible to conceive of things.[44] The lightness of the caress is an opening of the foldings of flesh to the point of nonsignifyingness, to the nothingness of matter. It is a sinking into a night where a woman lover, as much as a man, waits for light. The night of Eros is for her the future of matter, pregnant with the promise of a new day. The night is a nothingness that she cultivates for its grace. This grace is the bestowal of a renewed sense of vision, an assumption of flesh with the coming of light.

Whereas Lévinas associates a turning from light in eroticism with the loss of self and a descent into an unsignifiable carnality, Irigaray conceives of eroticism as the incomparable night of lovers absorbed in prolonging the threshold of illumination. Irigaray demonstrates that the expression of a carnal involvement in light has broader consequences for a feminine genre, a style of subjectivity that she attempts to articulate throughout her work. There is, Irigaray argues, a whole history that separates a woman from taking on the envelope of her own desire, the mater-ial garb of her own *jouissance,* of her love of herself, of her own love of light.[45] Rather than being an antivisual theorist, Irigaray confronts the issue of a woman's exclusion from her share of her act in illumination, in the dawning of (the implication of her carnality in the renewal of) light: "If we still have a chance, it lies in *confronting the night of man's act with that part of woman that still lies in the night.*"[46]

1 Martin Jay, *Downcast Eyes: The Denigration of Vision in Twentieth-Century French Thought* (Berkeley: University of California Press, 1993).

2 These include Julia Kristeva, Hélène Cixous, Monique Wittig, Michèle Montrelay, Catherine Clément, Margaret Duras, and Michèle Le Doeuff.

3 Luce Irigaray, *Speculum of the Other Woman,* trans. Gillian C. Gill (Ithaca, N.Y.: Cornell University Press, 1985).

4 Luce Irigaray, *An Ethics of Sexual Difference,* trans. Carolyn Burke and Gillian C. Gill (Ithaca, N.Y.: Cornell University Press, 1993).

5 Emmanuel Lévinas, *Totality and Infinity: An Essay on Exteriority,* trans. Alphonso Lingis (Pittsburgh: Duquesne University Press, 1979).

6 For example, in relation to Irigaray's theorizing of gender asymmetry in general as a consequence of a monological discourse, Judith Butler asks, "Is it possible to identify a monolithic as well as a monologic masculinist economy that traverses the array of cultural and historical contexts in which sexual difference takes place?" See *Gender Trouble: Feminism and the Subversion of Identity* (New York and London: Routledge, 1990), p. 13.

7 Luce Irigaray, interview in *Les femmes, la pornographie et l'erotisme,* Marie Françoise Hans and Gilles Lapouge, eds., (Paris, 1978), p. 50, quoted in Jay, *Downcast Eyes,* p. 493.

8 Irigaray, *Speculum,* p. 143.

9 Ibid., p. 224, quoted in Jay, *Downcast Eyes,* p. 536.

10 Rodolphe Gasché, *The Tain of the Mirror: Derrida and the Philosophy of Reflection* (Cambridge, Mass. and London: Harvard University Press, 1986).

11 Jacques Derrida, "White Mythology: Metaphor in the Text of Philosophy," in *Margins of Philosophy,* trans. Alan Bass (Brighton, Sussex: The Harvester Press, 1982).

12 Irigaray, *Speculum,* pp. 243–364.

13 Judith Butler, *Bodies That Matter: On the Discursive Limits of Sex* (New York and London: Routledge, 1993), p. 39.

14 Irigaray conceives of the body as a discursive reality that is irreducible to either physical or cultural determination. Morphology is the form of a body as it is lived and represented, as it is interpreted culturally. For a discussion of Irigaray's use of the term "morphology" in her work, see Elizabeth Grosz, *Sexual Subversions: Three French Feminists* (Sydney: Allen & Unwin, 1989), p. 111.

15 For an outline of the difference between an imaginary masculine body and a biological or essential body, see for example Moira Gatens, *Feminism and Philosophy: Perspectives on Difference and Equality* (Cambridge: Polity Press, 1991), pp. 115–118.

16 Irigaray, *Speculum,* p. 305.

17 Lévinas defines "there is" as the phenomenon of impersonal being. *Ethics and Infinity: Conversations with Philippe Nemo,* trans. Richard A. Cohen (Pittsburgh: Duquesne University Press, 1985), pp. 47–48.

18 See Edith Wyschogrod, *Emmanuel Lévinas: The Problem of Ethical Metaphysics* (The Hague: Martinus Nijhoff, 1974), pp. 118–119.

19 Joseph Libertson, *Proximity: Lévinas, Blanchot, Bataille and Communication* (The Hague, Boston, and London: Martinus Nijhoff, 1982), p. 32.

20 Emmanuel Lévinas, *Time and the Other,* trans. Richard A. Cohen (Pittsburgh: Duquesne University Press, 1987), p. 89.

21 Paul Davies, "The Face and the Caress: Lévinas's Ethical Alterations of Sensibility," in *Modernity and the Hegemony of Vision,* David Michael Levin, ed. (Berkeley: University of California Press, 1993), pp. 252–272, maps the caress as an alteration of sensibility rather than a break with sensibility in his analysis of Lévinas's movement away from vision.

22 Edith Wyschogrod, "Derrida, Lévinas, and Violence," in *Derrida and Deconstruction, Continental Philosophy II,* Hugh J. Silverman, ed., (New York and London: Routledge, 1989), pp. 182–200, discusses the relationship between work and the groping hand in Lévinas. For a discussion of the hand's action of differentiation, see also Jacques Derrida, "Geschlecht II: Heidegger's Hand," trans. John P. Leavey, Jr., in *Deconstruction and Philosophy: The Texts of Jacques Derrida,* ed. John Sallis (Chicago and London: The University of Chicago Press, 1987), pp. 161–196.

23 Lévinas, *Totality and Infinity,* p. 254.

24 Tina Chanter, "Antigone's Dilemma," in *Re-Reading Lévinas,* Robert Bernasconi and Simon Critchley, eds. (Bloomington and Indianapolis: Indiana University Press, 1991), pp. 130–146, maps the progressively more complex relationship between eroticism and ethical responsibility that develops chronologically in Lévinas's work.

25 Irigaray, *An Ethics of Sexual Difference,* p. 185.

26 Ibid., pp. 81–82.

27 Ibid., p. 197.

28 Ibid., p. 197.

29 See "Sorcerer Love: A Reading of Plato's *Symposium*, Diotima's Speech," in ibid., pp. 20–33. Irigaray discovers within the unfolding of Diotima's speech a form of love as a mediator of fecundity, which is excluded and passed over in the founding and of an operative, teleological love of things and, ultimately, truth.

30 Jacques Derrida, "Violence and Metaphysics: An Essay on the Thought of Emmanuel Lévinas," *Writing and Difference*, Alan Bass (London and Henley: Routledge & Kegan Paul, 1978), p. 91.

31 The term "sensitivity" as a form of sensibility is a nineteenth-century aesthetic term. Discussion of the political deployment of this humanist attribute is beyond the scope of this chapter. For example, Sander Gilman, "Touch, Sexuality and Disease," *Medicine and the Five Senses*, W. F. Bynum and Roy Porter, eds., (Cambridge: Cambridge University Press, 1993), pp. 198–224, describes the depiction of the sense of touch, conceptualized as the least discriminating of the senses, as the dominant sense of blacks and primitivism. The implication to be drawn from this insidious assertion was that dark-skinned races had no aesthetic sensibility. In using the term "photosensitivity," I am emphasizing the extent to which Irigaray's genealogy of light is directed at a rereading of sensitivity in her conceptualization of touch.

32 Irigaray, *An Ethics of Sexual Difference*, p. 80.

33 "How you looked in your morning, your sudden sparks and wonders of my solitude, you, my old beloved—*wicked* thoughts." Friedrich Nietzsche, *Beyond Good and Evil*, trans. R. J. Hollingdale (Harmondsworth: Penguin, 1973), p. 202.

34 For an account of Irigaray's reliance on the work of pre-Socratic philosophers in her development of the elemental, see Grosz, *Sexual Subversions*, pp. 168–172.

35 Irigaray, *An Ethics of Sexual Difference*, p. 14. The translators' note here draws attention to Irigaray's emphasis on the root meaning of "instance" as standing within the self, as opposed to "ecstasy," which is a standing outside the self.

36 Ibid., p. 9.

37 Ibid.

38 Ibid., p. 82.

39 The articulation of a morphology of such an opening is a key objective of Irigaray's ethics of sexual difference.

40 Margaret Whitford gives an itemized explanation of the way in which Irigaray uses the concept of the mucous repeatedly in her work. The mucous indicates a body whose morphology is neither exclusive to one sex nor a part-object separable from the body. Furthermore, the mucous cannot be reduced to the *maternal-feminine* body and an attendant container-like sexuality. Irigaray also defines the mucuous as the medium of the "two lips," a contiguity in which she articulates her controversial proposition of female sexuality and women's speech. See Margaret Whitford, "Irigaray's Body Symbolic," *Hypatia* 6, 3 (Fall 1991): 102–103.

41 Gaston Bachelard analyzes the ontological convertibility of radiation into matter and vice versa in contemporary physics. See "Matter and Radiation," *The New Scientific Spirit*, trans. Arthur Goldhammer (Boston: Beacon Press, 1984), pp. 61–84.

42 Irigaray, *An Ethics of Sexual Difference*, p. 193.

43 Luce Irigaray, *Elemental Passions*, trans. Joanne Collie and Judith Still (London: The Athlone Press, 1992), p. 13. Irigaray describes this text, with its shifting forms of address, as "some fragments from a woman's voyage as she goes in search of her identity in love" (p. 4).

44 For a discussion of different phenomenological accounts of depth, see Edward S. Casey, "'The Element of Voluminousness': Depth and Place Re-examined," *Merleau-Ponty Vivant*, ed. M. C. Dillon Albany: State University of New York Press, 1991, p. 11. Irigaray explores the concept of elemental depth as a state of immersion in "Speaking of Immemorial Waters," in *Marine Lover of Friedrich Nietzsche*, trans. Gillian C. Gill (New York: Columbia University Press, 1991).

45 Irigaray, *An Ethics of Sexual Difference*, p. 65.

46 Luce Irigaray, *Sexes and Genealogies*, p. 119, trans. Gillian C. Gill (New York: Columbia University Press, 1993).

10

The Gaze in the Closet

Mieke Bal

Much has been written about the confining, colonizing nature, or at least effect, of the gaze as a social force. This chapter presents a literary account of a different use of the gaze. Rather than working as a psychoanalytic or social concept, the gaze involved here is a mode of producing and communicating meaning. In other words the gaze I am discussing is a gaze that produces meaningful signals; it is a semiotic mode. Active but secretive, masking understanding with visuality, pursuing a knowledge that is more profound and new for being unacknowledged: such is the particular form of vision I want to put forward. What I mean is vision as an act of connecting, though potentially unacknowledged, silent, that others may not notice; a gaze that enables subjects to communicate without opening up. The gaze in the closet is a homosexual gaze, desiring, establishing contact with the object, hence communicative, yet *at the same time* able to remain silent about itself, silencing the homosexual connection.

This semiotic gaze has a double orientation, erotic and epistemological. Taking closeted homosexuality not as a negative, defensive attitude but as the model for a specific manner of "speaking" what cannot be spoken, I will map the features and possibilities of the closeted gaze as an epistemological trick. My case will be the use of the closeted gaze as staged in Marcel Proust's modernist masterpiece *Remembrance of Things Past*.[1]

I contend that the novel's most basic exploration is this erotico-epistemological experiment: the serial snapshot, which produces a contact sheet that allows the inside of the closet to become a knowable spectacle conveyed by a closeted gaze, accessible only to whomever is able and willing to handle such knowledge. The two central objects of desire in the novel, Albertine and Robert de Saint-Loup, exemplify the experiment. Their representations demonstrate that behind the surface of photographic light-writing there is neither depth, as Albertine's case demonstrates, nor inside, as Robert's does.

OUTSIDER'S SNAPSHOTS

There are two or three paths that take us to the notion of the closeted gaze. One is through locating what I call the focalizer's position. It is a position of the outside, and in its precision it produces the photographic effect of many visual descriptions in Marcel Proust's *Remembrance of Things Past*.[2] Some of these descriptions will be the object of this analysis. These passages refer to, or take their model from, particular kinds of photographs: snapshots, instantaneous arrests, random stills. They are narrative paradoxes: turning narrative into pictures, they subsequently turn a photo album back into a record of "life" while simultaneously emphasizing the immobility caused by the medium rather than by the object. This paradoxical character is necessary, I contend, to produce the specific epistemological mode of vision that I call, on the basis of the examples analyzed in this paper, the closeted gaze.

This snapshot effect often gets lost in the English translation. Thus, the following description, "taken" during a dinner at the Verdurins', renders the strangeness, the position as outsider of he who "sees," in narratological terms, the "focalizer" to whose visual mediation we owe this glance inside a milieu; but the translation obscures precisely those features:

> Et la [sa pipe] gardant toujours au coin de sa bouche, il prolongeait indéfiniment le simulacre de suffocation et d'hilarité. Ainsi lui et Mme Verdurin qui, en face, écoutant le peintre qui lui racontait une histoire,

fermait les yeux avant de précipiter son visage dans ses mains, avaient l'air de deux masques de théâtre qui figuraient différemment la gaîté. (I, 262)

translated as:

And by keeping the pipe firmly in his mouth he could prolong indefinitely the dumbshow of suffocation and hilarity. Thus he and Mme Verdurin (who, at the other side of the room, where the painter was telling her a story, was shutting her eyes preparatory to flinging her face into her hands) resembled two masks in a theatre each representing Comedy in a different way. (I, 286)

The translation, narratively adequate, emphasizes narrativity at the expense of visuality: the durative verb "il prolongeait" becomes "he could prolong," and the still visual description of the mimes is replaced by a parenthetical remark. In contrast, the suspended quality of the actions. The scene as a whole, theatrical like many of Proust's salon scenes, presents that well-known combination of mercilessly ridiculed conversations and characterizing gesture. But the two images represented in this passage, these two masks, isolate the two faces through framing. They also freeze the movement through the imaginary clicking of the camera, which turns this one description into a set of two snapshots: a contact sheet of serial photography.

Of course, Proust's work is literary, not visual in the material sense. My analysis of vision in it is predicated upon a distinction between (material) medium and (semiotic) mode. The language of narrative can produce vision. Where there is visuality, there is a viewer. The viewer within narrative may or may not be identifiable as the narrator. This subject of vision, the focalizer,[3] is often used to stage the position of the outsider as photographer. That position is a condition for the production of the snapshot. In the preceding case, the focalizer is Swann, who is new to, and already about to be cast out of, the "clan" of insiders. This position matters; it is crucial for our understanding of the mode of vision at stake. The discrepancy between the focalizer and the object makes for the gap, the slight mismatch, that allows the representation of strangeness. What the "photographer"-focalizer captures is what cannot be seen when one surrounds the gaze by the routine of affection.

Proust wrote about that estranging effect as photographic in a meditation on the estrangement in the sight of his ill grandmother, who doesn't know she is being watched. There, the outsider's positions bears the mark of deadly difference: the grandmother is beyond visual recognition because she is dying; he is not. The seriousness of the divide between insider and outsider casts its shadow on other visual encounters as well. In particular, the outsider position bears an obvious relation to the issue of the closet.

WRITING MOVEMENT

In preparation for the revelations of *Sodome et Gomorrhe*, vision is set up to serve as a door of access to the closet. While waiting for an excessively long time for the return of the Duke and Duchess of Guermantes, from whom he intends to ask a favor, Marcel has occupied a position from which, he feels, he can effectively look out for the return of the couple. From his "innocent" position he will "by chance" be able to watch the revealing encounter between Charlus and Jupien, who thus, unawares, come out of the closet for Marcel. So far, the narrative situation.

From his station the narrator, here also acting as the focalizer, produces twinned descriptions. The first one yields a series of successive "art" photographs that together form an imaginary museum of Dutch genre paintings. It consists of the focalizer's act of framing, of cutting out a portion of the spectacle of the world.[4] The view-taking is compared to painting, and the verb "framing" shows that the semiotic of photography is at stake: "framing silent gestures in a series of rectangles placed under glass by the closing of the windows, with an exhibition of a hundred Dutch paintings hung in a row" (II, 59). And the kitchen maid is daydreaming; the girl is having her hair done by an old woman who looks like a witch so as effectively to evoke the atmosphere of such paintings.

But there are moments where, rather than a thoughtful exhibition, the number of views suggests a random collection of snapshots, and not very successfully taken at that: "nothing but blocks of buildings of low elevation, facing in every conceivable direction, which, without blocking the view, prolonged the distance with their oblique planes" (II, 595). And when, in the afternoon, the hero resumes his watch, the descriptions of views taken from a distance alternate with those, detailed as if through a telelens, of the orchid and the humming bird. In between, at medium range, there are the snapshots of Charlus and Jupien, whose gestures succeed each other. These descriptions recall the serial shots made by the American photographer Eadweard Muybridge or by the French scientist Etienne-Jules Marey in order to "write" movement.

There are great differences among Proust's visual effects. For our purposes it is important to notice the difference between the "museum effect," the juxtaposition of pictorially pretty images with an obvious interdiscursive relation to a specific genre in painting—one based on voyeurism of domestic intimacy[5]—on the one hand and the "snapshot effect" of the emphatically random and vulgar kind on the other. This difference is explicitly theorized by the narrator. The Duchess of Guermantes, spokesperson of "*bêtise*," displays the blindness to this difference that enables the narrator to point the difference out:

> "What! You've been to Holland, and you never visited Haarlem!", cried the Duchess. "Why, even if you had only a quarter of an hour to spend in the place, they're an extraordinary thing to have seen, those Halses. I don't mind saying that a person who only caught a passing glimpse of them from the top of a tram without stopping, supposing they were hung out to view in the street, would open his eyes pretty wide."
>
> This remark shocked me as indicating a misconception of the way in which artistic impressions are formed in our minds, and because it seemed to imply that our eye is in that case simply a recording machine which takes snapshots. (II, 544)

The difference between the two visual domains, art and photography, is here exacerbated by the Duchess's denial of it in one of her characteristic exaggerations. The imagined situation—a tram ride as a worker's museum visit—also implies a change in social class, which in turn brings in the banality, the vulgarity, that the photographic snapshot also stands for, the record of everyday life as opposed to the paintings that varnish that life with aura. The misappreciation of artistic impression is simultaneously a misconception of the different visual domains. The word "snapshot" itself appears to summarize this philosophy of vision bound up with a class-specific aesthetic, indicating in its wake a notion that movement can be visually recorded. This visual recording mechanism produces serial snapshots as a form of writing.

THE ONTOLOGY OF THE SNAPSHOT: ALBERTINE

For Proust poetical, libidinal, and epistemological considerations are one and the same, and the problems of representation he raised tend to be problems pertaining to the integration of these three domains. For example, the reflection on the changing nature of beings, *êtres de fuite*, articulates the issue of ontology—what *is* the other?—as one of epistemology—how can I know that? Thus Morel, the love object of all the homosexuals in the novel, is compared to a medieval book full of errors: "He resembled an old book of the Middle Ages, full of mistakes, of absurd traditions, of obscenities" (II, 1066), a comparison that suggests an epistemology; but as a result, he is qualified as "extraordinarily composite," in other words, as *being* a series. The character who makes epistemology tumble into ontology, however, is Albertine. The entire *roman d'Albertine* is a quest for knowledge about her, but this epistemological anxiety is constantly fed by glimpses of her ontological difference: she is unknowable because, as a woman and as a lesbian, she *is* doubly other. This object of obsessive jealousy is a fugitive being because all she leaves behind is snapshots.

The ontology of the snapshot consists of the denial of depth, of existence behind or beneath the glossy, random surface of the accessible behind or beneath the glossy, random surface of the accessible visual present. Albertine is the figuration of this ontology. She was selected as a love object the moment she visually detached herself from the photograph of the girls on the beach, taking off on her bicycle and thus riding out of the picture, necessitating the change of photographic aesthetic from group portrait to quick snapshot.

Indeed, in *The Prisoner*, Albertine, who has lost her former fixed quality of beach photo, consists only of a series of snapshots: "... a person, scattered in space and time, *is* no longer a woman but a series of events on which we can throw *no light*, a series of insoluble problems" (III, 99–100; emphasis added). The shift from epistemology ("no light") to ontology ("is no longer a woman") announces postmodernism, and the phrase "scattered in time and space" (*disséminé*), with its Derridian overtones, articulates that shift.[6] That "woman" as "other" falls prey to this lunacy of the snapshot is, of course, no coincidence. This dissolution in visual, flat seriality is only aggravated as Marcel tries to counter it and "fix" Albertine by means of "light" thrown on her, and on paper. Thus she ends up *becoming* (ontology) the sheet on which the images (epistemology) of jealousy are going to be fixed: "For I possessed in my memory only a series of Albertines, separate from one another, incomplete, a collection of profiles or snapshots, and so my jealousy was restricted to a discontinuous expression, at once fugitive and fixed ..." (III, 145–146). With the word "*mémoire*" keeping the issue also on the level of epistemology, ontological "fugitivity" is presented here as a perversion of the former. The final words here, "à la fois fugitive et fixée," define quite precisely the nature of the series of snapshots and explain the specific use of this poetic in the novel. The importance of eroticism is crucial: the object of this fugitive fixing is the love object of whom the focalizing narrator is unable to fix the sexual orientation.

This is a philosophy of looking as fixing that is quite different from the standard theory of the gaze as control, which comes close to a paranoid iconophobia.[7] Most readings of Lacan's theory of the gaze emphasize the confining aspect of it, although it seems obvious that the "symbolic underpinnings of the visual imaginary"[8] also enable social intercourse through semiotic exchange. It is this more cheerful, in fact saving, aspect of the gaze that Proust explores in other passages, which will be discussed later. Here the snapshot produces unhappiness, but primarily for the photographer himself, who is forced into awareness of an incurable existential solitude.

But Albertine, ironed out ontologically, does not benefit from this at all. If looking is a form of killing, as horror films about voyeurism suggest,[9] looking away is what kills Albertine. The minute she turns from an *être de fuite* into a real fugitive, running away from the obsessive attempts to flatten and fix her, she is killed off by redundancy.

The ontology of the snapshot needs, and is predicated upon, the epistemology that founds it. During Albertine's presence at his side, the narrator composes an album in the vain hope of fixing the inaccessible other. But the photograph's flatness has yet another feature, one that hinders the very attempt that makes the narrator cultivate it: it encourages deceit, role-playing, masks. What is fixed is precisely the exterior, the appearance, which only hides more effectively the being that, in the case of Albertine, one is justified in assuming not to exist outside the album. If the serial picture-taking helps the subject to an epistemological trick, the fixing of image on paper bears on the object as well, and hence the endeavor cannot but fail: "And before she pulled herself together and spoke to me, there was an instant during which Albertine did not move, smiled into the empty air, with the same air of feigned spontaneity and secret pleasure as if she were posing for somebody to take her photograph, or even seeking to assume before the camera a more dashing pose..." (III, 146). The ontology is grafted upon the epistemology because what is at stake is not, or not exclusively, the fugitive being herself. The series of snapshots functions to reveal not the other's essence but the relationship between subject and other. It poses, and proposes to acknowledge, the limit of epistemic discretion when the object is another human being. In other words, it partakes of a methodological exploration of ethnography in which the other's being cannot be assessed without knowledge; yet knowledge infringes upon being. Albertine is the embodiment of this problem, and therefore it is crucial that she be gay, a woman, and literally fugitive. The symmetrical counterpart of Albertine-as-other is the selfsame object of desire. Here the challenge to the text's libidinal epistemology is even greater.

LIBIDINAL EPISTEMOLOGY

At the center of the novel's experiments with photography, in particular the exploration of the epistemology of the snapshot, stands the narrator's best friend, ego model, closeted homosexual, and closeted love object, Robert de Saint-Loup. His ontological status is like Albertine's: surface over depth, albeit a surface not characterized by photographic fixation but by fugitive mobility. Visions of him yield not a picture album but a contact sheet of rapidly taken photos of movement.

Photography in its specific guise of the serial snapshot provides the narrator with a uniquely suitable and efficient mode of representing this important character, of revealing the secrets he is invested with while at the same time keeping them. Saint-Loup is the most "photographic" character of *Remembrance* in three distinct ways. First, he is the most photogenic one, of a luminous beauty; hence, he is the ideal object of "art" photography. Descriptions of his beauty are plentiful and challenge the narrator's need to keep both his own and Robert's homosexuality a secret. Second, he is also the "official" photographer: he is the one who takes the famous photograph of the dying grandmother, who wished to leave her grandson a visual memory of her. Among a great number of its narrative and poetic functions, that "photo session"[10] narratively enables the revelation of Robert's homosexuality, as gossip has it that developing the photo in the darkroom was a pretext for him to make love to the liftboy in the Balbec hotel. But third, and more importantly, he is constantly being "photographed" in his movement. One such photo session constitutes the *mise en abyme*[11] of the poetics and politics of the snapshot in *Remembrance*.

Robert is a Muybridge character, a seagull of the kind Marey was constantly recording in its flight in his epistemic endeavor to understand movement. Speed characterizes this Proustian character; speed is the sign that signals him. This character of speed is a figurative being, opposed to Albertine. The difference between them is gendered.

Albertine is characterized by a certain passivity, an adaptation to the narrator's wishes so systematic that she entirely loses her consistency as a character. One remembers the repeated changes of plans to which the narrator subjects her: the day she intended to go to the matinee at the Verdurins' until the narrator discovers to his dismay that Mlle. Vinteuil—the feared evil spirit, since she is overtly gay—was supposed to be there. He forces Albertine to go elsewhere, only to discover that another "dangerous" woman, Léa, is to go there, so he sends his maid Françoise to fetch her home. This is pure insanity; but Albertine, lacking autonomy as a character, a paper doll at the service of the narrative, complies and does exactly as she is told. Albertine allows the narrator's desperate attempt to know her through fixing her, stenciling her on paper. The resulting snapshots reveal only the more painfully the impossibility, in principle, of "fixing" her.[12]

Robert, in contrast, escapes fixing in a different way, more actively and even more thoroughly visually. Since the beginning of their acquaintance the narrator has characterized Robert by quickness of movement as a trait that will pursue a character all through the novel as his or her determining, identifying sign.[13] This trait, however, develops into much more than the initial label or arrow, an index of identity. It is filled with narrative meaning, psychological characterization, physical feature, and, for the narrator, support onto which he can build his plot.

As is well known, the long novel is punctuated by a series of scenes of voyeurism, emphasizing by that rhythmic return of the "primal scene" the crucial importance of this particular visual libidinal epistemology. The series begins with the spying on an infantile "sadistic" scene between Mlle. Vinteuil and her female lover, typically centered on a photograph; passes through the literalization of the closet at the Hôtel de Guermantes; and ends on the "adult" sadomasochistic scene during the war. As an introduction to the last of this series of scenes, Robert's quickness serves to identify him but fulfills a number of other functions at the same time:

> ...when, at a distance of fifteen yards,...I saw an officer come out and walk rapidly away.
> Something, however, struck me: not his face, which I did not see...but the extraordinary disproportion between the number of different points which his body successively occupied and the very small number of seconds within which he made good this departure which had almost the air of a sortie from a besieged town.... This military man with the ability to occupy so many different positions in space in such a short time disappeared... (III, 838)

The relation between subject ("I"), vision ("saw,") movement ("come out"), and speed ("rapidly"), that hopelessly sense-based "*je vis,*" is what Muybridge and Marey, each with different goals, tried to fix *in* the image itself: the passage of time in a subjective perception whose center is void, without the unreliable help of the senses.[14] The denial of recognition on the basis of the face foregrounds the epistemological value of the snapshot *as such* because movement, conceived of as the occupation of points in space, determines the individual uniqueness of the character.

The description identifies Robert as a regular of the rather *louche* place, Jupien's hotel, where the hero-ethnographer finishes his travels of discovery and runs into himself. Robert "is one of them" (*il en est*) as well. He is a member not only of the cursed and elected "race" of inverts but also, more specifically, of the masochists whose ultimate joy is, according to the narrator's description, to be fixed on a flat surface, ironed out by beatings.

The psychological explanation of this characteristic quickness, rather "logical" after all, is suggested a bit before the just-cited passage: "the fear of being seen, the wish to conceal that fear, the feverishness which is generated by self-dissatisfaction and boredom" (III, 717), and later on another reason is added, a narrative-metaphysical one: the brevity of Saint-Loup's life. The earlier revelation marks the last Marcel will see of him, as if it makes Saint-Loup redundant. Just like Albertine, he can be killed off once the epistemology is worked out. This fact only adds a dimension to the fugitive nature of the character; paradoxically, in terms of the normative narratology of the Anglo-Saxon tradition where "round" characters are the superior others of "flat" characters, it "thickens" him.

Much more elaborate in its preparatory stages than the previous scenes of voyeurism, this scene definitely questions the subject of the gaze: the narrator's attempt to "cover" the object will be virtually successful here so that the act of looking, taking the inhabitants of the closet out in the open, will lock him in. The description of the military man is part of that preparation, and the principled detailing of the snapshot in almost geometrical terms underscores its importance. For, toward the end of the concluding volume of the immense novel, this scene constitutes an important step in the pursuit of the writing of time, goal and end of this work.

That this end, in the double sense, is staged in a closet and, importantly, doesn't have the hero come out, is, of course, relevant to the nature of the knowledge and the mode of knowledge production that the scene demonstrates. The nature of the gaze involved and the function of the serial snapshot to represent that gaze deserve closer attention in this respect. In the tradition of the metaphor of the camera obscura, instrument, after all, of inverted vision, of ideological distortion, and of exteriorization,[15] the closet occupies the same paradoxical position of allowing vision without having anything "inside" to show. This image suits the text perfectly: as I wrote at the beginning of this chapter, behind the surface of photographic light-writing there is neither depth, as Albertine's case demonstrates, nor inside, as Robert's does.

VIOLENT REVELATIONS

This argument brings me to the scene of revelation—of Robert, of Marcel, of Proust, and of the closet—which is best read as a contact sheet of a series of snapshots made at a distance, through a telelens, and extremely quickly. The description represents a much earlier stage of the slow discovery the hero is about to make, that dark night in Paris. The scene contains all the elements of the photographic poetics Proust deploys, and it enumerates all its different contributions to the particular visual epistemology that underlies Proust's text. It is the scene of the passionate stroller, "*le promeneur passionné.*"

The event, in all its simplicity, can only be reconstructed retrospectively: Robert is approached in the street by a man who propositions him; in response, Robert beats him up. Marcel has lingered and stayed a bit behind, a delay that motivates the vision at a distance, the specific discrepancy caused by the telelens, the "objectivity" of the object-glass. Here is the description that follows the meditation, which, I take it, essentially describes a contact sheet:

> I saw that a somewhat shabbily attired gentleman appeared to be talking to him confidentially. I concluded that this was a personal friend of Robert; meanwhile they seemed to be drawing even closer to one another; suddenly, as an astral phenomenon flashes through the sky, I saw a number of ovoid bodies assume with a dizzy swiftness all the positions necessary for them to compose a flickering constellation in front of Saint-Loup. Flung out like stones from a catapult, they seemed to me to be at the very least seven in number. They were merely, however, Saint-Loup's two fists, multiplied by the speed with which they were changing place in this—to all appearance ideal and decorative— arrangement. (II, 186)

The motif of quickness is here, as in the quote above, qualified by the drawing of movement in fixed points. The English "flickering" suggests cinematic vision; "instable constellation," in contrast, invokes the wavering camera hand, hard pressed to take so many shots in a row. The important point here is to realize the transformation of time into space; the fixation. The "*rapidité*" allows the inscription of the constellation *in front of,* hence detached from, Saint-Loup. The subject is detached from himself by the sense of sight, like the Lacanian baby in the Imaginary stage unable to coordinate, and proprioceptively recognize as his, the little hands and feet that fly by.

One sees several "copies" of the same body, successively. Numbered seven, the "ovoid bodies" provide Robert with many arms, of which the number seven is also an allusion to the holy number, necessarily uneven, of extremities dancing Hindu divinities have in Indian iconography. The combination of quickness and the distinctive position of each element in the description turns this passage into the description of a contact sheet rather than of a film. Perception is the real and only object of representation. Between the contact sheet of quickly made serial snapshots and cinema, the difference is of illusion: the greater success at writing movement makes the perception of movement, as well as of its writing, invisible. The device at stake here must produce not just a visual writing that is a trace of movement but also a movement that is a trace of writing. Pre-postmodern as the text sometimes is, it is also pre-poststructuralist, prefiguring Derrida's conceptualization of writing and the trace in *Of Grammatology*.[16]

The setting up of this photographic scheme in the introduction to the scene of the "*promeneur passionné*" warns the reader of the importance of things to come. The telelens with its discrepancy motivates the distance, the framing, the reduction to eyesight only as well as the incomprehension involved in this vision. As happens often in this work, incomprehension facilitates comprehension, for it helps to *see*: That point alone is a lesson in visual epistemology, specifically photographic: the routine of the senses loses its power over perception, the subject is evacuated from the center, and the notation—the writing proper—is the trace of the movement of which it grasps the essence. What there is to see, in its purest state, is the profound link between quickness spatialized as writing time, on the one hand, and the perception of desire in its purest state, that, purely visualized on the other.

For the stake here is desire, in this vision presented as an aesthetic. The revelation—exposure, in the photographic sense—of this desire is patiently mapped out in several progressive stages, the first of which operates the transition from distant look to close-up as if through a zoom lens: "But this elaborate display was nothing more than a pummelling which Saint-Loup was administering, the aggressive rather than aesthetic character of which was first revealed to me by the aspect of the shabbily dressed gentleman who appeared to be losing at once his self-possession, his lower jaw and a quantity of blood" (II, 186). The man seems to accept this triple loss like a fact of nature since he, "seeing that Saint-Loup had made off and was hastening to rejoin me, stood gazing after him with an offended, crushed, but by no means furious expression on his face" (II, 186). The man thus acts as visually as does the narrator: the one removes himself, the other comes nearer in this silent dance representing the figuration of an entire "instable constellation" whose meaning will be engraved in the monument that is the work.

The shift from visual epistemology to ontology and back recurs throughout the scene, most explicitly in the words "*dont le caractère agressif au lieu d'esthétique*." At close inspection, however, the agressivity, there lethal and due to homosocial desire, is here a cover-up and acting out of homosexual desire.[17]

The revelation of meaning is at first limited to the anecdotal level. This reporting has a relevant narratological feature. The interpretation is reported by the narrator, who qualifies his discourse not as free indirect discourse, which it might or even, realistically, should be but as a rendering of his own focalization. For this omission he has a good reason: "It was an impassioned loiterer who, seeing the handsome young soldier that Saint-Loup was, had made a proposition to him." Although, according to the logic put in place by the tele-objectivity of the presentation, this explanation should be coming from Saint-Loup, since the narrator had volunteered to take up a position of distant visuality only, it is the narrator who, equally "logically," endorses the evaluation of his friend as a handsome military—virile—man. The shift occurs in midsentence: from "seeing" to "being", image overrules thing. As a result, and third "logic," we must conclude that the narrator shares, at least visually, the photographed desire.

And indeed, the explanation of the event is immediately followed by an explanation by means of wild psychology, rather incomprehensible if one fails to take seriously the photographic epistemology that underlies the scene: "And yet the recipient of his blows was excusable in one respect, for the trend of the downward slope brings desire so rapidly to the point of enjoyment that beauty in itself appears to imply consent" (II, 187). In order to grasp what is at stake here, it seems important to acknowledge that this sentence is strictly incomprehensible. The inclining plane, one can *see*, was already visible on the contact sheet ("they seemed to be drawing even closer to one another"), but nevertheless it is at the same time a metaphor of the essential flatness/platitude of this scene that only reinscribes the importance of the particular manner of getting to know desire.

WRITING DESIRE

Three aspects of this scene invest it with central importance, thus turning it into a *mise en abyme*. First, the pure state of desire is a figuration in writing of time, visually accessible if one takes the indispensable distance to see it at the cost of not being able to satisfy it. "The closet" figures the irreducible incompatibility between knowing and acting. One remembers the mythical "kissing organ" that the narrator invented in order to enable him to integrate vision with the other senses, but that organ, precisely, described that fundamental lack.[18] Second, desire fixes itself visually onto Saint-Loup, the military man; a "category" of males whose virility had been staged very early on by way of the military parade at Combray, which also demonstrated its insurmountable visual-epistemic difficulties. The presence of the military in the final scene of voyeurism that will complete the hero's ethnographic knowledge through the revelation of inversion's "flatness" is therefore essential, beyond the anecdote and beyond the distribution of roles among the characters.

Third, and this aspect brings us to the crucial point about photography, this work in which desire is such a central, structural element demonstrates by way of this passage that desire is in turn subordinated to the writing of it that is possible. The contact sheet of seven ovoid bodies figures the work itself. As a sample of a writing, it is magically situated between space that makes flat and time that spreads out. It abandons linear sequentiality in favor of an instable architecture and constellation. And that constellation is just now parading before us. But as photography the contact on the sheet is only the "positive," the print between fugitive light and sheet of paper, whose negative, called "form and solidity" in the *madeleine* episode, is here defined as loss. Loss, then, is located in the unknown man, shabbily dressed, fugitive figure and *figurant*, but nevertheless indispensable as a screen.

The triple loss—of his self-possession, a jaw, and a lot of blood; in other words, his triple loss of face—is what I have elsewhere called a *disfigure*, a figure of rhetoric, a detail that is overformed and overinvested with meaning.[19] On the contact sheet, filled with Saint-Loup's astral and quick movement, one imagines that only one tiny image of the dripping *figurant* is visible. In the narrative, Robert pretends to be outraged by the man's proposition; he complains about the lack of sexual safety in the streets of Paris and dismisses Marcel: end of episode. The outraged reaction Saint-Loup displays provides the necessary transition to the moralism needed for the epistemological adventure to continue, which closes the passage.

That tiny snapshot of the bleeding man is, within the contact sheet and the episode, a detail, but one that is greatly disfiguring and disfigured. It figures a Lacanian responsiveness to the self-division of visuality as well as of desire, as Stephen Melville discusses it in chapter 7 of this volume. It also marks the profound need of visuality that this narrative demonstrates and that no literature without art translates into: no textual, linguistic intelligibility without vision.

The loss of self-possession can be situated on the "realistic" level, psychologically the level where Proustian characters appear to have a normal literary life. But the loss of the jaw is hardly plausible. The loss inscribes the disfiguration of the character's face into the series; *mise en abyme*, this loss disfigures the figure. The loss of blood, obscene, violent detail, "coloring" also, discolors the man.[20] As subject of this triple loss, the marginal object of serial photography is yet the exemplary subject of desire, the only one visible in pure state; a subject of desire who on a "downward slope" approaches while remaining visible, thus accomplishing, almost, the epistemic ideal pursued all through the novel.

The triple loss, however, is disfiguring in yet another sense—the sense that makes it a "logical" consequence of the closeted gaze. This loss figures, gives visible shape to, the loss of knowledge incurred by all subjects involved, narrator, focalizer-"photographer," character. The loss is, in addition, incurred by those critics who, eager to psychoanalyze the event, "forget" its specifically gay nature, thus maintaining the closet.[21]

What is not stated by any of the above subjects is something so banal that the term *platitude*, with its full ambiguity, is the only appropriate one. Saint-Loup, soon after, takes unexpected leave from Marcel, alleging the need to be by himself for a bit, and shows up hours later at the afternoon party they were to attend together. What remains unseen, then, is exactly what this strange photographic set-up has *revealed* and hidden at the same time, a knowledge that is a revelation and a hiding and that is also about these things. This is the closeted gaze "in action." Thus, in this crucial passage, the narrator is able to see and know what cannot be admitted to knowledge.

Staying at the proper distance for this particular focusing, Marcel declines to hear the proposal made by the stroller, hence declining to participate in the "impassioned" encounter of which he can therefore see only the downward slope. Saint-Loup, in turn, declines to say it. After the beating, however, he sends Marcel away, promising to join him shortly, so that the possibility of a date with the stroller is both inscribed and left uncertain, unknowable. Homosexuality loses its speakability.[22] The reader/critic who theorizes the downward slope in general terms partakes of the tabooizing of homosexuality, its being closeted, that is taking place at this very moment of revelation "in the (literary) act." Platitude—covering the homosexual event in a generalizing theory of desire—thus contributes to, repeats and endorses, the refusal to gain access to an "intimate" knowledge, a participating ethnography, access to the act. That too is a loss of self (-possession).[23]

The banal question of whether or not Robert will, after all, have a date with the stroller is, narratively speaking, totally irrelevant. Epistemologically speaking, however, the unanswerability of such an indiscreet and naively realistic question is absolutely crucial; it is the major flaw of Proust criticism to fail to take banality seriously. Like Albertine, Robert is unknowable, but the closest the narrator can come to knowing (him) is by exercising this closeted telegaze.

In Proust's novel the most successful erotic-epistemic pose, or act, is emphatically not penetration but "covering": instead of penetrating unknowable Albertine, the narrator's most pleasurable experience is to lie against her, covering as much of her skin as possible with his own. In the vision of the passionate stroller, the epistemological feat of "covering" has almost succeeded, but not quite. The trace left of the attempt is the contact sheet itself, on which is inscribed, hardly legibly, the very movement of approach, a writing pad where an infinitely tiny moment in time is spread out in space.

EROTO-GRAPHY

Proust and photography: the subject immediately evokes Roland Barthes. One remembers the opening of Barthes's *Camera Lucida*: "One day, quite some time ago, I happened on a photograph of Napoleon's youngest brother, Jerome, taken in 1852. And I realized then…, 'I am looking at the eyes that looked at the Emperor.'"[24] The conception of the photograph that Barthes will develop in the book is already present: it is a vision, by definition in the present, of a vision that is irrecoverably in the past. There is no exchange of looks, yet two looks confront each other, the one dead, the other alive. Between the two acts of looking the gap of time's passage has been dug.

Barthes developed this wonderful essay on photography out of this initial "snapshot"—quick, incidental vision—of a photo. From instrument of visual, spatial fixation, photography becomes the instrument of the definitive loss of time and death. Between one eye and another things happen: punctum is the word that, for Barthes, summarizes the thousand small happenings that he describes, modifies, criticizes, circumscribes, and specifies along the pages of the essay until the word only indicates the one experience of Roland Barthes before his mother's death. Along the way Barthes evokes the picture of Marcel's grandmother but to the involuntary memory that he compares the *tuché*, the happening of this-has-been of the winter garden photo. Strangely, while writing on photography he missed the closeted gaze as the most typical photographic specificity in Proust's writing.

One has not finished being astounded before photography, that glass eye that slides in front of the eye of the "operator" (Barthes's term) that is Saint-Loup in the anecdote of the picture-taking. But the narrator is the real photographer all through his writing. What photography allows him to inscribe, to fix like writing, is an essentially fugitive vision that is at the same time purely subjective and totally objective.[25] As Ann Banfield has demonstrated in a detailed analysis of Russell's epistemology by way of Barthes's essay, a photo is centered, but its center stays empty. Flat image, infinitely reproducible and manipulable, it provides an objectified image that remains nonetheless circumscribed by a total subjectivity. That paradox of photography enables one to grasp the punctum that is not of form but of intensity, an effect that emanates from an image irredeemably flat, in all senses of the word. Banality adds to its wonder.

"*Ce* quelque chose a fait tilt, *il a provoqué en moi un petit ébranlement, un* satori, *le passage d'un vide*," writes Barthes (81) about a detail-punctum that ravished his entire reading. *Tilt*: the downward slope that turned the impassioned stroller on yet another level into a *mise en abyme/*disfigure of the photographic stance that informs Proust's novel. That detail blows up with meaning (Naomi Schor); invades the text by its status as "instruction for use," which makes it into a self-reflection, overdetermined and disfiguring; and is the "downward slope" that caused the triple loss that disfigured the *figurant* but that, it must be added, continues to resist logical sense. Logic remains in the closet, just like Robert, even as the gaze discloses it.

The downward slope is the ultimate attempt to enforce Proust's narrator's epistemological desire, to stick, cover, map himself fully, like light on a sheet of paper, upon the object that therefore must be flat. If Barthes has so well succeeded in rendering the effect of photography—of the one photograph that mattered—it is first of all because he had the wisdom not to show it. Thus that photo remains as fictional as *Remembrance* is. That restraint is also a way of maintaining photography's flatness. But the photo of Barthes's mother rewrites, perhaps, the one of Marcel's grandmother; it is totally different from the photo session with the disfigured *promeneur*.

For one element, in Proust, is crucially specific. Before the objective eye, the impassioned stroller has to retreat. The slope is dangerously sliding, but the touch-*tuché* remains forbidden. That flatness/banality of generalized knowledge remains impossible. There is one narrative reason for this, the one that defines this work as modernist. In order for desire to continue all through this immense work, it must remain unfulfilled—the gaze must remain closeted. There is, however, also an erotic-epistemological reason for this restraint: the identification of the erotic with ethnographic epistemology. The closeted gaze, isolating perception from understanding, shows what cannot be known. If Albertine had to stay unknowable, and her unknowability had to be represented in her gay femininity, Robert has to stay away from the subject who desires him in order to prevent desire from losing face.

1 This analysis is part of a larger project that examines a variety of modes of vision in an attempt to oppose the unifying ideology of the gaze by pluralizing it. I am conducting the analysis on vision in *Remembrance (How to Read Visually: The Flatitude of Proustian Images*; trans. Anna-Louisa Milne (Palo Alto: Stanford University Press, 1996).) in parallel with a study of modes of visual exposition, of which elements have been published (e.g., Bal, "Telling, Showing, Showing Off," *Critical Inquiry* 18 [Spring 1992]: 556–594). On a pluralizing analysis of the gaze, see my "His Master's Eye," in David M. Levin, ed., *Modernity and the Hegemony of Vision* (Berkeley: University of California Press, 1993), pp. 379–404.

2 Marcel Proust, *A La recherche du temps perdu*, (Paris: Gallimard, 1954); Pierre Clarac and André Ferré, eds.) *Remembrance of Things Past*, trans. C. K. Scott Moncrieff and Terence Kilmartin (New York: Vintage Books, 1982). References in the text will be to the English translation, cited by volume and page number.

3 For all narratological concepts, see my *Narratology: Introduction to the Theory of Narrative* (Toronto: University of Toronto Press, 1992 [1985]).

4 Vincent Descombes, "Découper son tableau dans le spectacle du monde," *Proust: Philosophie du roman* (Paris: Editions de Minuit, 1987) p. 237.

5 See Norman Bryson, *Looking at the Overlooked: Four Essays on Still Life* (London: Reaktion Books; Cambridge, Mass.: Harvard University Press, 1990).

6 Jacques Derrida, "Différance," most accessible in *Writing and Difference*, trans. Barbara Johnson (Chicago: The University of Chicago Press, 1980). For this definition of postmodernism, Brian McHale, *Postmodern Fiction* (New York and London: Routledge, 1988). For a feminist critique of the concept of dissemination, see my *Reading Rembrandt: Beyond the Word-Image Opposition* (New York: Cambridge University Press, 1991), pp. 19–23; and "Light in Painting: Dis-seminating Art History," in Peter Brunette and David Wills, eds., *Deconstruction and the Visual Arts* (New York: Cambridge University Press, 1994), pp. 49–64.

7 See Martin Jay's seminal account of iconophobia in contemporary thought, *Downcast Eyes: The Denigration of Vision in Twentieth-Century French Thought*, (Berkeley: University of California Press, 1993).

8 See Chapter 7, Stephen Melville's contribution to this volume.

9 See Chapter 14, Parveen Adam's contribution to this volume.

10 The term refers, of course, to Lacan's theory of the gaze, especially as interpreted by Kaja Silverman, "Fassbinder and Lacan," *Male Subjectivity at the Margins* (New York: Routledge, 1992). Different but congenial views of the photographic gaze as related to gender, according to Lacan, are Parveen Adams, "The Three (Dis) graces," and Elisabeth Bronfen, "Death: The Navel of the Image," both in Mieke Bal and Inge E. Boer, eds., *The Point of Theory: Practices of Cultural Analysis* (Amsterdam/New York: Amsterdam University Press/Continuum).

11 *Mise en abyme*, a term from narratology originally borrowed from André Gide, refers to passages or elements that represent in a nutshell the entire work they are part of, or at least a relevant aspect of it.

12 This inaccessibility of Albertine is *represented as*, not a representation of, lesbianism. In Proust there is no lesbian gaze, no "lesbian as visionary" to use Renée Hoogland's phrase. Hoogland's chapter in this volume demonstrates the abysmal difference between the projected lesbianism as embodiment of the photographic sheet of light and the subjectivity of a lesbian gaze as she theorizes it.

13 See the chapter on characterization in my *Narratology*, pp. 79–92; also, Shlomith Rimmon-Kenan, *Narrative Fiction: Contemporary Poetics* (London, Methuen, 1981).

14 See Ann Banfield, "L'imparfait de l'objectif: The Imperfect of the Object Glass," *Camera Obscura* 24 (1990): 65–87.

15 See W. J. T. Mitchell, *Iconology: Image, Text, Ideology* (Chicago: The University of Chicago Press, 1985), especially the last chapter; and, for the aspect of exteriorization, Svetlana Alpers, *The Art of Describing: Dutch Art in the Seventeenth Century* (Chicago: University of Chicago Press, 1985); and Jonathan Crary, *Techniques of the Observer: On Vision and Modernity in the Nineteenth Century* (Cambridge, Mass.: MIT Press, 1990).

16 Jacques Derrida, *Of Grammatology*, trans. and with an introduction by Gayatri Chakravorty Spivak (Baltimore: The Johns Hopkins University Press, 1976).

17 These words evoke the aggressivity underlying aesthetic interest of another Robert, in Ian McEwan's *The Comfort of Strangers*, analyzed in this volume by

Ernst van Alphen.

18   Proust, *Remembrance*, II, 377–378. See Kaja
     Silverman's brilliant analysis of this description in
     terms of the particular form of homosexuality it
     figures, *Male Subjectivity at the Margins*,
     pp. 373–388.

19   See my *How to Read*, ch. 1. The argument is part of a
     reconsideration of the detail and especially of the
     opposition, proposed by Georges Didi-Huberman in a
     response to Schor, between *détail* and *pan*. Georges
     Didi-Huberman, "Appendice: Question de détail,
     question de pan," *Devant 1 image: Question posée
     aux fins d'une historie de l'art* (Paris: Editions de
     Minuit, 1990), pp. 271–318; Naomi Schor, "Le détail
     chez Freud," *Littérature* 37 (1980): 3–14 (Didi-
     Huberman's source), later also published in *Reading in
     Detail: Esthetics and the Feminine* (New York and
     London: Methuen, 1987).

20   It also triggers a reading of the final scene of *The
     Comfort of Strangers* and *its* coloring, painting, with
     lost blood. See van Alphen's analysis in chapter 12 of
     this volume.

21   Thus Charles Bouazis, characteristically imitating the
     incomprehensible discourse he is supposed to clarify:
     "*la jouissance qui est 'rapprochée' ne l'est qu'en
     vertu d'un 'plan incliné qui l'irréalise en la promettant
     (non en la 'consommant')*." *Ce que Proust savait du
     symptôme* (Paris: Méridiens Klincksieck, 1992).

22   This complicates the opposition Renée Hoogland sets
     up in chapter 11 of this volume between male and
     female homosexuality. Although she is certainly right in
     the cases she explores, her generalization ignores the
     specific problems that challenged me, for one, into
     writing this chapter and that must have motivated Kaja
     Silverman to write her book on the subject.

23   For a relevant account of loss of self as represented in
     the visual images painted by Francis Bacon, see Ernst
     van Alphen, *Francis Bacon and the Loss of Self*
     (London: Reaktion Books, 1992; Cambridge, Mass.:
     Harvard University Press, 1993).

24   Roland Barthes, *Camera Lucida*, trans. Richard
     Howard (New York: Hill and Wang, 1981), p. 3.

25   On the problematic of subjectivity and objectivity in
     photography, see the wonderful article by Ann
     Banfield, "L'imparfait de l'objectif," pp. 65–87.

The Gaze of Inversion: The Lesbian as Visionary

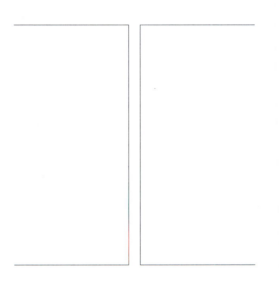

Renée C. Hoogland

In 1978, addressing the Midwestern Division of the Society for Women in Philosophy, feminist theorist Sarah Hoagland posited that the category of the lesbian falls outside the conceptual scheme of Western phallocracies. Such a position of nonexistence, she argued, provides the lesbian subject with a "singular vantage point with respect to the reality which does not include her," giving her "access to knowledge which is inaccessible to those whose existence *is* countenanced by the system."[1] By invoking the lesbian's cultural invisibility as a site of epistemic privilege, Hoagland underscores the central role of the specular metaphor in the discourse of Western epistemology; as has often been pointed out, the very term "theory" adequately reflects the ontological weight our culture traditionally attributes to the powers of vision. However, paraphrasing the Russian philosopher/linguist Mikhail Bakhtin, we could say that within the system of Western metaphysics, what can be known is only that which can be seen. If lesbian sexuality is not being "countenanced" by the general scheme of things, how is it that such invisibility, or "unknowability," can yet be argued to generate enhanced powers of vision with regard to that culture? Moreover, and perhaps even more pertinently in this context, the assumed connection between being and seeing alerts us to the crucial role of specularity in the Freudian account of sexuality, in which the perceivable absence or presence of a penis constitutes the mark of sexual difference, the founding structure of both subjective and objective reality. If its ontological "impossibility" renders lesbian sexuality culturally invisible, what could be the function of such a nonconcept in the unconscious subtext underlying the collective imagination that makes up these "realities"?

The purpose of this chapter is briefly to explore the paradoxical position of the lesbian in Western culture—a paradox, it will be clear, that centers on the notion of vision. By focusing on two modes of discourse in which specularity figures centrally, that is, Hollywood cinema and feminist critical theory, I will try to show that the particular cultural and theoretical configurations in which the lesbian is currently gaining apparent visibility succeeds in the final instance in reinforcing the impossible subject's invisibility.

My first intertext is one that has drawn a great deal of public attention on both sides of the Atlantic, a film that perhaps partly owes its box-office success to its prominent media visibility: Paul Verhoeven's highly controversial sexual thriller *Basic Instinct* (1992). Let me point out at once that it is not my intention to show that *Basic Instinct* is, as a female art critic put it on BCC's *Late Show*, so obviously a male fantasy that it does not need to be taken seriously. Nor do I wish to suggest that the film should be banned or condemned because, as several gay and lesbian activists in the United States have protested, it places lesbianism in an extremely negative light. Even so, though most contemporary viewers probably know that not *all* lesbians are psychopathic killers, I wonder if the majority of spectators would indeed recognize the mythical Oedipal scenario of the film for what it is—a male fantasy. Hence, even if the narrative is so clearly the fulfillment of a male wish—the film ends quite reassuringly with both murderous "lesbian" characters dead and the central bisexual female character falling into the protective arms of the male hero—I think *Basic Instinct* needs to be taken seriously precisely because of the *less* obvious ways in which it reinscribes oppressive structures of gender ideology by underscoring the founding myth of phallocratic reality that is, in Adrienne Rich's well-known phrase, the system of "compulsory heterosexuality." Paul Verhoeven's brainchild requires critical analysis because of the paradoxical manner in which the almost monstrously disproportionate visibility of the "lesbian" in this film effectively succeeds in rendering lesbian sexuality all but invisible.

The film's hero, Nicky Curran (played by Michael Douglas), is a San Francisco-based detective investigating the gruesome murder of former rock-and-roll star Johnny Boz. Also known as Shooter, Curran is not the stereotypical strong, unimpeachable defender of the law. It is implied that his alcohol and drug abuse have led to his wife's committing suicide, and it is furthermore suggested that he has been traumatized by a shooting accident in which he killed two tourists who "got into his firing line." A "wacko" tending to lose his temper and, it is repeatedly indicated, his sanity too, Curran is clearly a liability within the police force, which explains why he has been placed under compulsory psychiatric treatment. In one of the first scenes we see him in his therapist's office facing his "shrink," Dr. Beth Garner, an attractive dark-haired woman with whom Curran has been having an affair that—for reasons never fully made clear—he has recently broken off. On the face of it, the appearance of the figure of the female "shrink" suggests a reversal in terms of conventional gender relations: in her professional role, Garner naturally occupies a position of superior power over her patient. What is more, in order to be declared fit for his job Curran is ultimately dependent on her professional authority and expert opinion of his mental state. Such ostensible female power, over and above the anxiety provoked by the potentially emasculating effects of the psychoanalytic probing into the male unconscious per se, is at once neutralized by the fact that Garner is shown still to desire Curran, though he is no longer sexually interested in her. Bargaining with this libidinal inequality, our hero speedily succeeds in setting himself free from his guardian's psychic surveillance in order to carry on with the job.

While emphatically inviting us to approach the film from a psychoanalytic perspective, this early scene obliquely yet unmistakably also articulates the central motivating force of the narrative as a whole: castration anxiety. The case Curran is to investigate, the murder enacted in all its gory detail during the film's lengthy opening scene, represents the very scenario Freud considered to constitute the inaugurating moment of male sexuality. In what is apparently meant to be a thrilling sexual spectacle, we have witnessed Johnny Boz, lying helplessly on his back, his hands tied to the bedpost with a silk scarf, meeting his ghastly end when the blond female straddling him, at the apparent *moment suprême,* furiously and repeatedly plunges an icepick into his body.

Curran's investigations soon lead him to the beautiful Catherine Trummell (played by Sharon Stone), writer of successful crime novels. A *cum laude* graduate of Berkeley in both literature and psychology, this hundred-million-dollar heiress shares her life with a "lesbian" lover by the name of Roxy. In sharp contrast to Curran, who claims to have no money and is shown to inhabit a rather dingy apartment, Trummell lives in staggering wealth and luxury. Both her suggested insights into human psychology and her phenomenal financial power immediately render this woman an eligible object of Curran's fearful fascination. Obsessively attracted to the dangers of her superior power/knowledge, our hero is even more excited when Trummell, to his awe and delight, admits that she likes "fucking" men as well as women. During Curran's frequent visits to either of Trummell's opulently laid-out houses, her lover Roxy never makes any but rather fleeting appearances: she is either on the point of leaving, kissing Trummell on the lips while sending hostile looks toward Curran, or coming in when he is about to leave. Although Trummell at once becomes the prime suspect in the case—and Curran's buddy keeps telling him that this woman is "bad news"—he is irresistibly drawn to her. With the tension of the murder plot gradually building up, the intersecting love story soon reaches its culmination in what our hero is to refer to as the "fuck of the century." It is this—again protracted—heterosexual scene that I will closely look at.

Like the scene in the psychiatrist's office, this sequence begins by ostensibly confusing traditional gender roles. Although the camera focuses exclusively on the couple in the bed, as spectators we are led to infer the "lesbian's" covert presence outside our frame of vision, for on several occasions we hear Trummell point out that Roxy enjoys watching her have sex with her male lovers. This situation suggests a reversal of conventional subject/object positions: the voyeuristic pleasure feminist film theory generally assumes to be the male prerogative is here granted to a female character while the male hero *knowingly* inserts himself into the narrative as the object of her gaze.[2] On the face of it, this strategy would appear to be radical, if not subversive. But is it? What is the "lesbian" allowed to see? Her lover in the traditional heterosexual exchange with the male hero. What is more, as an audience we do not share the pleasure Roxy is assumed to derive from watching; indeed, we are expected to *experience* the same pleasure, our look being aligned with the camera's close-up shots of the "heady" scene on the bed. A glimpse of the voyeuristic pleasure itself, which the film suggests is part of "kinky" lesbian sexuality, is thus denied to us. This denial of course, is in line with the general invisibility of the lesbian: insofar as lesbian sexuality has a place in Western patriarchy, it is as a source of voyeuristic titillation in mainstream (straight-male) pornographic texts.

What may thus at first sight seem a reversal of traditional gender roles is no more than a reinscription of the phallocentric heterosexual scenario. In fact, what the sequence represents is, in psychoanalytic terms, the primal scene or *Urszene* of the parental coitus, either actually observed or construed by the (boy) child, the so-called primary scene that forms one of the *Urphantasien* underlying phallocentric reality. In his discussion of the primary scene, Freud explains that the observing (male) child perceives the act of heterosexual intercourse as an act of "aggression by the father in a sadomasochistic relationship." While giving "rise to sexual excitation in the child," the scene at the same time "provid[es] a basis for castration anxiety." Pointing up the repressed homosexual groundings of the fantasy, Freud continues by asserting that what is going on is interpreted by the child as "anal coitus."[3] In enacting one of the central fantasies of Western "hom(m)osexual" culture,[4] the film thus places the "lesbian" character in the position of the male child. Lesbian sexuality is therewith assimilated to the dominant sexual paradigm in that the operations of female non-normative desire are implied to mirror those of male heterosexuality almost—but not quite—exactly. Shown to be no more than a copy of "the real thing," the threat of otherness posed by the lesbian in her potentially destabilizing effects on the precarious "natural order" of things is hence effectively countered by the fact that Roxy is, stereotypically, set up as an "aspiring" male.

These suppositions are confirmed by the film's subsequent scene. To assert his masculinity, Curran has from the start insisted on positioning Roxy in the role of his competitor; not, however, as the female lover of the woman he wants to possess for himself but rather in the role conventionally assigned to the lesbian in patriarchy, the man manqué. The threat of lesbian otherness being contained in a copycat sameness, she has become a familiar and recognizable rival to him. The "fuck of the century" having come to its climactic conclusion, Curran gets up from the bed and steps into the bathroom to wash his face. As an audience we are looking over the hero's shoulder into the mirror when we see, next to his face, the "lesbian" lover entering the frame from behind. The confused division of the narrative space, resulting from the indirect and mirroring camera angles, produces a sense of disorientation whose threat is enhanced by Curran's nakedness, which stands in sharp contrast to the black leather gear of his interlocutor. But despite the suggested vulnerability in this disparity in protective covers, the hero's attitude is triumphant, self-assured, overbearing. His pleasure at this moment is evidently located in the fact that he has, so to speak, "defeated" the "lesbian" other and is gloating over the conquest he has just made. The apparent vulnerability of the exposed male body—already mitigated by the fact that it is never fully exposed: the frame of the camera limits our view to Curran's torso from the waist up while his (at this moment presumably rather flagging) genitals remain hidden from view—is effectively annulled when the victorious male turns around to face his opponent. Redistributing the space, he places his rival in the desired position by calling her bluff: "Let me ask you something, Rocky, man to man. *I* think she is the fuck of the century; what do *you* think?" Both times I sat watching the film in the theater, the audience around me broke into relived laughter at this point: here at last we were back on familiar territory. The stereotypical image of the lesbian as an imitation of the male, lacking what we are not allowed to see but which in its very absence proclaims its critical presence, that is, a penis, is undoubtedly reassuring, for what we are to infer here is that the "lesbian," as an inferior copy of the genuine article, is ultimately no match for the male hero, who in the end "wins" the battle quite conclusively.

The building up of this particular tension, that is, the introduction of an element of otherness that threatens to bring down the established system of power relations, only to be recontained when its potential effect seems to be most imminent, is initiated in the scene immediately preceding the one discussed above. Curran, continuing his pursuit in spite of his buddy's warnings, one night follows the object of his desire into a club. Once again our hero looks rather vulnerable, wearing not his usual layers of professional male attire but an open V-necked sweater, apparently with nothing underneath. The sense of insecurity of the (somewhat miscast) middle-aged hero is palpable when he starts moving about the rather freakish looking, frantically dancing crowd—easily recognizable as the fashionable crowd of artsy-tartsy, affluent, coke-sniffing baby boomers—amidst the overwhelming noise of amplified house music. When Curran finally spots his target, it is in an obviously nightmarish *tableau vivant*. Having followed Roxy into the men's room, he sees Trummell sitting on a toilet seat framed by the doorpost, on one side seconded by her "lesbian" lover, on the other by a black male—that is to say, by the two most threatening forces of otherness to male white heterosexual supremacy. Huddling over their cocaine, all three send defiant looks up at him (and us) until Trummell extends one of her elegant legs to smack the door closed in Curran's (and our) faces. Thus excluded from the secretive triangle made up by the mysterious female, the "lesbian," and the black male, the white male hero suffers extreme anxiety, a tension that the spectator, urged to identify with the latter's position, is invited to experience vicariously.

When the camera returns its look to the dance floor, we first witness Curran watching Trummell provocatively kissing her "lesbian" lover. As on earlier occasions, these kisses are obviously meant to mock the hero, representing a spectacle supposed to titillate and arouse him. The erotic energy invested in them is, in other words, not directed at either of the two women engaged in the scene but a the male watching it. When Trummell subsequently abandons Roxy and starts seducing Curran by dancing close up to him, the camera zooms in on her body rubbing his crotch, therewith directing attention away from the enigmatic sexually other to the self-evident primacy of the phallic. The remainder of the sequence is taken up by a visually rendered combat (in a series of shot-reverse-shots) between Roxy and the male hero, who is throughout holding his prey firmly clasped in his arms. The "lesbian" contender, dancing with the black man, is shown to be a conspicuously bad loser: she is angry, jealous, and humiliated. The visual focus on the rivalry in this sequence suggests that what is at stake is not so much the sexual object—Trummell—but rather the combative exchange itself: whereas the black male all but disappears into the background, the white male hero, by sexually appropriating the female, is shown to subject the "lesbian" to his power, therewith securing his masculinity. In this way, the sequence at once underlines and contains the threat and anxiety posed by lesbian sexuality to male heterosexuality, or rather to masculinity as such.

We recall that the battle between the sexual rivals comes to an end when Roxy gets killed in a car crash after a failed attempt to run down Curran in Trummell's car—quite obviously the victim of her own obsessive jealousy and murderous intentions. The other "lesbian" character who is finally blown to pieces is Dr. Beth Garner, for it is she who turns out to be not only a potentially emasculating shrink of the male brain but also the icepick-wielding psychopathic killer whose murderous impulses (which are repeatedly suggested to issue directly from repressed lesbian obsessions) lie at source of the film's narrative tract.[5] *Basic Instinct*, while pretending to render the lesbian visible on the big, slick Hollywood screen, in the final analysis confirms the continuing prevalence of the cultural scheme delineated by Marilyn Frye as early as 1983: what this film depicts is a reality in which the "lesbian" can only be and be seen as a bad copy of the straight male, a conceptual universe from which she must also, paradoxically, be violently erased.[6] Indeed, the actual word "lesbian" is not uttered once during the almost two hours to which the length of the film runs. It is such quite literal discursive absence that gives the lesbian subject a unique cultural position that differs radically not only from that of straight male and female subjects but also from that of gay males.

The lesbian subject's specific cultural position as compared to her male counterpart originates in the fact that homosexuals in Western culture serve as the exception to confirm the rule. Gay males occupy a discursive space within the heterosexual contract as "prohibited objects," in relation to which the law of Nature can assert itself. Whereas, as Judith Butler argues, "homosexualities of all kinds…are being erased, reduced, and (then) reconstituted as sites of radical homophobic fantasy," it is precisely as prohibited objects that male homosexualities are in effect perpetually (re)constituted by official as well as "reverse discourses" within the "grid of cultural intelligibility." Lesbians, in contrast, are "not even named nor prohibited within the economy of the law."[7] The mandatory falsification of lesbianism in phallocentric societies hence shows that it is not compulsory heterosexuality per se but compulsory *female* heterosexuality that is the condition upon which the "natural" order of things or, to be more precise, of what Monique Wittig defines as the social contract, depends.[8] Only by being relegated to, in Butler's words, a "domain of unthinkability and unnameability" can the lesbian be culturally present: as an "abiding falsehood," as a "copy, an imitation, a derivative example, a shadow of the real."[9] It is in its virtual discursive absence (effectively reinscribed by derivative terms such as "female homosexual") that the category "lesbian" must function as the abject of the cultural consciousness. By conspicuously performing the "unthinkable," the lesbian embodies a threat of exposure to both gay and straight upholders of the law, for the "monstrous" creature subverts what Butler calls the "ontologically consolidated phantasms of 'man' and 'woman'." The lesbian's alleged sexual "mimicry" is hence exactly the kind of drag that, as Butler contends, "enacts the very structure of impersonation by which *any gender* is assumed."[10] In order to ensure the self-presence of men and women as "male" and "female," that is, as genuine, authentic, real subjects, the lesbian's "abnormal" performance must be set off as an imitation against the real thing: "natural" heterosexuality, which, in an economy of the same, is in fact the term of "hom(m)osexuality." In what is so obviously a male fantasy, the narrative of *Basic Instinct* constitutes a precise enactment of this dominant cultural play; what may be less obvious, however, is that it also explicitly articulates this pervasively heterosexual scenario's underlying gender anxiety.

Before I move on to my second intertext, a final point about the significance of the film's title. Once a popular text has entered the domain of public discourse, its title usually starts to operate as a kind of icon: one tends to forget or just stop thinking about its so-called referential meanings. When I was writing this chapter and tried to bring up the film for discussion with my friends and colleagues, I repeatedly found myself groping for the words *Basic Instinct*. This led to the realization that there is something "wrong" with the phrase, for what if not an instinct could be considered basic? Whatever one would refer to as an instinct is already so basic that it does not require any modifier attesting to this quality. The consistent faltering of my memory suggested that the phrase is not merely tautological but indeed *illogically* so. And what is the "basic instinct" referred to: The lesbian monster's instinct to kill? The psychopathic and obsessive character of lesbian sexuality per se? Or is it, as I have argued, the myth of "natural" heterosexuality? By thus drawing attention to itself with its very insistence on the fundamental nature of the sexual drive lying behind the narrative, the film's title would seem to point up the very instability, the essential precariousness, of the heterosexual paradigm on which its underlying oedipal myth, and by extension the "natural" categories of sex, depend. If gender bending would not appear a rather foreign concept in this context, I would suggest that Paul Verhoeven's multimillion-dollar fantasy invokes that famous phrase from Shakespeare's *Hamlet*: "The lady doth protest too much, methinks."

The second mode of discourse I set out to address is feminist critical theory. Since the latter half of the 1980s, "mainstream" (i.e., white, middle-class, straight) feminism has sought to implement the lessons of "diversity" taught by poststructuralist theory by trying to incorporate multiple differences into our critical practices. However, as Judith Roof points out in her impressive book on lesbian sexuality and theory, the representation of female diversity in feminist literary critical anthologies published since 1985 ("bumper year for a crop of feminist collections edited by established scholars and published by prestigious presses") proves often no more than a reduction of difference to the "formula 'black and lesbian'."[11] A number of supposedly representative essays, usually positioned in these collections as a separate category and/or placed at the end of the volume, appear as mere "auxiliaries" in the sense that they are unexceptionally contained within (white, heterosexual, academic feminist) methodological debates. Mainstream feminists thus attest to their consciousness of diversity while foregrounding their claim to academic power by appearing to "correct feminist homogeneity."[12] However, as "displaced cast regular[s]," Roof argues, the incorporated instances of black and lesbian perspectives may well function as "the excess that disrupts the disrupters" of male culture. From the fact that distinctly "other" voices are at the same time placed within the "general" feminist paradigm, she correctly infers that various "minority" perspectives are granted a discursive space in a gesture of "critical separatism" so that excessive differences are "made the same, are kept separate but equal." In an attempt to account for both this insistent (token) acknowledgment of diversity and the reduction of differences (in class, ethnicity, and race in terms other than black) to the "combination 'black' and 'lesbian'," Roof suggests that the inclusion of deviant perspectives to "prove the efficacy of one or another mainstream critical philosophy" could be "construed as a fear that black and lesbian might upset that philosophy." Being programmatically inserted into the mainstream feminist paradigm, disruptive minority discourses become mere "players" in white, straight feminist scripts. As a result, the radical implications of the alternative theoretical paradigms articulated by black and lesbian voices can go unrecognized, nor do their contributions need to be accepted as "theoretical in themselves rather than as augmentative diversity."[13] Though ostensibly indicative of a willingness to confront the challenges of radically other perspectives, the mainstream feminist emphasis on cultural diversity since the 1980s has, we may conclude with Roof, on the one hand resulted in a newly articulated awareness of the pitfalls of a "totalitarian"—if this time feminist—vision and on the other in a seemingly generous "conciliatory takeover" of various othernesses so as to prevent the mainstream feminist applecart from being upset.

An even more curious development in this context, however, is the gradual dropping from sight of lesbian sexuality—and therewith of sexuality as such—as an epistemological and hence a political category. In her itinerary of feminist anthologizing practices of the 1980s, Roof astutely remarks on a shift in emphasis occurring during the latter half of the decade, an attempt at repoliticizing feminist literary criticism with the emergence of a "new combo, race and class" and a concurrent "de-emphasizing of lesbian sexuality."[14] Academic debates on "political correctness" as much as the reactionary backlash generated by the male establishment within educational institutions in response to "minority" demands, issue in an apparent need to side with the most visibly oppressed. Against the background of neocolonialist foreign policies operative in Euro-America during the Thatcher/Reagan years, multiculturalism and ethnic diversity become the passwords of a feminist project considering itself "coalesced with the range of diverse perspectives in a solidarity" against oppressive white male theory.[15] If the lesbian makes an appearance at all, it tends to be as a largely "apolitical category," while the effects of sexual orientation are only occasionally addressed, that is to say, only in relation to specific lesbian or bisexual writers.

That such a depoliticization of lesbian sexuality extends into the 1990s may be gathered from a recent (British) feminist anthology that, judging by its title, purports to constitute a move beyond the 1980s strategy of benevolent incorporation and/or assimilation with regard to radical perspectives. In their preface to a collection of commissioned essays titled *Destabilizing Theory*, editors Michèle Barrett and Anne Phillips embrace the joint challenges offered by a "politics of difference" to what they call the political project of "'1970s western feminism'" and the "theoretical undermining of many of its paradigmatic assumptions."[16] As motivating forces behind such challenges they identify "current work of feminists on post-structuralist and post-modernist themes," to which they parenthetically add "(the charge that the specificity of black women's experience and the racism of white feminists had been ignored)." Though conceding that their "book does not aspire to be a total account of 'feminism'," being "far from global in its reference points," they nonetheless claim to have addressed, from perspectives ranging "beyond narrowly national or regional boundaries," the "typical concerns of a western, academic feminist impulse…that has come to see 'western feminism' as an unstable and limited category." The virtual slippage of ethnic or racial differences in this claim to diversity is in itself remarkable; what strikes me as even more extraordinary is that any awareness of sexual diversity and the potentially destabilizing effects of a specifically lesbian theoretical perspective are left out of this preamble (to what presents itself as a project of "instability") altogether. To be fair, the question of lesbian sexuality is in fact addressed by one (token) essay. Even so, the editors' lengthy introduction that follows their preface shows that the lesbian's "curious habit of disappearing" (noted by Roof in feminist anthologies of the late 1980s) has by no means subsided in the present decade.[17]

For what are the "key elements" informing the breakup of an earlier feminist "consensus," according to Barrett and Phillips? In their sketch of a now diversified feminist project, they single out in the first place "black women's critique of racist and ethnocentric assumptions of white feminists." When they proceed by turning their focus to the problematical "distinction between sex and gender" and the concurrent "interest in psychoanalytic analyses of sexual difference and identity," the notion of lesbian sexuality is, strangely enough, elided. The feminist "unease" about the sex/gender distinction and the resulting interest in "sexual difference and identity" emerging in the late 1980s is said to have amounted to the "analysis of women's experience of mothering" and, "in its most essentialist moments, the celebration of Woman and her Womanly role." Bracketed by, on the one hand, an emphasis on ethnic and racial differentiation and, on the other, the feminist engagement with "post-structuralist and post-modernist ideas"—a third "element" of disruption— the notion of "sexual difference and identity" presented here does not even allow for a token appearance of lesbian sexuality.[18] The potentially destabilizing theoretical effects of diversity in terms of sexual orientation are thus also conveniently glossed over. Couched within this tripartite mapping of the forces of disruption, lesbian sexuality is both rendered invisible and split off from the other two "destabilizing" factors. Its covert positioning in this narrative prelude at once signals the (repressed) centrality of lesbian sexuality in the history of feminist theory and reinforces the prevalent notion of sexual deviance as an "intermediate" stage in the development to theoretical maturity—even if an otherwise destabilized maturity.

In her recent book *Around 1981*, Jane Gallop also points to the implicated position of mainstream feminism in the structures of (heterosexual) gender ideology.[19] She submits that the "internalized heterosexuality" of much feminist theory may indeed be read "symptomatically" as part of the "heterosexual teleology" implicit in both Western culture and the practice of literary theory.[20] Rhetorically asking whether "we prefer sexual difference because this particular difference conventionally promises narrative solution," Gallop analyzes the desire underlying much feminist theoretical practice as a fundamental desire for "a happy ending" within a cultural plot of otherwise irreducible differences. The feminist focus on gender can thus be seen to reinstate the promise of what Cora Kaplan has called the "inevitable resolution" to the plot of heterosexuality, the dominant cultural scenario in relation to which other social/theoretical divisions and deviations operate as mere "narrative backdrop or minor stumbling-block[s]."[21] Interestingly, Gallop's own text would appear to prove her point quite convincingly: in the afterword to *Around 1981*, which functions as a sort of retrospective impression of the years separating the completion of the manuscript (around 1991) from the period covered by it (up to around 1987), the lesbian significantly fades into the shadows of the narrative stage. The primary focus of the résumé is the successful contestation of the ethnocentrist bias of Euro-American feminism, first by African-American feminists and increasingly also by women of other ethnic groups and nationalities. This parting gesture redresses a relative neglect of issues like race and ethnicity in Gallop's earlier chapters, but it equally points up the very "symptomaticity" of lesbian invisibility in feminist discourse that she has been denouncing so insistently herself. Gay studies briefly make an appearance in relation to the perceived shift in feminist theoretical attention from "women" to "gender," but they are quite rightly identified as a field of (potentially problematic) intersection and overlap with feminist criticism and feminist critics' new interest in "men, masculinity, and even their own will to master."[22] At the end of even this extremely self-conscious story, lesbian sexuality has indeed, once again, been silently elided.

The various instances of feminist discourse I have (somewhat but not quite arbitrarily) singled out as intertexts to develop my own argument seem to suggest that one can only deal with so much otherness at once. It would require another essay to explore the precise relations between sexual and ethnic/racial "othernesses," but the evidence suggests that so far, where race is noted, sexual orientation is not. The current emphasis on multiculturalism and ethnic diversity within mainstream feminist theory almost unexceptionally leads to a marked lack of attention for, if not suppression of (lesbian) sexuality as an axis of differentiation and by extension as a structural aspect of diverse forms of signifying processes, including theoretical practice. This absence, it appears to me, cannot be explained away as a twist of fate or as the result of historical accident—fortunate or unfortunate as the case may be. As a site of discursive absence, such nonfigurations of lesbian sexuality should indeed be read symptomatically as precisely the kind of overdetermined ideological effect pointed up by Frye some ten years ago.

Within what is, then, still a predominantly lesbophobic cultural and theoretical context, lesbian theory and criticism continue to be a practice of re- and deconstructing our own stories of difference. Deconstructive reading/writing strategies and the postmodern foregrounding of (inter)textuality have enabled lesbians to chart the theoretical foundations to what Sally Munt has identified as an inherent aspect of lesbian culture per se: its "ability to be so *writerly*."[23] Forced to read between the lines of the texts of heterosexual culture, starting from the site of absence to produce our own alternative and deviant meanings, lesbians have, after all, always been "particularly adept at deconstruction."[24] In view of these considerations, it seems to me that the lesbian theorist may in effect be in an eminent position to exploit the "exciting epistemic privileges" that my various intertexts either implicitly or explicitly attribute to her. Such visionary powers would appear both to reside in and to derive from the fact that the lesbian's "gaze of inversion," when critically directed at phallocratic reality, threatens to disrupt the heterosexual teleology underlying both Western culture and the practice of literary theory—masculinist and feminist alike. Falling outside the dominant cultural scenario, the "unthinkable" concept of lesbian sexuality does not only call into question the binary system of a natural heterosexual difference but equally denaturalizes the very categories of sex, of man and woman. By exposing these as, in Butler's words, no more than "ontologically consolidated phantasms," the lesbian subject of knowledge poses a threat of disruption to any of the conceptual schemes that find their foundation, if not their ultimate destination, in these originary fictions, which, despite the growing and widespread recognition of both social and subjective fragmentation characterizing Western culture in these postmodern times, continue to be projected from the notion of an irreducible (hetero) sexual difference.

1 Cited in Marilyn Frye, *The Politics of Reality* (Trumansburg, N.Y.: The Crossing Press, 1983, p. 152.

2 On the distinction between scopophilia, or the perverse pleasure of the spectator, and *jouissance*, see Parveen Adams's enlightening account in chapter 14 of this volume.

3 Jean Laplanche and Jean Bertrand Pontalis, *The Language of Psycho-analysis* (London: The Hogarth Press/Karnac Books, 1988), p. 335.

4 "Hom(m)osexuality" is a term coined by Luce Irigaray. It is a diacritical pun on the French word *homme*, meaning "man," and the Greek *homos*, meaning "same," that serves to designate patriarchal culture as an economy of the same in which the female other merely functions as the object of exchange between male subjects. See, e.g., Luce Irigaray, "Commodities Among Themselves," *This Sex Which Is Not One*, trans. Catherine Porter (Ithaca, N.Y.: Cornell University Press, 1985), pp. 192–197.

5 The film's markedly ambivalent ending has given rise to considerable critical dissension. Though some have proposed that not Garner but Trummell is the "real" murderess in *Basic Instinct*, I take the closing scene as indicative of the fact that the castration anxiety posed by the figure of the lesbian cannot not be resolved by the killing off of individual lesbians. The appearance of the castrating icepick under the bed conveys that such anxiety endures precisely because phallocentric ideology ensures its inscription in the male subject's psyche.

6 In a chapter titled "To Be and Be Seen," Frye sets out to explore the "exciting epistemic privileges" of the lesbian, only to run immediately into the difficulty of defining the "exotic powers or special opportunities" of a category that conceptually does not exist. Finding the lesbian to be triply erased, to be, in effect, emphatically *excluded* from the phallocratic scheme, she contends that such "overdetermination," or "metaphysical overkill," signals a "manipulation, a scurrying to erase, to divert the eye, the attention, the mind." The totality and conclusiveness of the erasure, Frye infers, indicates that the lesbian's conceptual "impossibility" has to do with the "maintenance of phallocratic reality as a whole." Frye, *The Politics of Reality*, p. 162.

7 Judith Butler, "Imitation and Gender Subordination," in Diana Fuss, ed., *Inside/Out: Lesbian Theories, Gay Theories* (New York and London: Routledge, 1992), p. 20.

8 Monique Wittig, "The Social Contract," *The Straight Mind and Other Essays* (Boston: Beacon Press, 1992), pp. 21–32.

9 Butler, "Imitation and Gender Subordination," p. 20.

10 Ibid., p. 21. Butler rather loosely paraphrases Esther Newton's line of argument in *Mother's Camp: Female Impersonators in America* (Chicago: University of Chicago Press, 1972).

11 Judith Roof, *A Lure of Knowledge: Lesbian Sexuality and Theory* (New York and Oxford: Columbia University Press, 1991), p. 217. Roof focuses her detailed discussion in her chapter "All Analogies Are Faulty: The Fear of Intimacy in Feminist Criticism" on three "mainstream" 1985 anthologies, i.e., Elaine Showalter's *The New Feminist Criticism: Essays on Women, Literature, and Theory*; Judith Newton and Deborah Rosenfelt's *Feminist Criticism and Social Change: Sex, Class and Race in Literature and Culture*; and Gayle Greene and Coppélia Kahn's *Making a Difference: Feminist Literary Criticism*. She further considers Shari Benstock's *Feminist Issues in Literary Scholarship* (1987), Teresa de Lauretis's *Feminist Studies/Critical Studies* (1988), and Bella Brodski and Celeste Schenk's *Life/Lines* (1988)

12 Roof, *A Lure of Knowledge*, p. 223.

13 Ibid., p. 225.

14 Ibid., p. 230.

15 Ibid., p. 233.

16 Michèle Barrett and Anne Phillips, eds., *Destabilizing Theory: Contemporary Feminist Debates* (Cambridge: Polity Press, 1992).

17 Ibid., p. 230.

18 Ibid., pp. 4–5.

19 Jane Gallop, *Around 1981: Academic Feminist Literary Theory* (London and New York: Routledge, 1992).

20 Ibid., pp. 188, 199. Gallop explains the practice of "symptomatic reading" (p. 149), introduced by Gayatri Spivak in "French Feminism in an International Frame," by setting it off against "new critical close reading," which "embraces the text in order to more fully and deeply understand its excellences." Coming out of "psychoanalytic method by way of deconstruction…'symptomatic reading' squeezes the text tight to force it to reveal its perversities." Demystifying and hence diminishing the power of authoritative texts, a "symptomatic" reading practice

can at once be "respectful, because closely attentive, and aggressive, because it wrests secrets the author might prefer to keep" (p. 7).

21 Cora Kaplan, "Pandora's Box: Subjectivity, Class, and Sexuality in Socialist Feminist Criticism," cited in ibid., p. 196.

22 Ibid., p. 242.

23 Sally Munt, introduction to *New Lesbian Criticism: Literary and Cultural Readings* (Hemel Hempstead: Harvester Wheatsheaf, 1992), p. xxi.

24 Ibid., p. xiii.

12

The Homosocial Gaze According to Ian McEwan's *The Comfort of Strangers*

Ernst van Alphen

In this chapter I want to explore the specific nature of homosocial relations through the notions of the gaze and the glance. I will propose some reflections on intermale looking. The distinction between gaze and glance has been introduced by Norman Bryson (1983) in a discussion of modes of looking at painting. The gaze is for him the look that ahistoricizes and disembodies itself and objectifies, takes hold of, the contemplated object. The glance, in contrast, is the involved look when the viewer, aware of the bodily participating in the process of looking, interacts with the painting and does not need, therefore, to deny the work of representation. Mieke Bal, elaborating on Bryson's distinction, says the following about the glance: "The awareness of one's own engagement in the act of looking entails the awareness that what one sees is a representation, not an objective reality, not the 'real thing' (1991: 142). The gaze is a reading attitude that conflates model and figure in representation, an attitude that is encouraged by "transparent" realism, effacing the traces of the labor of representation. The glance, in contrast, is the mode that emphasizes the viewer's own position as viewer and the representational status of the object of looking.

...souvent les femmes ne nous plaisent qu'à cause du contrepoids d'hommes à qui nous avons à les disputer, bien que nous souffrions à mourir d'avoir à les leur disputer; ce contrepoids supprimé, le charme de la femme tombe.

Marcel Proust,
A la recherche du temps perdu (III, 413)

At first sight this distinction between gaze and glance does not seem inherently relevant to a reading of intermale looking. Bal and Bryson are discussing modes of looking at (visual) representations. It is not self-evident that intermale looking is a case of looking at representations. I will argue for such a conceptualization of intermale looking through a discussion of the social bond between men. This bond is not directly sexual in nature, nor are the modes of looking that shape it homosexual. Compare in this respect the specifically homosexual male gaze in Marcel Proust's novel (1954), as analyzed in chapter 10 of this volume by Mieke Bal. The homosocial bond does, however, delimit and determine the relationship between men and women. Like Eve Sedgwick, I will call that particular bond homosocial. First I will briefly evoke the theories on which Sedgwick has based her concept of the homosocial bond: those of the anthropologist Claude Lévi-Strauss and the literary scholar René Girard. Then I will call upon the novel *The Comfort of Strangers* by the British novelist Ian McEwan (1981), which will enable me to demonstrate the nature and consequences of this bond in their full complexity. The novel not only presents a sharp analysis of what happens "between men," but, significantly, it does so by way of visual motifs such as looking, spying, mirrors, and photographs. I contend that this overlayering of social relations and visuality is inherent to those relations, not coincidental. The question I will therefore address is: What is the point of all the picture-taking and mirror-looking in the novel in connection to the social relations between the male characters? *How* do they look? It is necessary to ask this last question not only because motifs of looking structure the novel so consistently but also because I contend that the nature of homosocial relations can be understood most keenly by an understanding of intermale looking.

In McEwan's novel one of the male protagonists, Robert, is spying as he follows another man, Colin. Robert secretly takes pictures of Colin. In these situations of watching, Robert is not looking at a painting, a representation, but at another man, Colin. However, the point I will try to make is that Robert's initial mode of looking at Colin turns Colin precisely into a representation. Colin is a live representation of a position within a system in which male identity is constituted. If I can make this point plausible, then Bryson's distinction between gaze and glance can serve as a concept to analyze the particular modes of homosocial looking as powerful forms of social agency and, by extension, as configurations of the homosocial cultural order as such.

In *The Elementary Structures of Kinship* (1969), Lévi-Strauss speculates about the beginning of human societies by examining the general structures of kinship relations. Two notions are central in his analysis: the gift and the incest taboo. These two notions together lead to an analysis of the practice of the exchange of women among men. According to Lévi-Strauss, the gift of women is of crucial importance for the emergence of culture, for the result of such a gift is much more fundamental than that of other kinds of gifts. By giving women, a relationship is created that is not just one of mutuality but of kinship. The men between whom the transaction takes place become relatives, and their offspring will even be blood relatives. Lévi-Strauss emphasizes the difference from other gifts by a quote from George Best: "'Two people may meet in friendship and exchange gifts and yet quarrel and fight in later times, but intermarriage connects them in a permanent manner'" (Lévi-Strauss (1969: 481).

Within this structure of exchange the distribution of roles seems fixed. Women are the gifts; men are the partners between whom an exchange takes place. The social organization that is thus taking shape is an organization among groups of men within which women are only objects. Lévi-Strauss claims that even in cultures where women can choose the men they marry, they do not necessarily form an alternative organization: "This remains true even when the girl's feelings are taken into consideration, as, moreover, is usually the case. In acquiescing to the proposed union, she precipitates or allows the exchange to take place; she cannot alter its nature" (1969: 115). The consequences of this view are far-reaching, for it could imply that organization on the basis of the exchange of women is still valid even within contemporary Western societies. My analysis of *The Comfort of Strangers* will present a statement on this issue.

The second important element in the transition from nature to culture is the incest taboo. Lévi-Strauss claims that the exchange of women provides a concrete elaboration of that taboo, which allegedly created the starting point of culture. If this elaboration is indeed the case, it sheds a disturbing light on the relationships of man to man and man to woman because it implies that the heterosexual relationship of man to woman is embedded within the relationship of man to man. The man-woman relation, a result of the exchange of women among men, is a *means* to create homosocial relationships. The emergence of homosocial relationships is then the starting point of culture.

René Girard depicts a less positive image of the relationships between men in his study of the novel *Mensonge romantique et vérité romanesque* (1961). His conclusion is based on European fairy tales and sagas about erotic triangular love relationships, and he subsequently applies it to the novel. In the dominant European tradition those triangles consist of male rivals competing for a female beloved. Girard concludes that the motive behind these triangles consists of a relation of rivalry between two active members of the triangle. The bond between these two rivals is at least as strong as the one between lover and beloved. Girard also discusses many examples where the choice of a beloved is determined by the fact that she was already selected by another person who is experienced as a rival. He even contents that the relationship between the two rivals is stronger and more defining of behavior and experience than the bond between lover and beloved.

Girard's theory shares with Lévi-Strauss's the notion that the relationship between man and woman is embedded in the homosocial one between men. The heterosexual relationship shapes the bond between men, a bond that in the end is much more important than the one between man and woman. The two theorists perceive the nature of this homosocial relationship differently, however. For Lévi-Strauss it is an idyllic bond, the starting point of culture, whereas for Girard it consists of rivalry and competition. Although space forbids me to develop this line, the difference between the two views can be understood in terms of Freud's theory of the Oedipus complex and can be explained in terms of the *phases* of that complex. Girard, then, theorizes the moment of the oedipal crisis of rivalry between father and son, whereas Lévi-Strauss deals with the situation of adaptation thereafter, when the son has renounced the mother, identified with the father, and quietly and good-naturedly collaborating with the father, awaits his turn.

Both Girard and Lévi-Strauss base their conclusions on material that is not necessarily identical to the situation of contemporary Western cultures. Lévi-Strauss examines structures of relationship in so-called primitive cultures, whereas Girard limits his analysis at first to tales stemming from premodern popular culture, then transfers his conclusions to the novel, which he thereby labels as fundamentally romantic. In contrast, I will use their theories as a searchlight to read a contemporary Western novel and ask how the homosocial bond is characterized there and how it relates to the heterosexual relationship. What, in other words, is the function of the homosocial within the heterosexual, or, the other way around, what is the function of the heterosexual within the homosocial? This chapter is *not* about homosexuality but about the foundations of heterosexuality. And, as I will argue, the relation between the homosocial and the heterosexual is grounded on an experience of similitude and difference that is best understood by means of visuality: ultimately, the connection of *a vision*.

McEwan's novel is about an English couple, Colin and Mary, who are vacationing in a picturesque Italian town with much water and many bridges and, as a result, many tourists. The town is never mentioned; the descriptions do not lead to identification of the place, but one does recognize Venice. When, late at night, Colin and Mary try to find a restaurant, they get lost. During their wandering they meet the Italian Robert, who leads them to a night cafe. After questioning them about their relationship, Robert is expected to tell about his own situation, a marriage: "When Mary asked how he met his wife, Robert said it was impossible to explain that without first describing his sisters and his mother, and these in turn, could be explained only in terms of his father" (1981: 30). After Robert's narrative of his family history, everybody goes home. Colin and Mary get lost again and spend the night in the streets. In the morning Robert finds them in a state of exhaustion and takes them to his apartment. They sleep their fill, and afterward they meet Robert's wife, Caroline. As a first unsettling motive of vision, Caroline confesses that she has watched them during their sleep. Robert resumes his narrative of his father and grandfather for Colin's sake. Unexpectedly, Robert punches Colin in the stomach when Colin makes an ironic remark about Robert's veneration of his ancestors. On the days following this encounter, Colin and Mary hardly leave their hotel room. They sleep, make love, and eat again and again.

After a visit to the Lido they pass the palazzo of Robert and Caroline, who notice and reinvite them in. Robert takes Colin to his bar, where he has to settle some business; the women stay behind. Caroline tells Mary about her disability. She has become an invalid because of Robert's sadistic lovemaking: her back has been seriously damaged. Subsequently she shows Mary the bedroom. The latter is totally flabbergasted and panicked when she is confronted by another visual event: the bedroom walls are filled with photographs of Colin that Robert must have taken secretly during the couple's wanderings through the city. But she cannot react; Caroline has drugged her tea. When the men come home, Colin wants a doctor called in to look after Mary. Caroline and

Robert refuse. Colin, already panicking because of Mary's sleepy state, begins to realize that Robert and Caroline want something from him, probably something sexual. He agrees on the condition that Mary is helped first. When Caroline starts to caress him, he beats her off. This blow wounds her, and she smears the blood on Colin's lips. At that, Robert starts to kiss Colin on the mouth and cuts his wrists. Over the dying body of Colin, Robert and Caroline make savage love. Mary, half unconscious and unable to intervene, has been forced to watch.

In what sense is this a novel about homosociality? Why is it not more obvious to interpret Robert's fascination for Colin as homosexual? All through the novel this issue seems confused. Robert is clearly not interested in Mary, even though she is called a beauty. He is exclusively interested in Colin. He takes pictures only of him, and whenever Mary is by chance included in the image, he cuts her out. Already, during their first visit to Robert and Caroline, Mary has seen a picture of Colin taken by Robert. When she tells Colin, she suggests that Robert might be erotically interested in him: "'Perhaps,' Mary said, 'he thinks you have a nice face'" (102). There are other moments in the novel that seem to confirm that interpretation. The bar owned by Robert is visited by men only; these men are described as identical to him:

> A number of young men dressed similarly to Robert, sat on high stools at the bar, and several more were arranged in identical postures. Everyone appeared to be smoking, or putting out his cigarette with swift, decisive jabs. Since they all wore tight clothes, they had to hold their cigarette in one hand, the lighter and pack in the other. The song they were all listening to, for no one was talking, was loud and chirpily sentimental. (28–29)

At their second meeting, Robert takes Colin again to this bar. The itinerary to reach it is described as follows:

> They were taking yet another unfamiliar route, along streets relatively free of tourists and souvenir shops, a quarter from which women too seemed to have been excluded, for everywhere, in the frequent bars and street cafes, at the strategic street-corners or canal bridges, in the one or two pinball arcades they passed, were men of all ages, mostly in shirtsleeves, chatting in small groups, though here and there individuals dozed with newspapers on their laps. Small boys stood on the peripheries, their arms folded importantly like their fathers and brothers. (108)

Based on this passage, two conclusions present themselves. Either this is a description of a homosexual pickup area, or this strict separation between men and women is typically Mediterranean. The text does not give a clue. On their way to the bar Robert has had several brief conversations, in Italian, with the men he meets. On arriving at the bar he asks Colin if he has understood the subject of those conversations. Colin's answer is negative. "Robert smiled again in simple delight. 'Everyone we met, I told them that you are my lover, that Caroline is very jealous, and that we are coming her to drink and forget about her'" (110). It is possible to read this remark as an indirect confession of homosexual desire. But this interpretation is not inescapable because Robert does not really express his desires. The effect of the remark, however, is obvious: he is trying to drive Colin into a corner, to put him in his place. I will revert to this idea below.

In the final confrontation between Robert, Colin, and Caroline, it is again possible to read clues of homosexual desire: "Caroline transferred more of her blood on the end of her finger till Colin's lips were completely and accurately rouged. Then Robert, pressing his forearm against the top of Colin's chest, kissed him deeply on the mouth, and as he did so, Caroline ran her hand over Robert's back" (129). This passage does suggest that both Caroline and Robert are in love with

Colin. That is why, one assumes, they hang his pictures in their bedroom. Husband and wife collaborate here in their violent conquest because they have a shared erotic object of desire. Yet I will ultimately contradict the notion that Colin is in the least an object of homosexual desire for Robert. Robert is in fact not kissing another man at all. Colin does not function as object of desire but as catalyst for Robert's heterosexual desire, whose object is Caroline.

Yet the lack of clarity in this matter must not be dissolved, for the question whether Robert's relationship to Colin is homosexual or homosocial is not only a crucial one for our purposes; it is also the question that turns the novel into a visual mystery. What is it, exactly, that Robert sees when he looks at another man; how is it that he looks; what is the nature of his gaze? This question determines his identity as a man.

Before returning to the subject of my argument, the nature of the homosocial in terms of looking relations, I will first make the same detour that Robert does. In order to understand his relationships to Caroline and to Colin, I must first present his relationships to his father, his mother, and his sisters; a full system of relations is in place and at stake. This family history is literally and figuratively the frame of the novel. In the film by Paul Schrader based on the novel, it is even more concretely the case. The film begins with a voice-over of Robert talking about his father. In the middle of the film he tells the same story to Colin and Mary, and the film ends with Robert's voice talking about his father at the police station, during the hearing.

Robert's father was a diplomat, a pure specimen of patriarchy both within and outside his family. His wife and four daughters, his son, Robert, and even the ambassador for whom he worked were all afraid of him. According to Robert, he was his father's favorite:

> He took my napkin from my lap and tucked it into the front of my shirt. "Look!" he said. "Here is the next head of the family. You must remember to keep on the good side of Robert!" Then he made me settle the arguments, and all the time his hand was resting on me here, squeezing my neck between his fingers. My father would say, "Robert, may the girls wear silk stockings like their Mama?" And I, ten years old, would say very loudly, "No, Papa." "May they go to the theatre without their Mama?" "Absolutely not, Papa." "Robert, may they have their friend to stay?" "Never, Papa!" (33)

The father gives his ten-year-old son the feeling of being a member of an exclusive club. This strategy is how the father manages to rule over the rest of his environment. Robert denounced the childish bad tricks of his sisters to his father, for "I believed he knew everything. Like God. He was testing me to find out if I was worthy enough to tell the truth. So there was no point in lying. I told him everything" (35). Of course, his sisters hated him and wanted to take revenge. One day, when the parents were away, the sisters presented Robert with a gift: two bottles of lemonade, chocolate, marshmallows, and cream cake. His father had absolutely forbidden him ever to eat candy or chocolate, believing those things gave one a weak personality, like that of girls. He was unable to resist the temptation and ate everything. When he fell sick, needed to throw up, and got diarrhea, the sisters locked him up in the father's study. He vomited and defecated all over the room. His father's reaction was: "'Robert, have you been eating chocolate!' And I said, 'Yes, Papa but...' And that was enough for him. Later my mother came to see me in my bedroom, and in the morning a psychiatrist came and said there had been a trauma. But for my father it was enough that I had eaten chocolate. He beat me every night for three days and for many months he did not speak kindly to me" (39). The relationship between Robert and his mother is in a sense the opposite of that with his father. If the latter relationship is characterized by fear and deference because of the father's absolute authority and the hierarchy that sustains it, the relationship with his mother is based on unconditional love and warmth. Until he was ten years old Robert slept in his mother's bed whenever his father was away. The sisters saw here another opportunity for revenge. When the Canadian ambassador came to visit the family with his wife and daughter, Caroline, the following happened between the children:

> Suddenly Eva said, "Miss Caroline, do you sleep with your mother?" And Caroline said, "No, do you?" Then Eva: "No, but Robert does."
>
> I went deep, deep red, and was ready to run from the room, but Caroline turned to smile at me and said, "I think that is really awfully sweet," and from that time on I was in love with her, and I no longer slept in my mother's bed. Six years later I met Caroline again, and two years after that we were married. (41)

The place that Caroline will occupy in Robert's life can best be characterized by the novel's title, "the comfort of a stranger." Robert is imprisoned in the relationship (of struggle) with his father, the ideal but feared reference point for his own identity. Deference and anxiety define Robert's experience of his father. In addition, he is involved in a struggle with his sisters; contempt, but also fear, define the experience of that relationship. In comparison with his father he is constantly afraid of not resembling him enough; in comparison with his sisters he fears too much resemblance, being like a woman. Robert's identity is shaped between these two extremes. Afraid of not being manly enough, he must distinguish himself from the opposite pole. His identity is in suspension: not enough like the one, he is constantly threatened with being too much like the other. This situation is emphatically not a matter of object choice but of a lack of subjecthood. It must be remembered that this experience of self and the lack thereof is the result of an imposed identification with the father.

The mother appears to stand outside this struggle. She loves her son unconditionally, yet she is unable to offer a solution for Robert's struggle precisely because she belongs to the respected father. Robert only sleeps with her when the father is away from home. Caroline, the Canadian girl, finds him "awfully sweet" just like that, just like his mother. She becomes his resting place and companion in his impossible struggle to build himself a masculine identity like his father's. Robert falls in love with Caroline because she is without conditions, because for her he need not prove himself because he *is* his own truth, as he was for his mother.

However, when they fail to have children and he turns out to be sterile, their marriage takes a different turn. Robert can forget his ambition to be a father, a patriarch. He sinks into the marsh of the other pole, his sisters', the nonelected, the nonmasculine. Now he struggles not to be the father but, more defensively, against the inferiority of nonmasculinity. And Caroline is no longer like his mother; she is, because of her sex and generation, also like his sisters. That is why he cannot but despise, humiliate, and hate her; that is why his love turns into extreme sadism. To Mary, Caroline recounts her marriage in the following terms:

> Robert began to really hurt me. He used a whip. He beat me with his fists as he made love to me. I was terrified, but the terror and the pleasure were all one. Instead of saying loving things to my ear, he whispered pure hatred, and though I was sick with humiliation, I thrilled to the point of passing out. I didn't doubt Robert's hatred for me. It wasn't theatre. He made love to me out of deep loathing, and I couldn't resist. I loved being punished. (117)

Sexuality and violence are here completely intertwined. Robert's sexual desire for his wife cannot be distinguished any longer from his contempt for and hatred of women in their quality of non-men. And this intertwinement of sexual desire and violence will further determine Robert's homosocial bonds with men.

McEwan emphatically does not present the intertwinement of sexuality and violence as a universal fact, as Bataille did, for example. The intricacy is the product of a specific organizational principle, perhaps most adequately described as the patriarchal order. Whereas Robert and Caroline are representatives of this order, Colin and Mary embody an alternative order, or rather the negation of that order. The novel stages the conflict between the patriarchal order and the tentative one that negates it. This conflict is represented spatially and visually. The whole city is filled with posters of a feminist pressure group that demands that rapists be castrated. Mary explicitly underwrites that demand. She has been a member of a women's theater group; she raises her two children by itself; her relationship with Colin can be termed modern, a kind of LAT relationship, based on mutual autonomy. The sadomasochistic relationship between Robert and Caroline stands in sharp contrast, based as it is on violent subordination.

The conflict between the two orders is shaped in a much more complex way, however, by the elaborate weaving through the novel of visual agency in the manipulation of camera and mirror, each standing for a way of looking. About Venice, the city where Mary and Colin are strangers, it is said that "two-thirds of the adult males carried cameras" (49). Robert himself, who is not a tourist, is nevertheless constantly walking around with a camera: "Over his shoulder he carried a camera" (26). Almost everyone in this novel carries a camera. Mary and Colin are the exceptions to the rule, which is remarkable, given the fact that they are tourists. When Colin begins to realize that Robert has been following him around with a camera, he looks around to see if Robert is somewhere near. He then sees so many cameras that their owners are reduced to negligible, meaningless items in the background: "There were cameras everywhere, suspended like aquarium fish against a watery background of limbs and clothes, but Robert, of course, was not there" (102).

Whereas the patriarchal order seems to be embodied by the camera and the *taking* of pictures, the order based on the negation of the patriarchal order is signified through the visual motif of the mirror. Mary and Colin find themselves quite often in front of a mirror. Realistically speaking, this simply mean that they pay more attention to their looks ("Colin stood in front of the mirror, listening, and for no particular reason he began to shave for the second time that day" [11]). But at the same time the mirror motif represents the nature of their relationship and a different relation between the sexes:

> They often said they found it difficult to remember that the other was a separate person. When they looked at each other they looked into a misted mirror. When they talked of the politics of sex, which they did sometimes, they did not talk of themselves. It was precisely this collusion that made them vulnerable and sensitive to each other, easily hurt by the discovery that their needs and interests were distinct. (17)

When we analyze the mode of looking that is at stake in terms of Bryson's distinction between gaze and glance, the collusion between Colin and Mary is the result of their looking according to the logic of the glance. Their involved looks dissolve the clear-cut difference between subject and object of their looks. The object of the look functions as a mirror, which means that subject and object are mingled and become mutually constitutive. The mirror functions here as the embodiment of a specific mode of looking: the glance.

The camera, the taking of photographs, embodies then the other mode of looking: the gaze. In this novel the taking of pictures comes to stand for the objectification and disembodiment of the contemplated object in the most literal and lethal sense. Robert's taking of pictures of Colin disembodies him, takes the life out of him. Colin is turned into a representation, with deadly effect.

In some respects, the order in which Colin and Mary stand is diametrically opposed to the patriarchal order of Robert and Caroline. This opposition does not mean, however, that Colin and

Mary's order is idealized. Mary and Colin are minors to each other; their situation entails the cancellation of sexual difference. In Robert's order, in contrast, the difference between man and woman is hierarchical and absolute. On the other hand, the equation of the sexes in light of the mirror suspends the properties of each sex, and that suspension appears to diminish sexual desire. The frequent lovemaking of Colin and Mary is described not as passionate but as pleasant.

The difference between photo and mirror as standing for the difference between the patriarchal order and the negation of it is also palpable in narratological terms. Colin, who is after all the main character of the story, hardly has an identity outside his relationship with Mary. We know nothing of his past, for example. In contrast with Robert, he never acts as focalizer of his own past. We get to know much more about the past of Mary and Caroline. He is not invested with the position to tell his story, nor does he wish to do so. When, at their first encounter, Robert interrogates the couple and thereby yields the narrating position to them, Colin, whispers to Mary, "We don't have to explain ourselves, you know" (26). In contrast, Robert talks all the time about his past, and in addition he has fixed his identity through an exposition of photos of his father and grandfather. Colin's identity is represented exclusively through the way he behaves in the present and talks, responds, acts, and thinks in relation to Mary.

As a man, Colin is not a representative of the patriarchal order. That becomes clear, for example, when Mary focalizes him sleeping naked on the bed. She takes pleasure in his beauty, but the terms in which she describes him stand in systematic contrast to some of current views of masculinity: "His arms were crossed foetally over his chest and his slender, hairless legs set a little apart, the feet abnormally small like a child's, pointing inwards.... His buttocks were small and firm, like a child's. Colin's eyebrows were thick pencil lines. His hair was unnaturally fine, like a baby's, and black, and fell in curls on to his slender, womanly neck (58–59). The description of Colin's body and face takes more than a page. It is entirely couched in terms of a baby, of femininity, or of the artificial beauty of sculpture. There is never any mention of "natural," organic masculinity.

Standing outside the patriarchal order, Mary and Colin have enough distance from it to have insight into its basic principles. When at the end of the novel Mary has to identify Colin's body, she mentally explains to him why he was murdered:

> She was in the mood for explanation, she was going to speak to Colin. She was going to recount Caroline's story, as closely as she could remember it, and then she was going to explain it all to him, tell him her theory, tentative at this stage, of course, which explained how the imagination, the sexual imagination, men's ancient dreams of hurting, and women's of being hurt, embodied and declared a powerful single organizing principle, which distorted all relations, all truth. (134)

Although Mary and Colin do not live in this order, narratively they get lost in it—with lethal consequences. This wandering into the patriarchal order is again represented in primarily spatial terms. Venice with its historical grandeur stands for that order. They wander in that city like strangers, and they get more and more lost. At the moment that Robert guides them through Venice they get entangled in the pitfalls of that order. We notice this entanglement, for example, after their first visit to Robert and Caroline's apartment. The text suggests that at that moment sex and violence become entangled for them too. When they leave the palazzo, we read the following: "As they descended the first flight of stairs, they heard a sharp sound that, as Mary said later, could as easily have been an object dropped as a face slapped" (80). This event closes chapter 6. Chapter 7 opens with this information:

> During the next four days Colin and Mary did not leave the hotel. Walking back from the

apartment to the hotel, they had held hands all the way; that night they had slept in the same bed. They woke surprised to find themselves in the same bed. Their lovemaking surprised them too, for the great, enveloping pleasure, the sharp, almost painful, thrills were sensations, they said that evening on the balcony, they remembered from seven years before, when they had first met. (81)

Although the connection between the end of chapter 6 and the opening of chapter 7 remains implicit, a casual connection is suggested between the encounter with Robert, the sharp noise, perhaps a slap in Caroline's face, and the four days of sexual pleasure. That violence brings pleasure is the implicit message.

When Mary defines the organizing principle of the patriarchal order as "men's ancient dreams of hurting, and women's of being hurt," eroticism and violence are presented as an inextricable knot within which no difference between cause and consequence can be noticed any more. It stops being a narrative process and becomes a static situation within which positions are not delimited but exist as a mixture of masculine and feminine positions. When Caroline described her marriage, however, she did so in terms of development and change, of a growing entanglement. Robert began to use violence at a certain point in time, not an arbitrary moment, but the one where he turned out to be sterile and therefore definitively unable to become a father. At first Caroline was afraid, terrified, of this development; only later did she learn to take masochistic pleasure in the violence. I am not interested in Caroline's development but in Robert's. His heterosexual desire for Caroline only became sadistic later, entailing the entanglement of sex and violence in a second round.

How do eroticism and violence interact in Robert's homosocial relation to Colin? I have already argued that Colin is not the object of homosexual desire for Robert, yet Robert constantly calls forth a homoerotic tension. Where does this tension come from, and what is its function? The epigraph that McEwan used for the novel helps to answer these questions. The epigraph consists of three lines of poetry by the feminist poet Adrienne Rich:

how we dwelt in two worlds
the daughters and the mothers
in the kingdom of the sons

The syntactical and formal structure of this verse emphasizes the embedding of the world of mothers and daughters within the kingdom of the sons. Moreover, it is striking that Rich mentions mothers but not fathers, as if she wants to say that the kingdom of the sons contains no fathers because the sons are still tasked with proving their own fatherhood in a continuous struggle, an endeavor in which they never entirely succeed. Never does a son reach the moment when he can say, "I made it; I am a father." Masculine identity remains the stake of struggle and must be proven time and again.

Rich's lines confirm my earlier assumption that Robert and Caroline's marriage is not a goal in itself but a function in a family history, in the development of a subject. Thus, a second meaning for the title begins to take shape, which at first sight seems to refer to the help Robert provides to the two strangers when they are lost and hungry. Now the relation is reversed. When Robert's subjectivity is shaped on a sliding scale between idealized man (the father) to nonmen, then his heterosexual love object, Caroline, is the comfort that a stranger can bring within this struggle. Because women stand outside the opposition of men and nonmen, they can be the means through which the man can prove his manhood or his fatherhood. Within this struggle Caroline is just a means, not a goal.

Robert's representation of the world is totally occupied by his ego ideals, his father and his grandfather: "My father and his father understood themselves clearly. They were men, and they were proud of their sex. Women understood them too. There was no confusion. Now men doubt themselves, they hate themselves, even more than they hate each other. Women treat men like children, because they can't take them seriously" (75–76). Robert says these things in a conversation with Colin. The latter, however, responds ironically. The subordination of women in Robert's world order is not chosen by the women out of deference and respect for the men but *because* they were subordinated. "Women did as they were told," says Colin. In response to Robert's nostalgic memories of the heyday of patriarchy, Colin says, "Your grandfather's day had suffragettes. And I don't understand what bothers you. Men still govern the world" (76).

The difference between Robert and Colin is enormous, and the reader is soon aware of it. Naturally, Robert sees Colin in a different light than the reader does. When Robert saw Colin stroll through the alleys of Venice in the company of Mary, Colin at first sight represented the other man's ego ideal. There was the man he would have liked to be. He sees Colin not as a beautiful man but as a *representation* of a position within the hierarchical system that constitutes male identity. The position that Colin represents, according to Robert's gaze, is a high position, higher than the one Robert occupies himself.

Robert's relation to Colin is initiated by a visual experience: he sees Colin walking in the streets of Venice. That's why his response to this experience is also visual. It's the reason why he secretly takes all the pictures of Colin, which he subsequently shows to Caroline, who also becomes fascinated by Colin. The issue of their fascination is, however, radically different for each. Whereas Colin is for Caroline an object of desire, for Robert he is the ideal with which he wants to merge. This difference between the desire to unite yourself to someone and the desire to become like something or someone also defines the difference between vision according to the photograph, or gaze, and vision according to the mirror, or glance. The taking of pictures is the taking possession of the other. Taking a picture is then an attempt to appropriate an object visually. In the mirror, however, subject and object of the look unify. One loses oneself in the object of the look when one sees the other as a mirror image.

At this point it becomes important to see the differences and the connections between "Colin" as (Robert's) visual creation and the character, a real person in the novel's fabula. When he has been made a representation, he is totally objectified but not real; hence, his representational status is absolute. On the one hand, one would expect the glance, that mode of looking that emphasizes representation, to be brought to bear on such an "image." On the other hand, Robert's response to Colin as representation ignores that unreality and "forgets" the unreal status of his (image of) "Colin." This forgetting leads to a crucial paradox. Robert's negligence of the representational quality of the image he has himself made enables him to practice the gaze, that mode of looking that neglects the representational status in favor of transparent realism. Thus, his self-made "Colin" becomes a "real" model. Signifier and signified are conflated; the representation and that of which it is a representation cannot be distinguished any longer. Whereas he wants to appropriate "Colin's position"—what he stands for—the act of appropriation consists of acts of disembodying the representation: he begins with *taking* pictures of Colin, and ultimately he kills Colin. Destroying the representation Colin, Robert tries to capture its content.

The difference in nature of Robert's and Caroline's desires for Colin becomes clear in the way they look at the photos. When Caroline meets Colin after knowing him only in pictures, she feels as if she is stepping into a mirror. For her Colin is the object of sexual desire, and his pictures are mirrors with which/in which she wants to unite herself. For Robert, the attraction is different. The passage that describes Robert for the first time demonstrates the difference between the two men. The comparison between Robert and Colin in the first sentence suggests that Mary, not Colin focalizes Robert:

> He was shorter than Colin, but his arms were exceptionally long and muscular. His hands too were large, the backs covered with matted hair. He wore a tightfitting black shirt, of an artificial, semi-transparent material, unbuttoned in a neat V almost to his waist. On a chain round his neck hung a gold imitation razor blade which lay slightly askew on the thick pelt of chest hair. Over his shoulder he carried a camera. A cloying sweet scent of aftershave filled the narrow street. (26)

Robert not only disposes of a whole range of cliché signs of organic masculinity such as muscled, long arms and much body hair, especially chest hair; he also displays those signs. His already transparent shirt is in addition open to the waist, and he is surrounded by the smell of aftershave. His presence shall not be overlooked. The description of Colin discussed earlier opposes this one in great detail. But if Robert wants to score as highly as possible on the sliding scale of true masculinity, he has a lack that warrants his choice of Colin as ego ideal: "He was shorter than Colin." Yet one could also argue that Robert's fascination with Colin stems from the fact that for him Colin is a true man without displaying any of the signs of traditional masculinity. Thus, Colin turns masculinity into a mystery, a sphinxlike problem that must be unraveled at all cost.

But, importantly, Robert is not only shorter than Colin, he is also older. Colin has enough experience of the intermale world to sense the relevance of age within homosocial relations. Colin displays his sensitivity to this issue not in a confrontation with Robert but earlier on, when he witnesses from his hotel room a confrontation between an old man and a group of younger men. He watches an old man trying to take a picture of his wife against the backdrop of a *terrasse* on which a number of young men are drinking. The old man, "with thin, trembling thighs" and "unsteady legs," wants these young men as background decoration, not as characters on the same level as his wife. The young men, however, turn to the camera and raise their glasses. The old man gets irritated and tries "to usher them back on the path of their unselfconscious existence" (15).

The street scene is clearly extraordinary to Colin. He tells Mary about it, but in doing so he exaggerates all of its elements, out of fear that Mary will not believe him "or because he did not believe himself": he describes the elderly gentleman as "incredibly old and feeble," his wife as "batty beyond belief," the men at the table as "bovine morons," and the husband as giving out "an incredible roar of fury" (16). The exaggeration Colin feels compelled to perform is itself important. It is a *mise en abyme*, a direction for reading that holds for the novel as a whole. The novel too is an exaggeration, necessary in order to demonstrate and make the readers believe. In order to get a clear insight into the mechanism Colin watches in operation between the old man, the young men, and the wife through whom it is structured, he must represent it with exaggeration, magnify it. Similarly, McEwan "exaggerates" when he makes Robert's striving for power end in murder. This exaggeration turns the novel into an allegory.

But if this passage can be taken to function as a *mise en abyme*, the visual theme that underlies the scene may also be taken as such. The old man *takes* a picture, appropriates his wife, and, in the act, circumscribes the young men's existence to mere figuration and decoration. They are not allowed to be partners with his wife, for that would make them partners with himself, too. Such partnership, in turn, would make all the men comparable. It would start the competition that older than the others, the old man can only lose. The little scene shows the visual underpinning of a situation of comparison as a structuration of social intercourse. It shows that homosocial relations are defined by the logic of the gaze.

Robert's deference to Colin later turns into jealousy. This change is the logical consequence of the patriarchal organization, the sliding scale that shapes masculine subjectivity. Since positions on this scale emerge through comparison, they are by definition exclusive; from the standpoint of one subject, each position can only be occupied by one man. Masculine identity is measured by the position other men occupy on the scale, either higher or lower than the measuring subject. At the moment that Robert admires Colin, the latter occupies the position on the scale that he would like to hold. Thus begins intermale competition. To become a man, some other man must be unmanned. This patriarchal rule seems to be symbolized by the golden razor Robert wears around his neck. The razor, a masculine attribute, will be used during the final scene to cut the wrists of another man. With Colin's life, his manhood must also be cut off.

But before definitively unmanning Colin, Robert alludes to this need in various ways. When Colin does not show enough respect for the museum Robert has erected for his ancestors, he receives a punch in the stomach.

> Robert stood up too. The geometric lines of his face had deepened and his smile was glassy, fixed. Colin had turned back momentarily to set down his empty glass on the arm of his chair, and as he straightened Robert struck him in the stomach with his fist, a relaxed, easy blow which, had it not instantly expelled all the air from Colin's lungs, might have been playful. Colin jack-knifed to the floor at Robert's feet where he writhed, and made laughing noises in his throat as he fought for air. Robert took the empty glasses to the table. When he returned he helped Colin to his feet, and made him bend at the waist and straighten several times. (77)

When Robert leaves the room after this incident, he first turns around and winks at Colin. In this passage Robert reverses the positions on the sliding scale of masculinity. Colin literally sinks down at Robert's feet. What is most striking, however, is the fact that all this happens *within* an atmosphere of comradeship, during drinks, with a wink. In his aggression Robert does not want to sever the homosocial bond; he only wishes to reverse the hierarchically ordered positions in which that bond exists for him. The moment the punch in Colin's stomach endangered the bond, the risk would be unbearable: Colin would stop providing a measuring scale for Robert's manhood. That is why the struggle must be fought out within an atmosphere of camaraderie. In order to be a man, Robert sorely needs Colin; at first to be able to shape an ideal of masculinity for himself; subsequently to elevate himself (literally) over that ideal—over Colin. But he needs Colin's comradeship so that the latter can recognize Robert's elevation. Without other men above or below him, Robert cannot be a man. This statement must be taken in all its ambiguity. The need of that verticality and that struggle implies violence, the violence that provides the intensity that will be erotically charged.

In a later passage, Robert's elevation over Colin and Colin's degradation takes shape in yet another way. Robert tries to humiliate Colin by saying that he told the men they encountered on the way to the bar that Colin was his lover and this wife was very jealous. As I mentioned before, I do not think this comment is an indirect declaration of love. Robert instead makes use of the taboo on homosexuality within the homosocial community. He makes use of homophobia to shape his homosocial relationship with Colin. Eve Sedgwick has argued precisely this point about homophobia in *Between Men* (1985). Homophobia, its horrible consequences for gay men notwithstanding (which Sedgwick elaborates further in her later *The Epistemology of the Closet* [1990]), is not so much directed against homosexuals as it is in the first place a means of channeling homosocial bonds. Sedgwick defines homophobia as a mechanism that must regulate the behavior of many by the specific oppression of a few (88).

A connection between homosocial bonds and homosexual feelings does exist, but this connection is much more complex than is usually assumed. Sedwick phrases it as follows: "For a man to be a man's man is separated only by an invisible, carefully blurred, always-already-crossed line from being 'interested in men'" (1985: 89). This formulation entails the notion that homophobic homosocial men are always already sexually relating to men. At first sight, the consequence seems to be that every man is slightly homosexual. That may be true, but it explains nothing. Sedgwick's statement describes a situation, the production of which I seek to understand with McEwan's help. The intensity of the involvement with other men that the homosocial struggle entails is threatening for homosocial men because it could become entangled with homosexual desire, the very desire that homosocial homophobia is meant to exorcise.

In Robert's homosocial world, violence and sexual desire stand against each other in reversed symmetry to the relation between them in his heterosexual relationship with Caroline. I have already argued that his sexual desire, already in place, entailed violence in his marriage in a subsequent phase. Now we see, conversely, that the intensity of a violent, competitive homosocial relationship gets entangled with homosexual desire. This entanglement is represented in McEwan's novel by extremely subtle recurring hints of an allusion to, or threat, of homosexuality. One is never sure whether or not situations can be interpreted as homoerotic. And that is precisely the point: because there is within a homosocial relation a constant "threat" of homoeroticism, such a threat must be violently exorcised. Because the distinction between "to be a man's man" and "to be interested in men" is subtle and in danger of disappearing, it must be forcefully reconfirmed time and again.

The murder of Colin allegorizes, in aggrandized and dreadful but symbolic form, one such reconfirmation. The climactic passage describes a meaningful sequence of actions. The murder, the unmanning of another man, is presented here as a condition for being a man. Robert and Caroline begin to make passionate love over the dying Colin. Mary, half unconscious with the drug Caroline has put in her tea, is forced to witness this hours-long lovemaking scene. Again, the concrete details produce the precise meaning. She must be half unconscious so that she cannot act because she doesn't participate, doesn't count. Yet she must not be totally unconscious because she must watch and see. As a witness to Robert's masculinity, she must bear testimony and acknowledge his position on top. Just as passive as the old man's wife whose picture was being *taken* with the young men as passive as she, Mary must photograph in her eyes the superiority of Robert: "All through the night that followed she dreamed of moans and whispers, and sudden shouts, of figures locked and turning at her feet, churning through the little pond [of Colin's blood], calling out for joy" (130). Mary's "dreaming" in this passage gives expression to the half-unconscious state in which she witnesses Robert's and Caroline's lovemaking. The importance of vision, of the homosocial gaze, becomes acutely clear in this final passage. The homosocially based masculine identity needed for heterosexual arousal must be seen, witnessed, or it cannot be.

The order in which these actions are placed in the sequence has a radical meaning. The implication is that Robert can only be sexually aroused with his wife, be a man to her, when he first humiliates—here, kills—another man. Heterosexual male desire is thereby placed in dependency upon homosocial relations; these relations are thereby defined as inherently violent and competitive. Homosocial violence is represented as the motor that operates male heterosexual desire.

The scene contains yet another crucial aspect. When Colin feels threatened and strikes back, Caroline is wounded and smears her blood on Colin's lips. This little scene is again symbolically charged. Colin's lips are painted red. He seems to have to be visually turned into a woman before he can be adequately murdered. Precisely because Colin was initially Robert's ego-ideal, he must now be transformed. Colin is not to be murdered in his quality of ideal man but in the form of a humiliated nonman. Thus, he is feminized. At the moment that Colin turns into the image of disabled masculinity, his murder is justified. Colin's earlier interpretation of the old man who tried to usher the young men into decorative background without agency when taking his wife's picture seems to apply here to Robert's behavior, of which he, Colin, is now the victim. The photographer, Robert, tries to usher him back into unself-conscious existence.

But then, Robert drinks his victim's blood with his kiss. Through that symbolic act Robert turns into Dracula. Dracula, in Western cultural history, is a figure in whom sexual desire and anxiety are mixed. Christopher Craft has argued that Dracula's desire is not heterosexual but homoerotic. Even if his victims are women, they are not the goal of his actions. At the end of Bram Stoker's novel, Dracula confesses that his female victims are just a phase toward his goal: "'My revenge is just begun! I spread it over the centuries, and time is on my side. Your girls that you all love are mine already; and *through them you and others shall yet be mine...*'" (cited in Craft 1989: 365, emphasis by Craft). Craft argues that Dracula's sexual object choice is homosexual, but in Robert's case I oppose such an interpretation. Perhaps there is enough reason to interpret Dracula as a closeted gay, but from the perspective of my reading it might be more revealing, more radical, to interpret his ultimate interest in his female victims' partners as homosocial desire. In spite of the difference between Craft's view and mine, there is a striking similarity between the two interpretations. In both cases women are only a provisional phase, a useable means within a "higher" desire, whether the latter desire is the wish to be a man's man or to be interested in men. Homosocial violence as the motive of male heterosexual desire is how I would like to define, with McEwan, the patriarchal order. This homosocial violence within McEwan's allegory is literal and lethal violence. But his visual motifs locate the violence of the homosocial realm in the unseen, in a mode of looking. The violence originates in the gaze that disembodies and objectifies it objects.

This homosocial violence as motive of male heterosexual desire must be *seen* in order to be acknowledged. Mary, reduced to eyes only, must register it: "Caroline was settling Mary in one of the two remaining wooden chairs, arranging it *so that she sat facing the man*" (124). It is too bad, for Robert and the order he stands for, that in the end this seeing is not what she does. Instead, she becomes the interpreter of the vision she has seen, thus retrieving the agency that was taken away from her. Within the allegorical reading of the novel, she becomes the embodiment of the ideal reader, a seer, seeing through a system that can thereby become an object of critique.

REFERENCES

Bal, Mieke. 1991. *Reading Rembrandt: Beyond the Word-Image Opposition*. Cambridge: Cambridge University Press.

Bryson, Norman. 1983. *Vision and Painting: The Logic of the Gaze*. New Haven: Yale University Press.

Craft, Christopher. 1989. "'Kiss Me with Those Red Lips': Gender and Inversion in Bram Stoker's *Dracula*". In Elaine Showalter, ed., *Speaking of Gender*. New York: Routledge, Chapman and Hall, pp. 216–241.

Girard, René. 1961. *Mensonge romantique et vérité romanesque*. Paris: Grasset.

Lévi-Strauss, Claude. 1969. *The Elementary Structures of Kinship*. Trans. John Doe. Boston: Beacon Press.

McEwan, Ian. 1981. *The Comfort of Strangers*. London: Jonathan Cape.

Proust, Marcel. 1954. *A la recherche du temps perdu*. Paris: Gallimard (Pléiade).

Sedgwick, Eve Kosofsky. 1985. *Between Men: English Literature and Male Homosocial Desire*. New York: Columbia University Press.

———. 1990. *The Epistemology of the Closet*. Berkeley and Los Angeles: University of California Press.

13

"Other's Others": Spectatorship and Difference

Irit Rogoff

THE POLITICS OF VISION

Intelligibility, the context and conditions for comprehending and identifying what is being heard or viewed, is a primary focus of current discussions of spectatorship and difference. "It is not difficult," says Chris Berry in *A Bit on the Side*, "to understand why hearing Suleri speak as a Pakistani would imperil…her listeners' self-perception…as the subjects of a two dimensional topography based on a dichotomy of subject and object positions…. [I]f one persists in viewing the world through the hegemonic metaphor of dichotomous desire in which one is only *either* empowered subject *or* disempowered other, *hearing* Suleri speak as a Pakistani means the listener is now the disempowered other."[2]

The discussion of spectatorship *in* (rather than *and*) cultural difference concerns itself with the possible contexts for understanding and misunderstanding; for being understood and misunderstood; and for the visual erasures, excisions, reifications, and objectifications that exist throughout the locus of seeing and being seen. Broadly speaking, two critical traditions have historically converged on the apparatuses and discourses of vision and spectatorship: first, the gaze as an apparatus of investigation, verification, surveillance, and cognition that has served to sustain the traditions of Western post-enlightenment scientificity and early modern technologies. Second, the gaze as desire, which splits spectatorship into the arena of desiring subjects and desired objects, a separation increasingly tempered by the slippages between the ever-eroding boundaries of exclusive objecthood and coherent subjecthood.

I know I've told you of how tired I was when I first came here of being asked where I came from. I say "Pakistan" and people think I am saying "Boston."

Sara Suleri, *Meatless Days*[1]

This chapter is rooted in one of the many analyses of spectatorship that have been facilitated by these two germinal critiques. Its subject is intelligibility at the level of vision at the more recently recognized intersections of both sexual and cultural difference. Its material field is the arena of what has come to be called visual culture; the information, desires, and encoded values that circulate throughout every level of culture in the form of visual representations. This insistence on a named arena, visual culture, serves to differentiate that culture from the epistemological fields of art history, film history, and so on, for it signals an understanding that conceptualizations of "other" or of "value" form part of the field of inquiry rather than being added as categories to interrogate and revise the status of existing corpuses of historical materials.

When training as art historians in the era of connoisseurship, we were instructed in staring at pictures. It was deemed that the harder we looked, the more would be revealed to us. Meanings, contexts, and values were submerged in the planes, textures, shades, and compositions that determined both canonical excellence and, of course, material value. Later on, when teaching in art history departments, every doubt and complaint voiced about a student's lack of intellectual curiosity or narrow or overly literal perception of the field of study was countered by the phrase, "Oh, but he/she has a good eye." Visual culture therefore replaces the regime of the "good eye" with an understanding of embodied knowledge, of disputed meanings, of the formation of scholastic discourses of material value, of viewing subject positions within culture, and of the role of vision in the formation of structures of desire. The term "other" functions here as a code that signals the conscious split within the formations of both discourse and desire, as it signals a viewing position situated outside the parameters of institutionalized epistemic structures. In the process of problematizing and theorizing the concept of the "other" we have developed a wide range of critical knowledge on culture, science, subjectivity, writing, visual representation, social institutions, and so on. This knowledge has been framed and furthered by postmodern theory which has examined the construction of the "other" in at least three overlapping forms: as an internal split in the subject, as the feminine other of sexual difference, and as the Third World or diasporic other mapped through colonialism and displacement—"the 'new' subject in history."[3]

It is, however, feminism and cultural/racial difference that represent the *lived* subjectivities that postmodernism theorizes and assists in deploying politically; in Teresa de Lauretis's words, "an active construction and discursively mediated political interpretation of one's history."[4] In order to avoid the vagueness, not to mention the stultifying binarism, that is brought about by designating as "other" all that is not self, it seems appropriate to return to Michel de Certeau's formulation of "intelligibility" when he argues in relation to the writing of any history that "a structure belonging to the Modern Western culture can doubtless be seen in this *(any activity of)* historiography; intelligibility is established through a relation with the other, it moves (or 'progresses') by changing what it makes of its 'other'—the Indian, the past, the 'people', the mad, the child, the Third World."[5]

This formulation means that we have at our disposal two major characterizations of otherness: sexual difference and cultural or racial difference, each accompanied by numerous models of analysis with which to interrogate the world, its visual structures of representation, and its institutionalized codes. How do these categories intersect, how do they inform each other's concept of difference, and how are the images of women within these categories of difference controlled? Those are the questions that I would like to ask here, viewed and organized within the framework of contemporary visual-arts practices.

The Kodak advertisement (Figure 13.1) deploys the woman of color as an icon of primitive savagery that presumably somehow serves to release true "color" from the constraints of civilization and onto the celluloid film being marketed. It is an example of double otherness in which the two categories of otherness enhance one another to a point of ludicrousness. Here geographical distance and cultural exoticism is further "othered" by the fact that it is an image of a woman whose face is marked by the artifice of brilliant, iridescent stripes of blue, green, and gold. The notion of captivity here functions via a long chain of sliding signifiers from the capturing of memories on film to captive natives to the captured status of aesthetic objects such as pictures. Identifying the spectatorial context in which the image becomes intelligible alerts us that this garish "coloredness" is equally the necessary construct for the establishment of whiteness. It brings to mind Julie Burchill's lovely and overlooked book *Girls on Film*, in which she says, "What does it say about racial purity that the best blondes (Jean Harlowe, Marilyn Monroe, Brigitte Bardot) have always been brunettes? I think that it means that we are not as white as we think, not as white as we want to be."[6] The construction of white women as a performative ultrawhite femininity functions within a structure of otherness in which the most profound anxiety is that one can never be white enough, masculine enough, heterosexual enough, or middle class/respectable enough.[7] As its other white-ness requires something just as fabulously, garishly, and artificially tinted and adorned as is the proverbial blond bombshell within its own representational structures. At the opposite end of the spectrum we have Carrie Mae Weems's *Black Woman with Chicken* from a series titled *JOKES* 1987 (Figure 13.2), in which the stereotypes of conventional representations of women of color in gen-eral, and African-American women within U.S. culture in particular, are confronted in their own terms by using the degrading and parodic stereotypes against themselves. The shift occurs with an *internal* splitting of a previously unified image: the woman in Weems's photo stares contempla-tively at the drumstick in her hand, thereby breaking the cultural link through which they previ-ously defined one another. In an essay titled "The Congo Floods the Acropolis," Sarat Maharj claims that "the drive behind Black Art's oppositional mode seems to be the desire to find some stance outside the prevailing system of representation from which to impeach or castigate it, from which to overturn and transform its way of viewing, of picturing self and other. But such an out-side standpoint, it would appear, is not so much found ready made 'out there' as it has to be con-structed from within. It has to be forged quite paradoxically, from the 'inside', out of the elements of the very system of representation it seeks to go beyond."[8]

Without assuming that the codes can actually be broken and that redemptive action can be taken against dominant modes of representation, it nevertheless seems clear that the need to appro-priate a gaze, a look that has objectified different groups in different ways, and the need to claim a place, a location from which to deploy that gaze, are the real issues at stake.

Among the many female investigators, bearers of a newly legitimate curious, investigative gaze, who are now flooding the world of detective fiction we find Blanche White, the heroine of Barbara Neely's recent mysteries. Blanche cleans houses in a small town in North Carolina; she is poor; she is large; she is black; and at the moment at which we first meet her she is also on the run from the police on a minor charge of bounced checks and is using her supposedly invisible cover as housemaid to hide out in the house of some bizarrely Gothic rich people:

> "And please remember, just a hint of starch in Mr. Everett's shirts."
>
> For one brief moment their eyes actually met. Blanche was the first to look away. "Yes, ma'am."
>
> After Grace left the kitchen, Blanche sat down at the table. Was it just the old race thing that had thrown her off when her eyes met Grace's? Her neighbor Wilma's father said he'd never in his adult life looked a white person in the eye.
>
> He'd grown up in the days when such an act very often ended with the black person's charred body hanging from a tree. For many years Blanche worried that it was fear which sometimes made her reluctant to meet white people's eyes, particularly on days when she had the lonelies or the unspecified blues. She'd come to understand that her desire was to avoid pain, a pain so old, so deep, its memory was carried not in her mind but in her bones. Some days she simply did not want to look into the eyes of people likely raised to hate, disdain or fear anyone who looked like her.[9]

A similar set of spectatorial dynamics is theorized by bell hooks in a recent article titled "The Oppositional Gaze":

> When thinking about Black female spectators I remember being punished as a child for staring, for those hard, intense, direct looks children would give grown-ups, looks that were seen as confrontational, as gestures of resistance, challenges to authority. Amazed the first

time I read in history classes that white slave owners punished enslaved black people for looking—the politics of slavery, of racialized power relations were such that the slaves were denied their right to gaze. Since I knew as a child that the dominating power adults exercised over me and my gaze was never so absolute that I did nor dare to look, to sneak a peep, to stare dangerously, I knew that the slaves had looked. That all attempts to repress our/black people's right to gaze had produced in us an overwhelming longing to look, to sneak a peep, a rebellious desire, an oppositional gaze, a "black look."[10]

Thus, the connection between legitimate ownership of a designated place, a location of belonging, and the right to look is made within these texts' very different voices. It is fairly clear to me that the shift from looking away, to hazarding a look, to looking on, to looking back within the structures of representation has taken place in direct relation to the processes of the naming of territories of identity, to the possession of an intelligible place from which to look.

What I would wish for is the possibility of taking up two of feminist theory's major concerns, the politics of location and the theorization of spectatorship, and positioning them at the intersection of the mutually reinforcing operations of racism and sexism. For as African-American feminist theorist Valerie Smith has said, "As gender and race taken separately determine the conditions not only of oppression but also of liberation, so too does the interplay between these categories give rise to its own conception of liberation."[11] The manipulation of such intersections surrounds us daily in the world of advertising and the fantasies it constructs. In order to establish what is at stake and to show that these two categories of sexual and racial otherness are used blatantly to construct one another, we must chart how these images deploy and visually encode the construction of sexual and cultural otherness as forms of commodity fetishism within the advertising and fashion industries. Having marked the uses of these conjunctions we can proceed to discuss the work of several women who occupy the position of "other's others" and who use it in order to formulate interesting questions regarding the conjunctions of gender, race, and representation; the processes of looking; and the processes of historicizing the self, a spectatorial repositioning at the intersections of two monumental critiques of Western patriarchal culture

In the numerous examples of advertising culture we can discern the conjunctions of female sexuality with ahistoricity and wildness. Jungle images and references work to position female sexuality as the irrational other, the seductive animating force, and thus to lend allure to such mundane products as hair depilatory cream, photographic film, and mustard. A wild, primitive female sexuality serves to extract the products from their normal habitation within a commodity hierarchy and position them outside the discourses of commodity advertising, as if to argue that there are products that are within the framework of Western consumer culture. Then there are other products with magical powers that stand outside the realm of the ordinary and that require a force outside the supposedly conventionally chaste Western female invitation fully to announce themselves. Similarly, the fashion fantasies that position white women models in relation to local black cultures in exotic island locations or present black women as the quintessence of sexual freedom unharnessed by the constraints of Western culture offer a combination of wild female sexuality and a product that will unleash it. These advertising campaigns crudely reproduce both the continental and the sexual relations of colonialism. First, woman is a colonized entity. Second, her sexuality and by inference the various products it endorses are the raw materials of the colonized other that are to be exploited for Western markets. Third, she is positioned as a lesser-developed entity that in her ahistorical intuitiveness serves to strengthen the West's phallocentric perception of its own rational and educated superiority. This elevated subject position, culturally gendered as masculine, exploits the excitement and fascination of the supposedly uncontrollable wildness offered by a half-naked female sexuality draped in jungle skins but simultaneously needs to control and master it by turning it into a commodity within a system of exchange values.[12]

These are the legacies of the old colonial world order reworked in today's system of global circulation, and we find them everywhere within our culture: for example, the recent advertising campaign for the West German cigarette brand "WEST," with its endless equation of "colorful" Caribbean locals with some touristic concept of freedom. Not only does this advertising campaign operate through binaries of extremely juxtaposed otherness but it also proposes a particularly clichéd notion of freedom—freedom from the contemporary disapproval of smoking constructed as freedom from Western cultural restrictions—in order to further its cause. Thus, colorful, "free," and extremely picturesque "others" support a touristic fantasy of escape through cigarette smoking as a form of slightly "oppositional," culturally deviant behavior.

In order to put into play a creative reworking of the uses and roles of such images, we need to rethink the relation among intelligibility, location, and spectatorship. Over the past few years, as the boundaries of the traditional old world empires have destabilized and shifted positions, we have seen an emergent preoccupation with the concepts of diaspora, exile, and consequent cultural displacements, what Salman Rushdie had termed "the empire within." Its consequences have been to make impossible precisely the type of global divisions that such popular cultural practices as those described above regularly exploit. Furthermore, it is not only the loosening of old-world colonialisms and the separation of the histories of enslaved peoples from those of their enslavers but also the concrete emergence of Second World identities as a consequence of the recent disengagement of the super powers in central and eastern Europe; the movements of peoples to North America; the immigration of European Jews into the Middle East; and the recent explosive reunification of divided European historical narratives that have contributed to the vast body of thought and work attempting to grapple with issues of cultural displacement and cultural discontinuity.[13] Some of the responses to these issues and conditions within the arena of visual culture have ventured to substitute an investigation of social spatialization and of positioned spectatorship for the traditional location of culture within linear and interrelated national/cultural histories. Geographies have thus become a great deal more than the scientific location and articulation of the natural world; they are now also a euphemism for concepts of "home," "emplaced culture," and "embodied identity," which need to be broken down if the complexity of current conditions is to be engaged with and problematized within visual culture.

Following on the work of Edward Soja, Neil Smith, Rosalyn Deutsche, and others in the so-called school of postmodern geographies, I share a preoccupation with "… critical sensibility to the spatiality of social life, a practical theoretical consciousness that sees the lifeworld of being creatively located not only in the making of history but also in the construction of human geographies, the social production of space and the restless formation and reformation of geographical landscapes: social beings actively emplaced in space and time in an explicitly historical and geographical contextualisation."[14]

Geography, then, is a cognitive system dealing with the established relations of subject and place: the theoretical analysis of space allows for subjective and noncognitive rewritings of those relations, and the discourses of spectatorship provide languages for the articulation and intelligibility of specific viewed and viewing subject positions. Thus, we might replace a discussion of geography or place with the notion of "site," which is fluid and contingent and in which discourses of place, space, positionality, and vision are mutually informing and constitutive. Contrary to readings that conflate geographies and identities and link both to a historical determination of the homogeneous, collective, and shared nature of cultural enterprise, the following discussion posits the strategic function of cultural displacement and dislocation and the ways in which these are pictorially constructed and signified. Furthermore, it argues that these processes of unsettling geographic, spatial, and spectatorial cultural identity are always, though with varying degrees of consciousness, gender coded and differentiated. This "site" is not only the one in which one is located and viewed in relation to the world but also the one from which one looks out at the world as bearer of a located gaze.

THE EMPIRE OF ART

The contingency of sites is always in relation to a fixity that they are working to oppose or to bring to critical vision and recognition. When Ana Mendieta positioned her works in the hills around Oaxaca or the caves in the vicinity of Havana, she was engaging with the perimeters of "the Empire of Art," that is, the colonial relations, mediated through a complex net of market, aesthetic, and national economies, between New York and the rest of the world. Mendieta was born in Cuba in 1949, emigrated to the United States in 1956, was educated in Iowa, lived in New York and Rome, and was brutally murdered in her New York home in 1985. Both her death and the subsequent trial and acquittal of her husband, the well-known minimalist sculptor Carl Andre, on charges of her murder were subjected to an exceptionally racist sensationalization by the New York press. "The art establishment," one article claimed, "is coming down on Andre's side." "There's a whispering campaign." "Here's this loony Cuban, and what can you expect?"

The possibility of suicide was also discounted by all of the articles that appeared immediately after Mendieta's death; the consensus was that she was "too ambitious, too pushy" to do herself in. From these articles and many others that have attempted since 1985 to deal with the unclear circumstances of Ana Mendieta's death, it would seem that both her life and her death have somehow been contained within a very particular geographical location, that of the art world. Though the art world cannot claim for itself a fixed and concrete location, a mapped terrain with distinct boundaries, it is nevertheless a world unto itself with a distinct cultural and linguistic tradition and a vehement sense of territoriality.

In attempting to spatialize the cultural narrative that has emerged around the work, life, and death of Ana Mendieta, I claim that these things have been constructed out of a set of territorial imperatives that continue to privilege a Eurocentric, urban, and commodity-oriented artistic culture whose center, it is claimed, is the New York art world. Mendieta herself, Cuban, female, a conceptual artist working in geographically peripheral areas, not only rejected such centrist organizing principles but sought to replace them with alternative sites and spectatorial positions that brought together natural topographies with the landscape of a female body imposed, inserted, or cast upon them. The press's folkloric location of her work and her life has served to characterize it in a particular way reserved for the defiant outsider. By using sensationalized versions of her biographical narratives it has served to make her work "unintelligible" in the terms that de Certeau proposes for the business of historical chronicling. By invoking the concept of geography, what Edward Soja terms "the politicized spatiality of social life,"[15] I am attempting to reframe or relocate her work within a cultural sphere that is polycentric and multicultural rather than centrist and hierarchical. Mendieta's process of deterritorialization had been affected through a framework of feminism, Third World cultural politics, and First World avant-garde art practices of the late 1970s and early 1980s. The relation of these elements to the great traditions and to her own work went through a series of sharp dislocations, which were brought to an abrupt halt by her violent death in 1985. The scope of the project she had begun was enormous, and it can only be seen as partially completed, but transience and discontinuity are inscribed in every aspect of the project, and its untimely ending does not in any way diminish or qualify its significance. Both her premature death and her declared state of exile can, in hindsight, work in a derogatory way to sentimentalize readings of her work rather than toward a recognition of the critiques of concepts of time and space as traditional cultural values, which she was working to deconstruct.

Mendieta's work in the last decade of her life had been closely bound to the earth. She worked through tracing the silhouette of her body on earth, sand, tree trunks, and fields in the environs of Iowa City, where she had done her studies, and in the Oaxaca region of Mexico and the hills of Jaruco near the city of Havana, Cuba. The works incorporate a rich variety of materials, including gunpowder, fire, wood, paint mixed with blood, cloth, metal foils, and many others. Some of these have been eased *in situ* with a great delicacy that works to echo the existent lines of rock or earth formations, and others have been etched through blasting with gunpowder or set up by fire with the intention of imposing their form on the landscape through extreme contrast. Free-standing silhouettes raised high against the skyline and set alight like the military banners of ancient armies on the march served to illuminate and transform the horizon for a series of eerie moments and then collapsed into small piles of ashes and charred fragments.

The transient status of the works, sites abandoned to either destruction or to change according to climatic and other conditions, echoes other states of transience linked to an earth that defines everything but cannot be adhered to in any way. They function like a contemporary production of site-specific archaeology that proceeds to play havoc with conventional notions of cultural time, of past and present; yet, in defying cultural time as a progressive sequence they do not attempt to impose some other nonspecific notion of timelessness.

The project that Mendieta embarked on could best be described through Deleuze and Guattari's introduction of a parallel concept to "Deterritorialisation," that of "Reterritorialisation." As Caren Kaplan understands this conception, its value "lies in the paradoxical movement between minor and major—a refusal to admit either position as final or static. The issue is positionality. In modern autobiographical discourses, for example, the self that is constructed is often construed to be evolving in a linear fashion from a stable place of origin towards a substantial present. In postmodern autobiographical writing such a singular linear construction of the self is often untenable or, at the very least, in tension with competing issues…. Much of contemporary feminist theory proposes a strategy of reading and analysis of positionality similar to Deleuze and Guattari's conception of 'becoming minor.'"[16]

If the status of works is determined by viewing and interpretative communities, what is the position of works that are strategically denied a predetermined viewing position? Are they contained within a culturally determined spectatorial regime, and is it possible ever to leave that regime in one form or another?

To begin with, Mendieta's works were made predominantly outdoors and remained there except for their photographic representations, thus negating the cultural boundaries in which works of art are produced and displayed: studios, galleries, museums. This placement was in clear defiance of the art world's obsessive concern with "the center" out of which small colonial offshoots could be tolerated, but no more. In the immortal words of art dealer Joe Helman, "If your work is traded in Prague, Bogota, Madrid, Paris and L.A. but not New York—you're a provincial artist. But if you're traded in New York and anywhere else, you're international."[17] Thus, the issues of cultural centrality and marginality take on a new twist with this emphasis on the siting of the work as an index of its value. Mendieta, who was culturally displaced between her Latin heritage and her American education and who increasingly attempted to employ models of analysis gleaned from Third World feminism in her own Western artistic practice, also displaced herself in relation to the art world by making ephemeral objects that were exhibited in distant and little-known rural spots. Mendieta's process of reterritorialization, of constructing what Edward Said characterizes as "a new world to rule," of making a collective gendered history rooted in a particular Latin American tradition and then consciously displaced again and again, is attractive precisely because it points to future possibilities rather than to closure. In "becoming minor," in exploring the potential that the recognition of difference and the negation of boundaries liberates at the heart of the great traditions, Ana Mendieta conferred a rich potential reworking on the condition of exile. This reworking claims the problematics of "intelligibility" as a mode for illuminating the relations between location, viewing, and the center's strategic conferral of value on those art practices that are either within its own paradigmatic boundaries or sufficiently distant from them to serve as a defining "other." The limitation of such strategic disruptions is their romantic entertaining of precisely "other worlds to rule," the possibility of shifting viewing positions but not the languages of representation themselves.

VISUALLY DISPUTED IDENTITIES

There are many radical differences between the artists I am discussing: some are generational, others have to do with media and artistic practices or with the access to and deployment of theoretically informed discourses. Not least, there is a considerable historical difference in the degree of self-consciousness now permitted by a cultural world in which, as Coco Fusco says, "the outside is in." But they serve the purpose of indicating the increasing understanding by several generations of artists that displacement, intelligibility, and the structures of spectatorship are mutually constitutive, and they also exemplify the processes by which these interventions have informed and sustained one another.

If the representations of geographies, as in Mendieta's codification of her own body as an index of a countergeography, Mitra Tabrizian's imaging of black culture in postempire, postsocialist London, or Yong Soon Min's meditations on the pressures on Asian women to assimilate into North American culture, do not work toward the signification of traditionally identified affiliations and locations, perhaps their resistance works toward a revised understanding of identity in the field of vision. Traditionally, coherent cultural identity has been seen as transcending such aspects of difference as gender or language while anchored in a shared participation in an overall historical narrative. Introducing these representations as further degrees of inherent difference with clear cultural manifestations may help to redefine positionality away from the traditional concept of rootedness within one specific and coherent given culture. How to make the invisible fragmentation of the subject, which works against traditions of cultural coherency, visible is the question being asked by many contemporary critics, and how to do so within the inherited language of signification and therefore disrupt its supposedly simple legibility is equally the subject of much contemporary artistic practice. In a recent piece which attempts to frame some of the issues related to the interrogation of identities between postmodern and postcolonial culture, Homi Bhabha speculates:

> It is this familiar, Postmodernist space of the *Other* (in the process of identification) that develops a graphic historical and cultural specificity in the splitting of the postcolonial or migrant subject. In place of the I'—institutionalized in the visionary, authorial ideologies of Engl. Lit. or the notion of 'experience' in the empiricist accounts of slave history—there emerges the challenge to see what is invisible; the look which cannot 'see me', a certain problem of the object, of the gaze which constitutes a problematic 'referent' for the language of the self.... What is transformed in the postmodern perspective is not simply the 'image' of the person, but an interrogation of the discursive and disciplinary place from which questions of identity are strategically and institutionally posed.'[18]

Mitra Tabrizian's series of the late 1980s, *The Blues*, comprises both large-scale photographs and enormous billboards commissioned by the city of Newcastle-on-Tyne to be displayed in its public spaces over a period of six weeks. Tabrizian, a photographer and currently a filmmaker, an

Iranian working in London, locates her images in the subterranean youth culture of the huge metropolis, in its postempire phase and its Thatcherite postsocialist culture of growing racism and indifference to the acute social problems that an interracial society is bound to go through in its first decades. The title *The Blues* is used here as a metaphor signifying the black voice—a voice of resistance, of disruption, of mood dominating fact. The work uses the codes of movie posters as a popular form, atmospherically staged in perfect moody detail, to construct in each "untold story" a critical moment in the confrontation between black and white. What the black man is confronting is the state of whiteness, the absence of an address, the fear and panic brought on by being viewed through stereotypes. "This stereotype," says Homi Bhabha, "is not a simplification because it is a false representation of a given reality. It is a falsification because it is an arrested, fixated form of representation…. [T]he legends, stories, histories and anecdotes of a colonial culture offer the subject a primordial Either/Or. *Either* the black is fixed in a consciousness of the body as representing a 'negative difference' to the white, *or* the black is fetishized disavowing that 'negative difference.'"[19]

The color blue is also an integral part of the mise-en-scène of crime movies, of the social and erotic disruption of conventional lives that characterizes the disturbing effects of "film noir." No matter what position the black man is put in in such scenes—under police interrogation, in prison, in a low-paid job, in being an invader—the black man questions the white man's identity. Yet the black voice is still a black man's voice, and the visually codified image not being looked at and the gaze being avoided are those of black men. Part of the insidiousness of the structure of the stereotype is that it contains its activity in relations between men positioned as an oscillation between knowledge and disavowal, pleasure and unpleasure. So the work begins with the confrontation between men and ends up with the encounter between the black man and the black woman. By setting up the unlooking, unpleasure, nonaddress as a mise-en-scène between a black man and a black woman on the move, a woman with a suitcase and an identity not fixed by stereotype but in the process of formation, Tabrizian is attempting to break up the binary and introduce difference; "difference takes us elsewhere," in Tabrizian's words, "since difference is also the deferral of meaning."

What Tabrizian is working with throughout the series are theoretically informed attempts to understand the numerous layers and projections through which the "other" is constituted as the object of desire, as focus of the gaze, and as unpositioned object of spectatorial regimes and thus as the agent of an identity, that of the "one," in the process of constant formation and affirmation. Tabrizian says,

> A challenge to any racist ideology must begin with making 'visible' what is usually 'invisible'; in this case those racist traits woven into the unconscious of white society to expose the fiction of identity. What is at stake here is the crisis of identity (the ability of white culture to construct a black identity which serves its own purposes and its position of power which allows it to control the representations of that identity). And what is important is the process of subjectification rather than the identification of images as positive or negative. This is certainly not the only kind of intervention. But it is one strategy that attempts to question any absolute definition of the white and of the black, the meanings of which are polarized around fixed relations of domination and of subordination, displaced from the language of history onto the language of 'nature.'[20]

At the end of *The Blues* project, in the image of a woman moving out of a space with a suitcase, we find the double bind of "other's others." Operating along the same lines that require difference as a necessary component for defining separate identity, the black as the necessary other against which white identity can come into being means that white desire in the form of racist aggression is visited upon the black by the white in pursuit of its own identity. Its parallel model, as articulated in

The Blues, is a condition in which desire is projected *onto* woman rather than being provoked by woman. What happens then when one figure, the figure of the black woman, occupies both of these positions simultaneously? Does this double loading of the visual image actually enable the production of a split sign? The spectatorial and interpretive community is left to unframe the contained narratives and to accept the visual unintelligibility of the images contained within them. What has been set up is the exact opposite of the notion of "another world to rule," a series of staged tableaux in which each language—filmic, iconographic, and spectatorial narrative—is at profound odds with the others, demanding that we relinquish the habitual dependence between narrative and vision that conditions cultural intelligibility.

Subtly different fragmentations of the female "other" as sign emerge in the work of Korean artist Yong Soon Min, who works in the United States. She is positioned between her own female identity (Asian), the dominant culture (U.S.), and the imperatives of assimilation. Min's video and photo installation *Make Me* (1990) is a play on words between the notion of a cultural remaking and the colloquial expression for possessing a woman sexually. The work explores images of women within dominant popular culture and shows them to be the exotic representatives of a fiction called "Oriental mystery" (as in a Joan Chen amaretto advertisement) as well as the embodiment of the clichés of subservient and accommodating Oriental femininity. At the same time, mass culture holds out the opportunity to "become American," to conform in every way to visual and behavioral codes of supermarket and fashion-magazine signification that belongs everywhere and no where in particular. To enact the illusory promises of assimilation is to arrive at the dubious prize doled out by dominant culture of having become a "model minority." But, as Yon Soon Min shows, even one's features are themselves constantly under attack as the visual marker of difference, and they do not go away however strong the external veneer of conformity. The combined dynamic results in one's inscription into the culture only to be used by it as a signifier of otherness. Doubly other, features and stereotypes of feminity are thus at odds with dominant visual and cultural codes. Min states,

> There is much at stake in an attempt to address the identity of a marginalized group such as Asian Americans and especially the artists and the cultural workers of this group who may perhaps be considered to be doubly marginalized. It is not simply a matter of describing the make-up or characteristics of the individual and/or collective identity of Asian Americans and their cultural production. Our cultural identity has become ever more a contested entity inundated with complex and contradictory claims of authority, authenticity, and ownership from a myriad of sources, expected and unexpected. Insofar as much of the primary struggles of Third World people are about land rights and self determination, our own determination of cultural identity here necessarily also involves a struggle—claiming a place and asserting a position in relation to dominant cultural forces—for our own cultural integrity and well being.[21]

As the site of that erasure and of the resistance against it, Yon Soon Min focuses on the female body, her own female Korean body, colonized and migrated, endlessly mystified, and celebrated for its conflicted identity until it ceases to be in any way hers. The "model-minority" project not only describes split signs by layering visual and linguistic codes, linguistic approval on top of visual unease, but makes strange the assumptions of significatory unity required by spectatorial communities.

Intelligibility, spectatorship, and the establishment of meaning and identity cannot be separated, nor can they be empirically objectified. The absolute and uncompromising confrontation of Carrie Mae Weems's photographs (*Four Black Women*) insist that a white subject looking at the image of a black subject sees "whiteness" in the process of being established through negative differentiation. Simultaneously, a black subject looking at an image of a black subject sees it through structures of identification, through the desire to negate cultural stereotypes, or through a sense of pleasure at mobilizing what bell hooks called a "Black Look." The confrontation between these two structures of spectatorship is what provides these images with their acute tension. The spectatorial regime is (re)turned onto the bearer of the gaze with questions regarding which meaning is being established and which framework of intelligibility anchors the position of viewing. The resulting self-consciousness includes both a dramatic restaging of circulating representations and narratives that sharply draw the gaze to acknowledge their familiarities as well as simple acts of removing those referents. Walking recently through an exhibition of works by Lorna Simpson (Figure 13.3) I was confronted by a taxonomy of abject gestures—the figures in these large-scale photo installations are all viewed from the back, and the spectator becomes intimately familiar with napes of necks, backs of shoulders and hands, and headless figures of supposedly generic "black women." These images of turned-away figures do not simply defy or avert the gaze of the viewer. Rather they create an acute perception of what is missing, of the inability to continue the processes of identification through the fixated forms of "negative differentiation." Not only the conditions but, more importantly, the uses of intelligibility are withdrawn from the spectators, who are consequently required to begin producing another relationality to these images of black women who are simultaneously invoked and denied.[22]

As Griselda Pollock says, "Neither veiled as enigma and mysterious other, nor punished by our foolish desire to 'assimilate' to the figures of power, we have to return a steady and resilient look at our culture. The game is not to strip away the veil and expose the truth—it is to know what masks we wear, to define the texts we perform and to accept the necessity for critical knowledge as the condition for new pleasures, a 'new language of desire.'"[23]

13.1 Kodak advertise-
ment, Exhibition guide,
Documenta 9

13.2 Carrie May Weems,
"Black Woman with Chicken"

13.3 Ana Mendieta, "Untitled"

13.6 Mitra Tabrizian, "Exchange"

13.4 Ana Mendieta, "Untitled"

13.7 Mitra Tabrizian, "The Interior"

13.5 Ana Mendieta, "Guanbancex & Guanaroca"

13.8 Mitra Tabrizian, "Her Way"

13.9 Yong Soon Min, "Assimilated Alien"

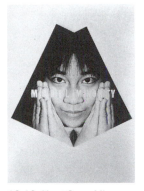

13.10 Yong Soon Min, "Model Minority"

13.11 Amaretto advertisement, *Interview* 1990

13.12 Fashion advertisement, *Allure* 1990

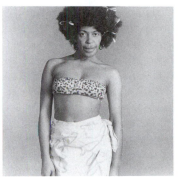

13.13–16 Carrie May Weems, "Four Black Women"

1   Sara Suleri, *Meatless Days* (Chicago: University of Chicago Press, 1988).

2   Chris Berry, *A Bit on the Side—East West Topographies of Desire* (Sydney: EM Press, 1994).

3   Abigail Solomon-Godeau, *Mistaken Identities* (Santa Barbara: University of California Santa Barbara Art Museum, 1992).

4   Teresa de Lauretis, "The Essence of the Triangle or Taking the Risk of Essentialism Seriously: Feminist Theory in Italy, the U.S. and Britain," *Differences* (Summer 1989), pp. 3–38.

5   Michel de Certeau, *The Writing of History* (New York: Columbia University Press, 1988), p. 3.

6   Julie Burchill, *Girls on Film* (London: 1979).

7   I am grateful to Vincente Raphael, my colleague in the UCHRI research project "Minority Discourse" for his constant insistence on the instability and the mutual interconnection of the aspiration to whiteness, heterosexuality, and middle-class stability.

8   Sarat Maharj, "The Congo Is Flooding the Acropolis: Black Art, Orders of Difference, Textiles," *Interrogating Identity* (New York: Grey Art Gallery, 1991).

9   Barbara Neely, *Blanche on the Lam* (New York: Penguin Books, 1992).

10 bell hooks, *Black Looks—Race and Representation*, (Boston: South End Press, 1992).

11 Valerie Smith, "Black Feminist Theory and the Representation of the 'other'" in Cheryl Wall, ed., *Changing Our Own Words* (New Brunswick, N.J.: Rutgers University Press, 1989).

12 The most rigorous and insightful analysis of advertising culture in this context remains that of Judith Williamson in *Decoding Advertisements* (London 1978) and "Woman Is an Island" in Tania Modleski, ed., *Studies in Entertainments* (Bloomington: Indiana University Press, 1986).

13 See my "Terra Infirma—Geographies, Positionalities, Identities" *Camera Austria* 42 (1993).

14 Edward Soja, preface to *Postmodern Geographies— The Reassertion of Space in Critical Social Theory* (London: Verso, 1989), p. 2.

15 Ibid.

16 Caren Kaplan "Deterritorializations: The Rewriting of Home and Exile in Western Feminist Discourse" in *Cultural Critique*, 6 (Spring, 1987), pp. 187–199.

17 Richard Woodward, "For Art, Coastal Convergences," *New York Times*, July 16th, 1989, p. 33.

18 Homi K. Bhabha, "Interrogating Identity" *Identity—The Real Me*, ICA Documents 6 (London: 1987), p. 5.

19 Homi K. Bhabha "Interrogating Identity—Frantz Fanon and the Post Colonial Prerogative," *The Location of Culture* (London and New York: 1993), p. 40.

20 Mitra Tabrizian, *Correct Distance*, (Manchester: Cornerhouse Publications, 1991).

21 Yon Soon Min, exhibition statement, *The Decade Show*, The New Museum of Contemporary Art, 1990.

22 *Lorna Simpson—For the Sake of the Viewer*, (Chicago: Museum of Contemporary Art, 1993). The catalog contains exceptional essays by Beryl Wright and Saidiya Hartman that discuss Simpson's project in great depth and in somewhat different contexts, those of African-American cultural politics, than I have chosen for my own discussion.

23 Griselda Pollock, "Veils, Mask and Mirrors," cited in Tabrizian, *Correct Distance*.

14

"Father, Can't You See I'm Filming?"

Parveen Adams

A version of this chapter was published in *Supposing the Subject*, ed. Joan Copjec (New York: Routledge, 1994).

What is it to watch a film about perversion? Does such a scenario invariably call up the scopophilia of the spectator? Indeed, does a perverse scene have an advantage over others in achieving this effect? Clearly, much cinema thinks so and plays with a repertoire of incitement not just to look but to look at a perversion. It is in general a supplementary feature of any perversion to incite a spectator, as if the aura of the perversion is made up of a consumption of vision that demands that a spectator restore the visual energy that is exhausted in the scene. "Look at me," says any representation of perversion in a structure of fascination. One's eye does not fall on such a representation; it is seized by it. It is clear that our horror and enjoyment go together. If we turn away because it is "too much," we have to ask "too much of what?"

This question leads to the thought that the enjoyment of the film spectator is perverse insofar as it obeys a regime of scopophilia, and even to the thought that perversion is enjoyable insofar as it can be compared with the pleasure of the spectator. But it seems to me that this comment precisely fails to distinguish between a pleasure and the question of *jouissance*. In order to try to sustain these distinctions I will speak about just one film—Michael Powell's *Peeping Tom*. It concerns a young man, Mark Lewis, who films women as he kills them. At the time it appeared, the film constituted something of a scandal; one reviewer suggested that it should be flushed down the

sewer. But since then it has acquired a certain critical status. Linda Williams has called it a "progressive" horror movie insofar as the woman is permitted a look.[1] And indeed, the regime and the economy of "looking" within the film and for the spectator are central issues that I want to address. How are we incorporated into the structure of looking that constitutes the story of the hero?

I want to situate the question of looking within the question of perversion and its relation to *jouissance*. The real title of the film should be "Father, Can't You See I'm Filming?" For I shall argue that the deadly filming by Mark Lewis is both a defense against and a fulfillment of the *jouissance* of the other. The film that starts by including us within the perverse scenario gradually creates a separation between us and that scenario by representing the sight and looks of two women. Yet this very representation of the women that separates us from the perversion merely hastens Mark Lewis into the enactment and culmination of its logic.

I have already referred to the Lacanian category of *jouissance*. *Jouissance*, of course, is not something that exists, or rather it exists as that which is not there, which is lost and gone forever. It is the Real, that which Lacan famously announced is impossible. But that doesn't mean it is irrelevant. It irrupts and disturbs the life of the Symbolic order. That which comes to the Symbolic from the Real, Lacan calls the *objet petit a*. It functions as a hole and as the cover for a hole; to describe it is to chart the vicissitudes of the lost object. The lost object is the connection between the symbolic and the Real, and its stake is *jouissance*. The Symbolic and the Real are two heterogenous orders, and yet the Real appears in the Symbolic; this means that though there is no direct, different relation to *jouissance*, we have to deal with the object that is the leftover of *jouissance*. I will add that that *jouissance* isn't very nice and that, unlike Mark Lewis's mother, your mother should have warned you against it.

Now, the *objet petit a* can be misrecognized and can be sought for in different ways. You can hanker after the object, thinking you can have it, in which case you fail to know that the object comes *before* desire, that it is the cause of desire. Or you can hanker after the object thinking that the other has it, which can be seen in the analysand's expectations in the analytic situation. Or the relation to the object can be one of identification, as in the perversions, most clearly exemplified by masochism where the masochist becomes, or rather therefore *is,* the object that ensures the jouissance of the other: you are, in other words, that which ensures that the other has the object. This is where analysis comes in—you can recognize, as at the end of analysis, the lack of the object in the other, in other words, that the other is incomplete and does not have the object either. En route to that point, you can identify with the fall of the object as in the *passage à l'acte,* as did the young homosexual patient of Freud's when she jumped onto the railway cutting. Or by contrast, in acting out, you can seek direct access to the object and to *jouissance,* seeking to have the object in reality. This approach differs from merely hankering after the object in reality because it partakes of that strangeness that made Lacan identify the presence of the Real in the Symbolic.

This discussion shows that the subject is partially determined by these relations to the object. Hopefully, analysis undoes many relations to the object and permits a separation from the object. Perversions such as that which the film unfolds would resist any such separation, so the spectator of such a film may well be placed in an interesting relation to the object.

First, let me tell you something about the film. *Peeping Tom* is the story of a young man, Mark Lewis, who films and who works in a studio as a focus puller. His own cinecamera, from which he is never separated, is a special object. With it he can film the scenes that he cannot put into words. In these scenes the camera films a murder and is a murder weapon, for one of the tripod legs has a concealed blade at its tip. A victim is filmed as the blade approaches her, the subject being a study in terror. The expression of terror is amplified by the addition to the camera of a reflector, a concave mirror in which the victim watches her own terrified, distorted image and which fixes a look upon her that, as the detective remarks, far surpasses the terror normally found on a victim's face. Yet this act never quite works; *something* is not captured that would mark his own assumption of the role of director. Such a triumphant documentary eludes him; "the lights always fade too soon."

This partial and schematic story will readily support your worst fears about the kind of film *Peeping Tom* is. Is it, as Mary Ann Doane asked a decade ago, the kind of film in which, to the detriment of women, "the dominant cinema repetitively inscribes scenarios of voyeurism, internalizing or narrativising the film-spectator relationship?" In this argument the man looks and the woman isn't allowed to. Presumably the man looks at the woman, and presumably he finds satisfaction in the target. But Mark Lewis is looking for a *look* that will satisfy his looking, and yet it will not give him this satisfaction. Certainly his looking is inscribed in scenes of voyeurism and exhibitionism, but there are other inscribed scenarios of looking that are narratively constitutive of the film. In these it is the woman's look that counts, or rather, the woman's relation to the look. For the look is the object look, and it is the vicissitudes of this object that I want to follow through the film.

The title of the film, *Peeping Tom,* and the appearance of a psychiatrist who speaks of scopophilia are both necessary and misleading. If anything, at the beginning the film peeps; we peep. But Mark Lewis is primarily an exhibitionist. This is partly to do with his murdering camera with its phallic blade, but it is also because of what he aims to do, which is to produce and to steal a look. For what is the terror he produces? What does it do? It effects the division of the other to show that the other has the object. That is to say, the scene ensures the *jouissance* of the Other, which is the aim in all perversion. Now, in exhibitionism and voyeurism the object at stake is the look. When a peeping Tom looks, the circuit of the drive only closes when, by a rustle or a movement, he finds himself surprised as pure look. By contrast, the exhibitionist forces the look in the other through the division of the other. In the end, in the Lacanian doctrine the exhibitionist too identifies with the object. But its mechanism allows us to make sense of the distorting mirror in

Mark Lewis's scenario and of two crucial scenes later in the film.

It is important, whether it concerns exhibitionism or voyeurism, that the pervert's partner has an eye that is complicit, a fascinated eye. This reminds me of a story of a failed exhibitionist act told by Theodore Reik, in which the woman exclaims, "My good man! Won't you catch cold?" She looks and refuses. But what happens when the look is captured? For in seeking to divide the Other, the pervert is mounting a challenge against castration. The lack that would appear in the Other will be filled with the object. The exhibitionist's partner with the fascinated eye is complicit in this denial of castration; the look completes the other; it secures the jouissance of the other. However, it doesn't work with the woman in Reik's story, and as we shall see it doesn't work with one woman in the story of *Peeping Tom.*

So Mark Lewis, in his exhibitionist murder scenarios, attempts to experience *jouissance* directly and in this the film invites our participation. As he stalks his first two victims, we are enclosed within his camera's point of view. At this point we are one with a thousand horror films relishing the threat to the victim at the very moment we identify with her. Then the film veers away from his documentary; it cuts before the murder, and it repeats his documentary as an act of repetition and projection in his darkroom. But he does not capture what he had hoped to capture. The film shows us that, as indeed in sadomasochism, what is at stake is something quite different from pain, painful though it is. His aim is to document what Lacan calls the *angoisse* of the other, that anxiety that touches the Real and puts it in relation with the barred subject. This aim is what puts this film at the level of the problem of *jouissance* rather than the imaginary system of pleasure and unpleasure. We as spectators are implicated in this as we are put in the position of wanting to see what it is that Mark Lewis wants to see, though we do not know what he wants to do. Not only do we see through his viewfinder in the first two murder scenes but at times we share his re-viewing of the scene with him in his darkroom. Usually we see his broad back first, and the part of his body gives way to the content of the documentary that he has made, which sets up an explicit relay of looks in which we are looking together at our shared victim. However, the screen is sometimes dominated by his back at the end of his documentary, at the moment when he recognizes that he has not captured the ultimate look he wants. Then his body functions to block off the prior scene of perverse anticipation; it operates as the block on perverse seeing. In the display of the second murder there is an additional figure who acts as a second block. She has this effect for another reason, as we will see—she is blind.

The film provides part of the unfinished documentary as another related documentary. Old footage shows Mark Lewis as a boy filmed by his father, who also made documentaries. Strong lights awake the boy, who is deprived of sleep and privacy by being filmed in states of fear. His father is represented as a scientist whose study of fear has led him to film his child—awakening to find a lizard in his bedclothes, at his mother's deathbed, watching a courting couple. The footage ends with this happy monster leaving home with a second wife, leaving the boy with a gift—a camera. Obviously the camera can only shoot his father's film, and the son sets off to document a scene that essentially repeats the scene his father documented. The scene Mark Lewis tries to film, his own primordial mise-en-scène, has to do not with the usual senses of primal scene but with intolerable *jouissance.* The promise is that this production will free him once he has captured it on film. But each murder can only be a rehearsal, for the lights always fade too soon.

In effect Mark Lewis wants to make a documentary that will free him from the torment of his own life. If he can capture something on film, he will free himself. The film would document the look of terror that someone about to be murdered would exhibit if the victim not only faced death but also faced her own face at the *momento mori.* In this scenario we can see the promise of looking and its impossibility. It rests upon the idea of the *completion* of terror in which the subject and the other, killing and being killed, seeing and being seen, are incarnated in a single object, in a single impossible moment. Mark Lewis's murders rest upon the hypothesis that by killing a victim he will have enacted a sufficient sacrifice. But this is impossible, and the documentary is only a simulacrum of the documentary that awaits *him* as its completion. The attempt to mimic the Other in order to flee the other returns him to the place of victim in these sacrifices to the other. It is a scene that can only be completed when it is correctly cast, when he himself finally takes the lead.

The drama concerns the fulfillment of this logic. Two figures, a daughter and her blind mother, live in the flat below Mark Lewis and his darkroom. They precipitate a crisis in the drama and in the spectator's relation to the object look. The daughter (insofar as she mobilizes a romantic wish that is split off from his primordial scene) produces the wish in him *not* to make a victim of her; he must not see her frightened or her fate would be sealed. It is this problem that highlights the inescapability of his perversion, and it finally makes us look differently. Meanwhile, his encounter with the mother propels him into his suicide scenario and allows a break in the relay of looks the perverse scenario sets up. I will talk about the daughter first and her first meeting with Mark Lewis, which produces this something new that means that he does not want to make a victim of her. However, this something finally simply highlights the inescapability of his perverse desire. The film is not explicit about how this situation comes about, and I will try to elucidate it.

So, the first meeting. We find ourselves looking at a birthday party in full swing and at Mark Lewis looking in through the window at it. The daughter, Helen, whose twenty-first birthday party it is, rushes ingenuously into the hall to invite him in, but he pleads work and goes upstairs. We see him watching part of his unfinished documentary (the film of the first murder we have already seen) when there is a knock at the door. It is Helen with a piece of cake for him. She comes in, accepts milk to drink, and precipitously asks to see the films he's been watching—as a birthday present. They go into his darkroom, and there she learns more than she bargains for from this stranger: not only that he is the landlord of the house but that it was his father's house, and that this father was a scientist who studied the development of fear in the child. In fact, he studied it in *his* child, in Mark Lewis, and Helen is shown black-and-white documentation of this. She sees the scene with the lizard. She is frightened and demands to know what the father was trying to do. Finally a party guest comes to take her back, leaving Mark staring at the slice of cake on the table.

Something has happened of which this description gives no idea. Visually, the scene, set in his darkroom and projection room, is quite remarkable. It is dimly lit, with high contrast between shadowy, blurred spaces and the sudden violence of spotlights, with deep reds and yellows, a certain grainy quality predominating. Our eyes stumble around it just as Helen does in the dimness, and we too react to the lights Mark Lewis focuses on her with sudden violence. The scene plays upon the machinery of lighting and filming, the elements producing an echo of his scenario and a faint threat.

This interplay is far from his intent. He sits Helen down in his own director's chair, with his name on it, to watch the films of his childhood. Something makes it hard for her to be his victim, something that this scene itself produces. Despite the threatening echo, it is something other that is happening: a mutation amongst the partial outlines, shapes, dim spaces, and volumes, a mutation to do with what's happening to Mark Lewis, which we register through what is happening to us. As in a dream, our position is, as Lacan says, "profoundly that of someone who doesn't see." Which is to say that we merge with this scene just as Mark Lewis merges with Helen within it. We could say that this identification founds Mark Lewis's ego and saves Helen from his scenario.[2]

Helen is also associated with a matrix of things to do with his mother. There are clues scattered about—the milk that figures again, the knowledge that Helen's room was his mother's—but they only fall into place when we take other things into account that are less obviously about the mother, things that refer to what we might call the time of the mother, a time of the reflection in the mirror, before triangulation, a time of a nascent relation to others and its promise of tenderness. Let us call it the promise of the humanization of this monster, Mark Lewis.

These scattered clues include Mark Lewis looking in through the ground-floor window of his own house at the party—what is so familiar to all and so desperately foreign to him—looking in at chatter, laughter, gaiety. He is looking into his childhood home. He finds Helen in his childhood home, literally and symbolically in the place of his childhood. But more explicit still is the gesture with which Mark Lewis, caught up in the scene in front of him, seems suspended in a response from the past. It occurs twice: once in the second meeting, when he gives her his very first twenty-first birthday present, a dragonfly brooch, and again on their way to dinner when he stands transfixed before a kissing couple in the street. In a strange gesture, he slowly and tentatively touches his chest almost without knowing it, caught up in another world. In the first scene the gesture occurs as a mirroring of Helen's movements when she holds the brooch up in one place and then another to see where it should go (and it is in the middle of this scene that he strangely asks the question, "More milk?"). It is a gesture that includes the breast, feeling, and some fledgling relation to others, a gesture that gives us the little there is of Mark Lewis outside his compulsive and near-psychotic perversion.

So Helen has a special place. He risks killing her if he photographs her, and it is a risk he cannot take. It is not just that she is linked to the faint recollections of his mother; it is that these recollections have been incorporated into something new. The romantic wish does not emerge in a direct way from these links but from an identification with Helen, an identification that founds Mark Lewis's ego. It is the type of identification that is made with someone who has the same problem of desire as oneself. This is true here insofar as the Other is absent in both cases. Helen and her mother, two women, and the absence of the father, on the one hand, and on the other Mark Lewis and his father, two men without the mother.

The way the film conveys something of this founding identification of the ego is by situating Helen at the point of intersection of the Imaginary and the Symbolic. Helen functions as the place of demand, first for a present, then for an explanation of his childhood films and also for help with photographs for the children's book she has written. She is curious and full of questions about him, an appropriate place where the Imaginary and the Symbolic might intersect. It is a place where Mark Lewis might try to tell his story, dividing himself between his ego ideal, which is the place of the camera, and this alternative place in which his nascent ego might flourish.

In this way Helen stands for normality, the release from the constant repetition of his scenario, the peace for which Mark Lewis longs. He risks killing her if he photographs her, which we can now see would also be to lose that little bit of himself that he has built through her, alongside the perverse structure. Despite this beginning of an ego, the project of making the documentary is not displaced. Rather, the effect of the encounter with Helen adds an urgent necessity to the task of finishing the documentary. It remains the only way Mark Lewis can conceive of finding his way to peace. So we must note that Helen is not the place of Mark Lewis's desire. His desire remains elsewhere; it remains coordinated with the camera and with fear, his master signifiers. Helen kisses him goodnight after dinner; he stands there and slowly raises his camera until the lens touches his lips and his eyes close. Helen kisses Mark; Mark Lewis kisses the camera.

What of the spectator in all this? These scenes with Helen work in a quite different way to capture the spectator in a play of perverse looking. They include Helen watching the films of Mark that his father made, and this time it is Helen's voyeuristic pleasure and her own recoil from it that implicate the spectator. Reynold Humphries has pointed out that when we see the father handing his son a camera:

> The child immediately starts filming those who are filming him, i.e., he points the camera at

their camera and, by extension, at the camera of the *énonciation*: at Helen, at us. For her it is too much and she asks Mark to stop the film. Her voyeuristic status is even more clearly revealed to her than at the point where he started to set up his camera to film her. Now the screen is doing what it is not meant to do: it is looking back at her/us, returning her/our look...[3]

Which is to say that the object look falls. The mechanism that produces this effect is just one of the number of ways in which Michael Powell harasses us into a certain spectatorial vigilance, a harassment that extends throughout the film. Though this vigilance concerns the separation from the object, a final intervention in the relay of perverse looks is necessary, and it is Helen who will figure narratively in the film's definitive intervention.

If Helen is the motive to hasten the complete documentary, her blind mother is the one who is the determination of its suicidal form. This mother can be quite frightening; certainly she produces panic in Mark Lewis, and there are two uncanny scenes that I want to comment on. The first is her first meeting with Mark Lewis as he calls to collect Helen for dinner. I say "uncanny" because in dwelling upon it, we dwell upon Mark Lewis's dwelling, from which he is estranged and yet in which he dwells. It is the uncanny of the maternal presence re-presented within his madhouse. It is worth dwelling on the opening moments of the scene, which Powell has organized with great care. We see Mark Lewis's face in the hall, and then we are almost aware that a veil in front of the camera is being lifted off toward the top righthand side of the screen, first revealing the mother in focus on the sofa on the bottom left of the screen and then Mark Lewis standing on the right. Watching the scene in slow motion reveals something very interesting—what we see through the veil is the face of Mark Lewis in the hall, and superimposed within that the image of the mother seated on the sofa in the living room. It is astonishing; it's there, though you can hardly see it in real time. There follows a handshake and paced heartbeats on the soundtrack as she holds on to his hand, and the beats continue even after she releases it. Again, before leaving, he looks at the back of her head knowing that she knows he is looking at her. She troubles him deeply, but we've seen nothing yet.

In his projection room, Mark Lewis is watching the film of Viv's murder; he hears a sound, and he switches on the spotlight to reveal the blind mother tripoded against the wall with her stick. This provocative presence in his inner sanctum is threatening. Mark Lewis panics in front of this woman castrated by her blindness but armed with her weapon with its pointed tip. This much is fairly obvious. But what can we say of the look? It is too simple to say that the blind cannot look. What makes the mother a terrifying figure is that she also stands for the object look, for it is not the look the pervert seeks. The aim of the pervert is to make vision and the look coincide; here, we have instead the blind woman as the look, the look when vision has been subtracted. The look is not locked into the Other; the look falls there. This, of course, is the Lacanian idea of separation.

Now, the spectator does not remain unaffected by this woman who stands for castration and the fall of the look. She interrupts our desire to see what Mark Lewis wants to see, by threatening us just as she threatens him. In or out of the perverse structure, we too are threatened by castration and the noncoincidence of vision and look. Usually, as Lacan remarks in Seminar XI,[4] the look is the object that most completely eludes castration. Here, the separation of the look unveils castration.

This woman knows and "sees." She has "seen" the darkroom through the nightly visits as she lies in her room below, and Mark Lewis remarks that she would know immediately if he were lying. Her "seeing" is the screen of knowledge that he must pierce through in order to attain his *jouissance*. When she taunts him about what it is he watches all the time, he switches on the film of Viv's murder that her abrupt entry had interrupted. Following the injunction, "Take me to your cinema," he leads this blind woman toward the screen. Perhaps this is a test: Will she see his secret or will the murder documentary bring reassurance of the truth of *jouissance* and the lie of castration? The test fails him, for the documentary reveals the failure of another "opportunity" and he moans that the lights always fade too soon.

But this test also fails the spectator, though not for the same reasons. Remember, we have just seen Mark Lewis take the blind woman to his "cinema." We are there as before, looking at him looking at the screen. Usually his broad back gives way to the documentary scene he is replaying, but in this scene this does not happen, and he does not open up the space of perverse seeing and share his victim with the spectator. His unseeing back continues to occupy a large part of the screen, and the usual relay of looks is interrupted. Moreover, this time there is one more spectator—we are in fact also looking at the blind woman's back as she faces the image of the second victim at the point of death on Mark Lewis's screen. So what do we see? On the upper part of our screen is the upper part of the victim's face with its staring eyes, on the lower left Mark Lewis's back, and on the lower right the large, coarsely patterned cardigan and hair of the blind mother. It is with this image that the object falls. Paradoxically, we are too much in Mark Lewis's place—the victim is looking straight out at us, identifying us as the place where the camera originally was. Yet he himself is no longer in that place, since we continue to see him on the screen. Moreover, we see the woman who cannot see, yet who has her head turned inevitably to the documentary screen. The circuit of the look then is doubly disturbed. We do not occupy the place from which Mark Lewis now seeks to see what he wants to see, and the blind woman *cannot* occupy that space either. While in the place from which the film was shot, we find the perverse loop of seeing intercepted. The look falls and releases us from perverse looking by disrupting any identification with the two viewers on the screen. They become the blind spots in our wish to see. *The position of the object affects the nature of our desire.*

I cannot but develop my example from Lacan's notion of the fall of the look, which he famously illustrates in his account of Hans Holbein's *The Ambassadors*. Lacan does this through considering the anamorphic moment that allows a glimpse of the reality beyond the illusion of the painting. At the moment of turning away from this painting of worldly success, the strange shape in the foreground suddenly takes on the aspect of a skull, a reminder of mortality. The painting is shown to be merely a signifier; for a moment it fails to elude castration. Now, for Lacan anamorphosis always concerns a certain stretching and distortion, but I have argued elsewhere that Lacan's idea of anamorphosis is governed by a phallic metaphor that unnecessarily restricts the conditions under which the reality beyond the signifier is indicated.[5] Here there is no question of a perspectival distortion of any kind, but nonetheless the look falls; the separation of the look unveils castration for us.

But what we learn is not for Mark Lewis. Having failed once more to document the murder scenario, he panics and grabs the available opportunity to film, which is of course the mother. He starts the camera and unsheathes the blade, but it won't work. He cannot put this woman into his exhibitionist scenario; her blindness refuses inclusion in the documentary that he continuously seeks to complete. In her case the lights have always already failed. Yes, she is frightened, but he cannot get a blind woman to *see* her own terror. How can he escalate the terror and produce the ultimate division without a response to his distorting reflector? She will always be the incomplete Other who is not invested with the object. This marks the moment when he registers that all future opportunities will end in failure. One could say that he realizes that the object will not be realized, that the *jouissance* of the other cannot be guaranteed.

On leaving, the mother talks of "instinct," and she notes dryly that it is a pity that *it* can't be photographed. Here is an other who gives him a consultation and says that "all this filming isn't healthy" and that he will have to get help, will have to talk to someone.

What is the consequence of all this? Mark Lewis tried to film and kill the mother—"It's for Helen," he says to her—in order to finish his documentary. But the encounter with the mother alters only one detail. It is still urgent to finish the documentary, but this encounter determines him to put into operation something he had known he would have to do for a long time, namely, to include himself in it as the victim. I have not mentioned the strand of the narrative that introduces detectives into the plot following the murder of a stand-in in the studios. But it is clear, psychically as well as in support of the narrative, that Mark Lewis does not commit suicide because the police are closing in on him, but rather that he ensures they close in on him because he has decided to commit suicide. They are to be included in the final documentary.

The mother and daughter have interrupted the logic of looks that prevailed for us through the murders and have served the narrative function of hastening the final suicide scene. So what about Mark Lewis? Is his last act different from the preceding ones? Does he not stop the chain of murders, the endless series of failed "opportunities," by sacrificing himself? Does he not bravely turn the cameras and the blade point on himself to face what he has hitherto avoided, his own division? Isn't there some psychical shift, some ethical step?

Let me state my thesis: there is no drama of separation from the object here, only the movement of acting out, which by itself changes nothing but which in fact completes it. Mark Lewis does not extricate himself from his dilemma by giving up the hope that after one more time his project will work. He just makes sure the one more time will be the last time; the last time *as* the one more time that works. Now, in acting out as it is understood in analysis there is a particular relation to the object. It is at one and the same time an acting *out*, outside, the scene of analysis and an acting for the Other, that is, the analyst. Something in the analyst's discourse propels the analysand into acting out. When there is a break in the analyst's discourse, the analyst is no longer there qua analyst, and we get what Lacan, in his Seminar on anxiety, calls wild transference. Acting out is transference without an analyst; when there is no one to speak to, there is only the Other to act in front of. When the analyst qua object leaves the analytic scene, the analysand looks for the object in the real.

Lacan elaborates the concept around a patient of Ernst Kris, the man who thinks he is a plagiarist. Kris reads his book and assures him he is not, but the patient goes straight out to eat cold brains and returns to tell the analyst about it. It is a piece of acting out directed at the Other, which takes place in the real and is only secondarily put into language. The only point I want to emphasize here is that Lacan reads this acting out as the patient's comment to the effect that everything Kris is saying is true but beside the point, for what concerns him, the patient, is cold brains, the remainder, the *objet petit a*. Acting out could take the form of smelling your analyst. Lacan alludes to smell *(l'odeur)* as object. What is happening if you smell your analyst is an acting out, for the Other doesn't smell.

The question of whether Mark Lewis is acting out in the suicide scene is a complex one. One could argue that all perverse scenarios are acting out and that Mark Lewis's last scenario is not essentially different from all the others. Certainly acting out in analysis can produce innumerable transitory perversions. Acting out is to a large extent like perversion not only in relation to the object but also in relation to knowledge. J.-A. Miller, in his unpublished seminar *Extimité*,[6] talks of acting out as the short-circuiting of the discourse of the analyst. The diagram for this discourse shows the four places of agent, other, product, and truth occupied respectively by the analyst as the object, the barred subject, S_1 the master signifier, and S_2 unconscious knowledge. The discourse is short-circuited when the analysand tries to obtain the object directly, in reality, without any reference to knowledge (S_1 and S_2). So acting out is by definition acting outside knowledge, and it involves a real object. The difference with analysis is that though it too involves an object as real, it also concerns knowledge, so the object has a relation to knowledge. This difference means that in analysis there is the loss of the object, and in acting out there is a solidification of the *bouchon*, for the object in Lacanian theory is both the hole and that which stops it up.

The pervert has also pierced the screen of knowledge, and in a more constant way. For the disavowal that is at the heart of all perversion, as Freud showed, is not just a disavowal of the fact that the mother does not have the penis. It is also a disavowal of the lack of knowledge that preceded the sight of that absence. Jean Clavreul has elaborated this point with care in his article "The Perverse Couple." He argues that a lack of knowledge causes the child to look in the first place: the lack of knowledge as the cause of the scopophilic drive. What is disavowed is that the child did not know and wanted to know, which in turn means that the father is not recognized as having the knowledge before the child. This is how the pervert occupies the position of one who will never again be deprived of knowledge, particularly knowledge about eroticism. Then, as Clavreul says, "This knowledge about eroticism feels assured of obtaining the other's *jouissance* under any circumstances."[7]

We saw earlier that what the pervert seeks is an eye that is complicit with him, that will turn a blind eye to what is happening, that will remain fascinated and seduced. It is made possible precisely by the short-circuiting of the dimension of knowledge that is coordinated with the Other.

So in a sense the pervert is already, always, in the place of the analysand who acts out outside the Other and yet for the Other. The last scenario is not distinguished from the others by virtue of being a piece of acting out. Mark Lewis remains a pervert to his deadly end. If anything marks the final scenes, then, it must be its *difference* from acting out. Now, if the suicide scene is pure acting out, the scene with Helen that immediately precedes it is quite different. It is the revelation of the distorting mirror, not just to Helen but for the first time to us. Helen has changed something in Mark Lewis concerning what he desires his relation to knowledge to be. Mark Lewis is doomed, yet there was something in his life he managed to preserve outside this doom. It is in this scene that Mark Lewis, at the limit of temptation, even while utilizing the very instruments of his enjoyment, does not seek complicity from Helen. Hers is an eye that he wishes *not* to fascinate and seduce. He tells his pervert's secret, and he knows she will not turn a blind eye. There is no threat to Helen in this scene when he holds the blade at her throat. It is his telling his story in the only way he can—fitfully and in large part in images and actions; but it is a telling all the same, a telling the blind mother had bade him do. So in addition to the documentary he is about to complete, he leaves a story behind. The pity of it is that it in no way diminishes his own disavowal of knowledge. His acting out remains a one-way ticket with no way back to the Symbolic. Perhaps if Mark Lewis now knows something new, it is that his documentary can never be his return ticket to the Symbolic. The intervention of the women represents the fact that his act, killing, is only a postponement of his destiny. So he goes to meet his solution, his death, and thus to meet his maker, his father. As the screen darkens, a small voice says, "Goodnight daddy; hold my hand."

These are the last words in the film; mine, however, must be about Helen and her part in the scene where she is told the story and confronted with her own distorted reflection in the mirror. Clearly, she survives castration. The mirror is like the Medusa's head, and though Helen has to look at it, she then turns her head away. The fascination of the image fails; Helen is not petrified. She is not stiff with either terror or enjoyment. She fails to be the pervert's partner; she effects a separation from the perverse scenario. The way in which this is achieved also means that we, as spectators, are freed from Mark Lewis's scenario. Once again this freeing occurs through the fall of the object. Helen awaits Mark in his darkroom, and curious as she is, she turns on the projector. We realize what she is looking at as her face registers first disbelief, then dawning horror, and finally a choking fear. Mark Lewis enters and fiercely demands that he not see her fear. He agitatedly turns on a whole bank of sound tapes to satisfy her curiosity with his cries and screams when he was five, seven.... This is the first time that the sound that complements his father's documentary footage has been referred to. And he further tells Helen that all the rooms in the house were and still are wired for sound. Then, on her insistence, he shows her the secret of his scenario—not just the blade but the concave mirror in which we clearly see Helen's grotesquely distorted image. Simultaneously we hear a dreadful cry such as his first victim had emitted. But Helen is mute, and the cry resounds as his own childhood terror in his father's "scientific" scenarios. It is in the gap between her terror and his, between her grotesque reflection and his bloodcurdling cry, that the object falls. A space bursts open in the seamless scenario, which is too close, too present, too full. Our drama is over. Mark Lewis no longer threatens Helen or the spectator. What is left is his enactment of the remnants of the perverse scenario, starring an old Mark Lewis.

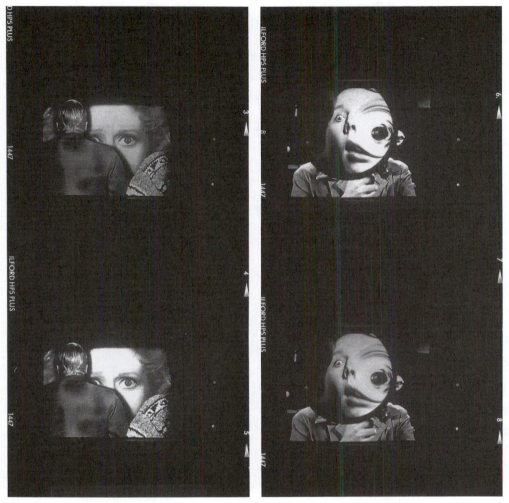

14.1   14.2

1   Linda Williams, "When the Woman Looks," in Mary
    Ann Doane, Patricia Mellencamp, and Linda Williams,
    eds., *Re-Vision* (Washington: American Film Institute,
    1984).

2   I am grateful to Gerry Sullivan for drawing my attention
    to the passages on André Gide and his choice of love
    object in Lacan's unpublished Seminar, " The
    Formations of the Unconcious," *Seminar V,*
    1957–1958.

3   Reynold Humphries, "*Peeping Tom: Voyeurism, the
    Camera and the Spectator,*" *Film Reader* 193–200
    (1980).

4   Jacques Lacan, *The Four Fundamental Concepts of
    Psychoanalysis,* trans. Alan Sheridan (London: Hogarth
    Press and the Institute of Psychoanalysis, 1977).

5   See "The Three (Dis)Graces," in P. Adams, *The
    Emptiness of the Image* (London: Routledge, 1995).

6   The *Extimité* seminar was given by J.-A. Miller in
    1985–1986.

7   Jean Clavreul, "The Perverse Couple," in
    S. Schneiderman, ed., *Returning to Freud* (New Haven:
    Yale University Press, 1980).

In the standard positivist account (which nobody, not even the positivists, believed for very long) the eye is a passive organ that receives information and honorably transmits it. The contrasting view is that sight is shaped culturally and linguistically and that there is far more to seeing than meets the eye. There are some who hold the not unreasonable belief that both are true. One such is Martin Jay.

At the beginning of his *Downcast Eyes*, Jay suggests that some physiological explanation of human visual experience needs to sit alongside the culturalist one. In fact, everyone Jay discusses is culturalist, but some are more culturalist than others. The most culturalist of all is Marx Wartosfsky, who believes that all perception is shaped by historical changes.[1] Jay opts for the more modulated view, which allows for some physiological explanation of vision within a cultural one. Still, he notes that there are difficulties in specifying the relation between the physiological and cultural accounts. I suggest that these difficulties become especially acute when it comes to the notion of the gaze.

The gaze may be a powerful force, and yet it is not a force at all. It is immaterial, symbolic indeed, "metaphorical." There has been no physical account of the gaze, in the West at any rate, since the theory of extramission was set aside. This idea held that rays were emitted from the eyes: the eye did not only receive light rays; it gave them out. Jay, in his encyclopedic study, notes that while the theory

> has long since been discredited, it expressed a symbolic truth. For the eye...can clearly project, signal, and emit emotions with remarkable power. Common phrases such as 'a piercing or penetrating gaze,' 'melting eyes,' 'a come-hither look,' or 'casting a cold eye,' all capture this ability with striking vividness.[2]

But how is it that only a symbolic truth is expressed here? Precisely how does the eye convey what it conveys if it does not do so by active physical means? My interest here is not in defending the theory of extramission but in suggesting, as I will later, that it was dismissed on grounds that were far too thin. Moreover, the theory of extramission (and with it notions of an active eye) was dropped at a specific historical moment (although it resurfaces in a different guise in Freud's discussion of sight and Lacan's of the gaze). It was the demands of the moment as much as the rigors of experimentation that decided the fate of extramission. My main concern is with situating this historical moment in a broader process whose contours I have tried to explain elsewhere.[3] This concern makes this chapter less of an "afterword" than an idiosyncratic reflection on certain contributions to this collection as well as on Jay's own book, *Downcast Eyes*. If I give more weight to the contributors who offered historical perspectives, it is because my focus is on historical process.

From the standpoint adopted here, modern Western history has profound consequences for how we view the physical, energetic existence of things. In the modern era, psychical and social processes, by some strange alchemy, have an immaterial existence. If one mentions the material or physical force of psychic or social processes, one is assumed to be some kind of reductionist who thinks that the "biological" or the "physical" determine said psychical and social processes. The fact that psychical and social processes also shape more overtly physical ones is neglected.

The theory of extramission may have been a lousy theory. But in some of its manifestations, it was also a theory that did not split psychical and physical effects, as we shall see in the next section. After that I turn, through Freud, to how visual matters have come to be treated metaphorically rather than physically. Freud's work is relevant here because he also disputes that the eye is a passive receiver, and he effectively credits the active eye with a physical force. But he, like Lacan, sees the cultural eye not as an active transmitter of light; it is more an agent of darkness. The eye, or one side of the eye, to be precise, becomes something that stops us seeing. It does not, as in the extramission theory, enable us to see. In the last part of this chapter, I will situate this shift in the historical terms mentioned before. As Jay shows us, the denigration of vision means that other perspectives on sight have faded. But the paradox may be that the denigrated vision of twentieth-century thought is no metaphor but a reflection of a physical, historical reality in which we see less and disavow more.

THE THEORY OF EXTRAMISSION

The idea that there are two sides to sight is as ancient as extramission. In fact, it was a weighing-up of these two sides that predisposed Galen, the best known of the extramissionists, toward that theory rather than intromission or reception. For Galen, it was either the case that what we see transmits to us, or we know it "because our sensory power extends towards the perceived object." Meyering, in his excellent discussion, notes that as the former alternative was untenable, Galen opted for extramission. Galen's elaboration

> involves the Stoic conception of *pneuma*, an all pervasive agent composed of a mixture of air and fire. The optical pneuma flows from the seat of consciousness, the *hegemonikon*, through the (hollow!) *nervus opticus* (or optical nerve) to the eye. Upon its emergence from the eye, it immediately combines with the adjacent air and assimilates it instantaneously (just as sunlight only has to touch the upper limit of the air in order to transmit its power directly to the whole). This double instantaneous assimilation of the air to the sensitive pneuma as well as to the light from the sun transforms the air itself into a homogenous instrument of perception for the eye (just as the nerve is for the brain)...[4]

Galen was building on the Stoical tradition. He was also, despite the fact that Aristotle had founded a rival school of vision (according to Meyering), building on Plato.[5] Simon Goldhill, in his dissection of the complexities of classical vision, takes things further back, to when "the new intellectuals" (usually known by the misleadingly disparaging term 'sophists') began an inquiry into vision itself. Democritus's materialist objects, for example, based on the reception in the eye of *eidola*, 'little images,' emanating from an object, established the notion of a physical ray connecting viewer and viewed, a notion that founded an extensive intellectual tradition of optics as '*une analytique du regard*' (to use Simon's phrase)."[6]

Extramission, light from the eyes, was believed in for almost two thousand years. In the seventeenth century, the idea of extramission came to be considered absurd. The key event here was Johannes Kepler's 1604 analogy between the eye and the camera obscura.[7] Now, the camera obscura concept had been around since at least 1521,[8] and a few words on it are in order. It is the simplest image-forming system: an enclosed empty space with a small opening through which light enters. Such devices form an inverted image of relevant external objects on the internal surface opposite the opening. Relevant objects are those whose image is refracted by the light as it enters.

Until Kepler made the analogy, it was unclear whether the eye was an emitter or a receiver. But the balance of public opinion was in favor of extramission. According to Smith, "The sixteenth-century inventor of the camera obscura had to defy current opinion and state that the eye was always a receiver, never a transmitter, of rays. Ever since then the science of optics and an understanding of the eye have run parallel."[9] Kepler recognized that inverted vision held true for both eye and camera obscura and then assumed that both operated on the same receptive principle. In fact, as Gillian Beer shows in chapter 6 of this volume, the eye fell well short of the actual camera, or at least had radical differences from as well as major similarities with it. But for this knowledge we have to wait for the nineteenth-century invention of the camera proper, together with the "great advances in microscopes, telescopes.... Even as the domain of sight advanced by means of such instruments, the evidence was mounting that the eye was an uncertain instrument and men of science insecure observers."[10]

In the seventeenth century, however, before Helmholtz's evidence (which Beer dissects) showed that visual perception was inherently unreliable, the notion of the purity of the passive eye was accepted. It was thought that light, to vary Krauss's metaphor, "passes to the human brain as if it were transparent as a window pane."[11] In one of those shifts that characterizes the evolution of normal science together with conventional wisdom, the concept of extramission was rejected, and it was taken for granted that eye and camera obscura were the same—passive receivers alike.

As if sensing that an analogy was not really enough to dispense with the theory of extramission, an experiment "disproving" it would occasionally be invoked. Jay mentions this experiment in a footnote, suggesting that the belief in extramission was due to the way light shines off the eyes. "This is especially evident in certain animals. Descartes, as late as *La Dioptrique*, credited the cat with extramission for this reason. In 1704, however, an experiment showed that if a cat is immersed in water, the lack of corneal refraction prevents the eye from shining."[12] Unfortunately, though the experiment is mentioned in the literature, it is difficult to find any details of it. Anthony Smith, to whom Jay refers, is typical. Smith says that he too was unable to find a source for the experiment, but he regards it as significant, although he gives us no more information than that the cat's eyes did not shine when it was immersed because there was no corneal refraction.[13] So we do not know if the cat was alive or dead, swimming or scratching; just that it was put in water, its eyes did not shine, and the theory of extramission was discarded accordingly. Like the conviction that the eye was a camera, the willingness to believe that the immersion of the cat simultaneously doused the theory of extramission owes something, probably everything, to the historical dynamics, the contextual shifts, under discussion here. We will come back to this.

SEEING AND NOT SEEING

No sooner had extramission hit the bucket than it resurfaced in theories that emphasized the worrisome side of it (Mesmer's rays from the eyes, the anthropologist's relocation of the evil eye) and neglected the theory's concern with how perception is shaped. For, as we have seen, part of Galen's point was that the light from the eyes joins with *and shapes* the view we have of reality. This notion of perceptual modulation (which is what I think it is) of course stayed with us in various forms, but it was no longer thought of in active physical terms. The irony here is that by the mid-nineteenth century, as Beer tells us, "the invisible, instead of being placidly held just beyond the scope of sight, was newly understood as an energetic system out of which fitfully emerged that which is visible." Beer concludes her analysis of the nineteenth-century world of the invisible, and of the climate in which the human being was discovered to be "unbounded because pulsed through by process," with a prescient note on Freud's positive response to the great physicist Helmholtz. In the context of Beer's analyses of "energetics" and wave theory, "Freud's response becomes evidence of his capacity to catch the reverberations that sound most intimately in many lives of his time."[14] And in this context, we might allow that Freud's account of sight repeats something of the logic of extramission, a logic of waves and rays and invisible energetic forces that reemerges in the left field of psychoanalysis (good psychoanalysis is always in left field). Paradoxically, "sight" was the one field excluded from the nineteenth-century recuperation of the concept of waves and rays.

In Freud's account, and Lacan's after him, there are literal blind spots, things we refuse to register on our retina or which, having registered, we refuse to receive consciously. We disavow or sco-tomize them. How exactly do we do this? For Freud, seeing was an activity "that ultimately derived from touching."[15] This derivation meant that sight was an active sense. It reached out and followed the contours of its objects. It penetrated (on occasion). In Freud's writings on hysteria, the impli-cations of this view are extended. Freud always saw hysteria as a physical problem. The body expressed a symbolic truth in a hysterical symptom, but the symptom was precisely a physical expression. The question that initially fascinated Freud (and prompted his *Project for a Scientific Psychology*) was the mechanism of this physical expression. To say the same thing, he was fascinat-ed by the mechanism of repression in hysteria, for this mechanism expressed itself in a physical "turning back" against the subject's own body.

In Freud's early published work on hysteria (with Josef Breuer) he pursued the physical path of hysteria through the mechanism of the daydream. It was the *images* of the daydream, as well as the drowsy, affective state that accompanied it, that so often paved the way for the symptom. He went on to pursue hysteria through the *release* of the image of the symptom into language. But let us stay for a little with the role of the image in symptom-formation.

I have argued elsewhere that there is a necessary relation between the inward-turning imagery of hysteria (the archetype of femininity) and the aggressiveness of the gaze. In the first case, a fantasy is held before one's own eyes; it is one's own product, and it is turned inward against the self. In the case of the gaze, the fantasy is projected onto the other. It is an aggressive projection because, in Freud's terms, active seeing, the type of projective, external focusing Lacan was to call the gaze, is an expression of the drive for mastery. The drive for mastery, in turn intertwined with sadism, is also constitutive of the drive for knowledge, which Freud mentioned occasionally. Mastery, knowledge, and seeing are grouped together by Freud. He terms them the "less organic" partial drives, as distinct from the more familiar oral, anal, and phallic drives.

These "less organic" drives constitute a problem for Freud's view of reality. On the one hand, they are properties of the ego, part of the ego drives. Seeing especially is critical in perception and reality testing, and these functions pertain to the ego. On the other hand, the theory of the less organic drives was first propounded in the *Three Essays on the Theory of Sexuality* of 1905. Like all the sexual drives, seeing, knowledge, and mastery are thus fantasy-imbued. We see what we desire (hope and fear) to see as much as "what is there." Freud of course wished to keep the ego and real-ity testing clean of fantasy. As is well known, he did not succeed. What is less well known is that he first introduced the distinction between the ego drives and sexual drives in an article on hysterical blindness. In a letter to Sándor Ferenczi (December 4, 1920) Freud writes dismissively of this paper; it was no more than a contribution to a Festschrift.[16] Actually, it has something to tell us.

But my immediate interest lies in the inescapable energetic aspect of the "less organic" dri-ves, for though they are less organic, they are no less energetic. They are precisely *drives*. Like all drives, they are also directional: they have an aim. Still, the idea that the projected gaze is an ener-getic force is one thing; it is another really to think of it in physical terms. It is easier somehow to do this in the case of the inward-turning gaze because we can see the physical results of the inward-turning gaze taken to an extreme in hysterical symptoms of paralysis. When the capacity for phan-tasmatic visualization, for projected gazing, is turned back against the self it can, quite literally, hold one still.

The inward turning, or turning back against the self, of the drives of mastery, knowledge, and seeing is constitutive of femininity. It is a turning back that overlays an earlier one, when the ego is first formed. Lacan termed this process passification, understood in terms of a mirror stage. In more detail, my argument is that the ego is first formed at the hands of the mother or other through taking her imagined capacities (mastery, knowledge, and seeing) as one's own. But pre-cisely because they are her capacities, they are directed not outward but inward against the self. Just as the other looks at one, so one looks at oneself. One does not look out actively. The reversal of passivity into activity occurs when one does look out. This reversal characterizes the latency period and continues to characterize masculinity. In femininity, one looks back yet again. From this standpoint, femininity is a passification that overlays an earlier passive state; masculinity is the active state in between.

The very stillness, this constructed passivity, that marks hysteria in an extreme form and femininity in a more diluted dose, means that it would be well here to qualify the notion that Freud picks up on a Galenic, extramissionist thread that had been dropped in the seventeenth century. Freud, or rather Freud's theory, does indeed imply that a physical light of perception comes from within and shapes what we see. This theory implies this much insofar as it implies that we see everything through constructed realities, realities that are colored by the fantasies that construct us in turn. But Freud's theory also implies that this physical, perceptual force can curtail our active agency in the world as much as it can extend it. For the extramissionists, the emphasis was on the vision that comes from within. Galen himself did not have it both ways; he did not believe that the eye was passive. The light from within took us out and up to the unending stars. What I want to propose now is that there is something else that lives alongside these historical shifts, an alternative vision altogether. Freud directs us to it in a remarkable observation:

> Appropriate experiments have shown that people who are hysterically blind do nevertheless see in some sense, though not in the full sense. Excitations of the blind eye may have certain psychical consequences (for instance, they may produce affects) even though they do not become conscious. Thus hysterically blind people are only blind as far as consciousness is concerned; in their unconscious they can see (*die hysterisch Blinden sind also nur für Bewusstsein blind, im Unbewussten sind sie sehend*).[17]

Once the ego is implicated in the withholding of sight, the idea that hysterically blind people still see—"in their unconscious"—can only be explained if an alternative source of information about reality coexists with the information the ego receives through "reality testing." We have to remember here that Freud was writing in German. Strictly, "in their unconscious" means "in that of which they are unconscious." It is not that we have an unconscious; rather, we are unconscious of what we have. And "it" can be busily registering another reality, a reality other than the constructed one. I want to propose this other reality as the alternative vision that is overlain by a constructed, fantasy-imbued sight.

This other reality has been observed across time. Freud was in line with a fine tradition in outlining his two simultaneous sets of vision. Kant, in that wildest of books, *The Critique of Judgement*, said that we observe the world through imposed categories most of the time. But sometimes, for some reason, the categories are suspended. When they are, we have an experience of the "supersensible," a perspective that is not confined to a personal standpoint. This other perspective is receptive, but it is not passive. The passive and the receptive may sound the same, but they do not look alike. The heart of the difference is that the passive is historically constructed, whereas the receptive is not. By this account, the other, receptive vision becomes a symptom of another reality, a point of connection with it. It is in all of us, but we resist it. It is outside time and therefore the only thing that can disrupt time and timeliness. It is in us as an alternative to our egocentric, categorizing visual standpoint. (Today we call this standpoint the subject-centered position.)

THE VISUAL TURN (AGAIN)

If we survey the various turns in the fortunes of constructed vision, a survey prompted by Jay's own book and the chapters in this one, a fairly clear pattern emerges. When the notion of the active eye went underground it was replaced, in the seventeenth and eighteenth centuries, by the eye as passive receiver. This passive eye was not meant to be constructing anything; it received nothing less than the virtual truth. Thereafter, the predominance of this passive eye was disputed by the power of the invisible in the nineteenth century (Beer) and the power of construction, understood by some in the nineteenth century (Crary) and stressed in the twentieth (everyone).[18]

Eventually, we arrived at a position where we could recognize once more that vision was constructed, but the construction was now an inward-turning one as well as a projected gaze. This position was an advance, but its cost was the rejection of any notion of *constructed* physicality. Together with this rejection, I will suggest, goes a loss of the other reality, the alternative receptiveness manifest in another way of seeing. These things go together because the power of the constructed fantasy, the projected gaze, becomes stronger and covers over that other reality.

It remains to trace these turns in more detail. Everyone seems to agree that the seventeenth century marked a new turn. Lacan describes it as the shift from self-definition based on identification with the other: "that is I," to a definition based on assimilating all that is other to oneself: "that is me." That assimilation included the visual world. The subject did not go to visual objects; visual objects came to it. The subject did not emanate to the object; the object performed this service for the subject. I am putting things this way because in the seventeenth and eighteenth centuries there is a visual turn from active to passive seeing. On the face of it, it can seem that this turn is a move away from subject-centeredness, that it is an abdication of the subject's power if it no longer imposes its view but rather humbly receives it. However, this passive move makes the subject the center of the world: however passively it sees, it does so from its own standpoint, which also happens to be the world's center.

As Tom Conley shows us, this passive centrality is not without its critics. By building anamorphosis into his painting *The Ambassadors*, Holbein mounted his own critique of the new subject-centered perspective. Anamorphosis means having to abandon the central position in order to see something else altogether. From the central position, the subject's standpoint, *The Ambassadors* looks like two ambassadors. From the side, crouch down a little, and the painting becomes a portrait of a skull. Conley draws this perspective out in a discussion of Holbein and Lacan and the famous Renaissance discovery or rediscovery of three-dimensional perspective. On the one hand, Conley suggests that the subject-centered fixed point was born in the Renaissance with Brunelleschi's and Alberti's discovery of perspective, and that we have been trying to stand out of our own light ever since. On the other hand, there was the practical anamorphic critique of the idea that the subject's standpoint revealed all there was to be seen.

Conley uses my argument in *History After Lacan* as well as pointing to a fine critique of it. I underestimated the complexities of visualization (I am trying to redress the balance here by looking at the other "unconscious" vision, which sits alongside the constructed one). I had only considered the vision involved in fantasy and how passivity is constructed in the first place. I call this construction the foundational fantasy. At the risk of presuming on the reader's patience with more summary, I will outline this theory briefly, as it is relevant to the visual turn under discussion.

The construction of passivity depends on the construction of "fixed points." The first fixed point is brought into being by the repression of the first hallucination. On this repression depends one's sense of oneself as a subject with one's own standpoint. This repression and any subsequent repression constitutes a fixed point because repression runs counter to the hypothetical flow of energy into which we are born and of which we remain a part.[19] It is essential to the birth of a subject not only because it constitutes a fixed, still point but because of the contents of the hallucination that is first repressed. This first hallucination is that of commanding the breast (or the mother attached to it), and from this fantasy come the foundations of our being. When we imagine that we command the breast, we arrogate to ourselves the functions of intelligence, planning, and calculation and imagine the other as dumb, passive matter, an object to be directed and patronized by the subject, oneself. In other words, the foundational fantasy is also the occasion whereby ideas and matter, or (subjective) mind and (maternal, objective) body, are split. This split, paradoxically, is why we think of "fantasy" or any thought process as immaterial. Any visual fantasy of course involves images and therefore a distribution of light. That one thinks of an image in the mind's eye as somehow immaterial reflects the very prejudice I am attempting to analyze. In this connection, it is worth noting Janet Soskice's analysis of the weight given to the sensual in medieval Christian thought. She argues that this emphasis reveals a regard for the body that is lost in later writing. It is moreover a regard that extends to a regard for other physical things. In discussing that favored image of the time, the icon, she writes:

> The icon is in its own way a transformation, remaining wood and paint yet being image and saint at the same time. The physicality of the surface, the wood, the pigments, is an emblem of the physicality of the God whose veneration the icons serve. Aesthetics are informed by theological conviction. The icon is furthermore not passive to the gaze. If anything, and explicitly with the icons of the Virgin and Child, it is the worshiper who is looked upon.[20]

The tendency to think of mental processes (fantasies or pure thought) as immaterial increases over time. It remains to see why. The foundational fantasy is not only a subjective, psychical affair; it is also an historical, monolithic, or totalizing force. To state this idea more clearly: as a subjective, psychical event, the foundational fantasy is ancient, in the West at least. But there are other psychical possibilities. Until the visual turn or thereabouts, the foundational fantasy is not dominant as a belief system because its pretensions to direction and control are held in check by religious and political forms. It only becomes dominant psychically when human beings begin to deny their indebtedness in various forms: one was born free and equal in the marketplace; one owes nothing to nature, to the other, occasionally there is some debt to one's father but most certainly not one's mother. With these denials is born the illusion of autonomy. In this context, perhaps the most significant thing about the dematerialization of the active eye is that it makes us really separate from one another. If the way we see one another is no longer a way of touching, it makes us truly independent and alone.

Janet Soskice, in discussing the shift from the late medieval period to early modernism, notes Eco's argument on the move from Albertus Magnus to Saint Thomas Aquinas. For Albertus, beauty is there regardless of whether people exist or not. For Aquinas, the object's beauty is constituted in relation to a knowing subject.

Though the relevant mind-set (one's subjective standpoint is all) was critically reinforced during the Renaissance, the foundational fantasy, as a force in human affairs, only gathers steam when it has the technological means to make itself come true. The actual means to the domination of nature (as object) are necessary before the fantasy can act itself out on the larger scale, replicating and reinforcing the microcosmic version that governs our individual, highly competitive psyches. This parallelism extends to the construction of fixed points. Just as fixed points are constructed psychically through the repression of energy, so they are constructed technologically through the "repression" of nature. I mean that when nature is bound into technological forms (commodities) that cannot reenter reproduction, it is bound into fixed points. Critical for our purposes is the idea that the proliferation of fixed points on the outside, in the built environment, reinforces the fixed points, and the need for fixed points, in the psyche. Thus, this argument is dialectical. On the one hand, the subject's psyche is altered by its physical environment. On the other hand, the subject's imposition of a foundational psychical fantasy alters that environment.

But let me back up a little to Conley. Conley discusses Lacan's theory of the fixing of the letter, how we need to be tied to a certain word or sound in order to stop language perpetually sliding (and our self-concept along with it). Lacan's theory of the *point de capiton* says nothing of fixed visual points in the psyche (as in the energetic repression of hallucination) or the parallel fixed points of technology which are constructed out of and against the reproducible flow of nature. Nonetheless, the desire to fix the sliding of the signifier is symptomatic of a broader social process to which Holbein was superbly sensitive. After the seventeenth century, the new perspective was more or less fixed—so to speak—and for a time any notion of a constructed vision disappeared.

In that most visual of centuries, the eighteenth, seeing was mainly perceived as passive. This view contrasted not only with the position of the extramissionists but with the rationalist insistence (Descartes was preeminent here) on the importance of innate intuitions and, of course, reasonable deductions. In other words, while Descartes may have limited responsibility for the dualism of consciousness and matter, he at least retained the notion of an active consciousness that could construct ideas. These ideas were not all the result of perceptions imposed on the passive receiver, as they were for Francis Bacon, John Locke, Isaac Newton, whose "sensationalist" perspective gained the ascendancy in the eighteenth century. As Jay writes:

> What we have called the visual tradition of observation thus largely replaced that of speculation, once the residual active functions of the mind assigned by Locke to reflection were diminished, as they were by David Hume, Etienne Bonnet de Condillac, and other *philosophes*. Although all elements of the Cartesian attitude toward vision were not abandoned in eighteenth-century France...they were fighting a losing battle with the more uncompromising sensationalism that gained ascendancy in the late Enlightenment.[21]

Peter de Bolla, in his chapter on the *siècle des lumières*, shows that there was nonetheless a reflective notion of the gaze operating in that key philosopher of the Enlightenment, Adam Smith, who possessed a sense of positioning and perspective that parallels that of Lacan. While one sees, one is aware of oneself being seen. This awareness acts as a guarantor of one's existence, a hidden guarantee that makes it possible to occupy the phantasmatic "objective standpoint." Otherwise, I might add, the weight of passive reception might be altogether too much for the active subject. In the eighteenth century mind-set especially, this newly born narcissistic subject needs to control the action at the same time that he insists he knows the object as it really is. He knows it because he passively receives information from it. He does not try to impose his own view upon it. As I have suggested, he manages these apparently contradictory ideas by passively receiving from his own standpoint. This theory is reflected in the new obsession with landscaping and other devices which enable him to shape and enlarge the parameters of what he sees from that standpoint. From his enlarged and dominant perspective, accepting that his actual mechanism of sight is passive is not so hard.

At the same time, knowing that the object is *watching* him encourages his paranoia. Bryson's observation on the essentially paranoid nature of some Enlightenment painting is relevant here, especially when one recalls the dialectic engendered by passification. When one is the recipient of the gaze and rendered passive by it, one feels trapped and confined. One is also anxious about the intentions of the image-giver, the watcher. This anxiety is the wellspring of aggressiveness (Lacan's *aggresivité*), which relieves the subject of anxiety by projecting the affect of fear outward onto another. This projection is how we go from the inversion of capacities and drives (mastery, knowledge, seeing) to claiming them as our own—unless we are corralled into the feminine position, in which case they are once more inverted.

It would seem that by the beginning of the nineteenth century, the subject had had enough of the pressure of visual passification; never mind the fact that it had made him the center of the world. In the context of charting the waning of the Enlightenment trust in sight at the end of the eighteenth century, Jay observes, "One mark of the change was the replacement of passive sensation by a more active will as the mark of subjectivity in the philosophies dominating the early nineteenth century."[22]

This dialectic of passification and aggression intensifies as the foundational psychical fantasy makes itself materially true, physically altering how we perceive ourselves and our environment. It achieves this alteration because the physical environment we inhabit is also, quite literally, changed by our technological interactions with it. Our need to project outward changes the environment, which increases the objectifying pressure on us and in turn increases the paranoid need to control an environment which is felt as more and more threatening. What can be visually identified can be most readily controlled (see also Burgin).[23] This is Heidegger's point, and it is developed by Lacan and Foucault alike.

Part of the nineteenth-century fascination with the invisible is, I suggest, a desire to increase the sphere of control. Part of the anxiety about the invisible is that it cannot be controlled. Part of what gives a theory like extramission its paranoid feel is that it purports to describe something that cannot be seen or identified and that might even, in the case of the "evil eye," be out to get us. The trend is always to insist that whatever cannot be seen and controlled is not real. The idea that the instrument for seeing, the eye itself, has invisible properties is beyond bearing. The idea that the eye *touches* others threatens autonomy and atomism alike.[24]

The truth about paranoia is and always will be that it is prompted by the projection of one's own aggressive desires. Our paranoia increases, together with our need for visual control (of all those invisible rays), as our real aggression toward the other, and the natural world, increases. The unconscious fear is that one will be *touched* by what one has harmed. The passification dialectic has real effects on us, just as we have effects on others, and on the *physis*, the natural world.

"Vision" is denigrated in the twentieth-century thought under discussion in Jay's book and in this volume. As Jay shows us, the denigration is unjust: "sight" has not been universally privileged. But if I am right about the effects of the dialectic on the *physis* and the related tendency to think in terms that split mind and matter, it may be that we are looking past what the denigration of vision really entails. In other words, if the gaze has a physical component, if the aggression in the gaze increases in circumstances such as these in which we live, then "vision" has been physically affected and deserves its denigration. In other words, how we see changes over time. Different theories of perception and of sight may have been more true for their times than they appear with hindsight.

The idea that we see the same way at all historical points is of course untenable. Even so, we persist in thinking that, say, the Egyptians painted the eye the way they did because they were a bit thick, or the medievalists showed perspective the way they did because they were a bit slow.[25] We do not credit them with their own critiques of a subject-centered perspective, even though we are quick to spot, say, cubism's relation to subjectivity. Is it a critique? Or is it a revealing of the object to the subject in all its aspects—a revealing that saves the subject the work of walking around to look at the object's other side?

It is plain enough that the dominance of the vision that would subordinate everything to one's own standpoint is recent. Still, there is more than one vision. Freud's "unconscious" vision is an alternative to the passive ins and active outs of constructed vision. It is worth reiterating that this receptive vision is not the same as a constructed passive one. This point can be difficult to grasp. For instance, when Heidegger eulogizes the receptive passive relation to Being when compared to the activity that rules in the West, he often elides two senses of the word "receptive" (see Scheibler).[26] Once a distinction between these two forms of receptiveness or passivity is made, it becomes easier to grasp both the nature of the passification dialectic and the source of the alternative to it.

Human beings did not and do not always see out of self-centered eyes. There is another receptive vision, whose very existence disrupts the subject-centered standpoint. The point is that this other vision is at risk, it depends on unbound energy. It becomes less the more that energy is bound in a proliferation of fixed points within and without the psyche. The more such binding occurs, the less we receive of that which disrupts. Somewhere we know this, so we denigrate the constructed vision that blinds us but mistake it for all there is to sight.

One can read Jay's book overall, as one can read many of the essays in this book, as mappers or markers of how a different, receptive vision was lost, covered over by a dominating gaze. In an earlier essay of Jay's, he postulates an alternative positive vision to that described in Foucault's negative panopticism.[27] But in accord with the anti-dualist temperament of the times, he backs away in *Downcast Eyes* from the implied dualism. By the end of that fine book, Jay has enjoined a plurality of vision, a mixed bag with some goodies as well as rotten eggs. He enjoins this as an alternative to the negative notion of the gaze, the denigrated vision of twentieth-century French thought.

Of course, I have nothing against pluralities. I am prepared to say feminisms, masculinities, and even contexts. However, the theme of the duality of vision warrants more investigation. The wish to go beyond dualities does not stop a given duality from existing. Moreover, the duality, let alone plurality, of vision is something of an endangered species. One of its poles is in danger of disappearing, leaving us with a monolithic vision that is precisely negative and depressingly totalizing. We no longer receive much that disrupts, so we denigrate the vision that stops us receiving but mistake it for all there is to vision. If I am right, the disjunction between a receptive and a constructed vision (active or passive) is the source of all disruption of received views. It is the condition of pluralities. But it is a condition that depends on the existence of things that are beyond our control.

15.1 Garlic skin (detail)

15.2 Jean Fouquet, "Madonna with Child," ca 1475 (Musée Royale des Beaux-Arts), detail

15.3 A medieval gaze: Eve of Autun (cathedral of Saint-Lazare)

15.4 A medieval reflection: Statue from tomb of Saint-Lazare, Autun, detail

1 Martin Jay, *Downcast Eyes: The Denigration of Vision in Twentieth-Century French Thought* (Berkeley: University of California Press, 1993), p. 5.

2 Ibid., pp. 9–10.

3 See Teresa Brennan, *History After Lacan* (London: Routledge, 1993).

4 Theo C. Meyering, *Historical Roots of Cognitive Science: The Rise of a Cognitive Theory of Perception from Antiquity to the Nineteenth Century* (Dordrecht, Kluwer Academic Publishers, 1989). p. 26.

5 The theory of reception opposed to the theory of extramission also had to deal with the mechanism for the transmission of the visual image. One of the most imaginative solutions was that posed by Lucretius. He posited an "onion-skin" theory of perception in which the objects' "skins" floated toward the subject. Lucretius, *On the Nature of Things*, trans. R. Latham (Penguin, 1951) p. 131. (see illus 15.1)

6 See Simon Goldhill, "Refracting Classical Vision: Changing Cultures of Viewing," chapter 2 in this volume.

7 See the discussion in Nicholas J. Wade and Michael Swanston, *Visual Perception: An Introduction* (London and New York: Routledge, 1991), p. 42. The best source on the decline of the camera obscura model is Jonathan Crary *Techniques of the Observer: On Viison and Modernity in the Nineteenth Century* (Cambridge, Mass.: MIT Press, 1990).

8 See the discussion of Leonardo da Vinci's use of the device in Jay, *Downcast Eyes*, p. 65.

9 Anthony Smith, *The Body* (London: George Allen and Unwin, 1970), p. 385.

10 Gillian Beer, "'Authentic Tidings of Invisible Things': Vision and the Invisible in the Later Nineteenth Century," chapter 6 of this volume.

11 Rosalind E. Krauss, *The Originality of the Avant-Garde and Other Modernist Myths* (Cambridge, Mass.: MIT Press, 1985), p. 15.

12 Jay, *Downcast Eyes*, p. 9, n. 26.

13 Smith, *The Body*, p. 387.

14 Beer, "'Authentic Tidings of Invisible Things.'"

15 Sigmund Freud, "Instincts and Their Vicissitudes" (1915) in Sigmund Freud *The Standard Edition of the Complete Psychological Works of Sigmund Freud,* ed. James Strachey, trans. James Strachey *et al.* (London: The Hogarth Press, 1957) *SE*, vol. 14.

16 Jones, *Life*, vol. 2, p. 274. But this "*pièce d'occasion*," "On the Psychogenic Disturbances of Vision," tries to blame hysterical blindness on the sexual drives and thus keep the ego clean. However the same article will, on examination, reveal that it is also the "ego" that withholds visual information from consciousness. This means that in hysteria the ego and the sexual drives are in some way intertwined. Obviously this article predates Freud's eventual recognition of the common origin of ego-libido and object-libido in that it tries to separate the ego and sexual drives for the first time. Freud, "On the Psychogenic Disturbances of Vision" (1910) *SE,* vol. 11.

17 Ibid., p. 212.

18 Crary, *Techniques of the Observer.*

19 The theory of fixed points was already in the air in the Renaissance. For Dante, the still point of the universe was Satan's anus, which presumably held in what it had and refused to give anything out as well as refusing to let anything in.

20 Janet Martin Soskice, "Sight and Vision in Medieval Christian Thought," chapter 3 of this volume.

21 Jay, *Downcast Eyes*, pp. 84–85.

22 Ibid., p. 107.

23 Victor Burgin, "Paranoic Space," in Lucien Taylor, ed., *Visualizing Theory: Selected Essays from V. A. R. 1990–1994* (New York: Routledge, 1994).

24 It is, I would suggest, exactly because of this atomism that the idea that the eye touches can also be felt as reassuring (see Merleau-Ponty, *The Visible and the Invisible*).

25 See Phillip Rawson, *The Art of Drawing: An Instructional Guide* (London: MacDonald, 1983); and Fred Duberty and John Willats, *Perspective and Other Drawing Systems* (London: Herbert, 1983).

26 Ingrid Scheibler in Verena Conley, ed., *Questioning Technology* (Minneapolis: University of Minnesota Press, 1993).

27 Martin Jay, "In the Empire of the Gaze: Foucault and the Denigration of Vision in Twentieth-Century French Thought," in *Foucault: A Critical Reader*, ed. David Couzens Hoy (London: Basil Blackwell, 1986), p. 196.

CONTRIBUTORS

Parveen Adams is senior lecturer in psychology, Brunel University. She is the coeditor of *The Woman in Question* and has written numerous influential articles on feminism and psychoanalysis. Her *Emptiness of the Image* is to be published by Routledge in 1996.

Mieke Bal is professor of the theory of literature, University of Amsterdam. Her most recent books are *Death and Dissymmetry: The Politics of Coherence in the Book of Judges* and *Reading "Rembrandt": Beyond the World-Image Opposition*. Her *Murder and Difference* won the 1991 Award for Excellence of the American Academy of Religion.

Gillian Beer is the Edward VII Professor of English at the University of Cambridge and president of Clare Hall. Her books include *Darwin's Plots*; *Arguing with the Past*; and *Forging the Missing Link: Interdisciplinary Stories*.

Peter de Bolla is Fellow of King's College, Cambridge. He is the author of *The Discourse of the Sublime: History, Aesthetics and the Subject* and *Harold Bloom*. His forthcoming book is titled *The Education of the Eye*.

Teresa Brennan is visiting professor of philosophy at the New School for Social Research and also teaches in Cambridge. Her most recent book is *History After Lacan*.

Tom Conley is professor of French literature at Harvard University. He has written *Film Hieroglyphs* and *The Graphic Unconscious in Early Modern French Writing*. Forthcoming is his *Self Made Map*.

Helga Geyer-Ryan is associate professor in the Department of Comparative Literature, University of Amsterdam. She is coeditor of *Literary Theory Today* and is the author of *Fables of Desire: Studies in the Ethics of Art and Gender.*

Simon Goldhill is lecturer in classics, Cambridge. He is the author of *Language, Sexuality, Narrative: The Oresteia*; *Reading Greek Tragedy*; and *The Poet's Voice.*

Renée C. Hoogland is lecturer in lesbian cultural studies at the University of Nijmegen and post-doctoral research fellow with the Department of Comparative Literature at the University of Amsterdam. Her publications include *Elizabeth Bowen: A Reputation in Writing.*

Martin Jay is professor of history at the University of California, Berkeley. Included among his books are *The Dialectical Imagination* (1973); *Marxism and Totality* (1984); *Adorno* (1984); *Permanent Exiles* (1985); *Fin-de-Siècle Socialism* (1988); *Force Fields* (1993); and *Downcast Eyes* (1993). He most recently edited, along with Anton Kaes and Edward Dimendberg, *The Weimar Republic Sourcebook* (1994).

Stephen Melville is associate professor in history of art at Ohio State University. His publications include *Philosophy Beside Itself: On Deconstruction and Modernism.*

Irit Rogoff teaches Visual Culture and Critical Theory at the University of California, Davis. She is the editor of *The Divided Heritage: Themes and Problems in German Modernism* (Cambridge 1991) and *Museum Culture: Histories/Theories/Spectacles* (Routledge 1993) and the author of *Terra Infirma: Geography and Spectatorship* (Routledge 1996).

Janet Martin Soskice is lecturer in the Faculty of Divinity at Cambridge and fellow of Jesus College, Cambridge. She is the author of *Metaphor and Religious Language.* Her edited books include *After Eve: Women, Theology and the Christian Tradition.*

Ernst van Alphen teaches comparative literature at the University of Leiden. He has published widely on ideology, theories of reading, and relations between the arts. His most recent book is *Francis Bacon and the Loss of Self.*

Cathryn Vasseleu has published papers on animation, medical imaging technology, virtual reality, and sexual difference and has made a film, *De Anima*, about medical images of conception and sexual reproduction. She has recently completed a doctorate in philosophy at the University of Sydney on vision and embodiment in the work of Irigarary, Lévinas, and Merleau-Ponty.